MULTICULTURAL SOCIAL WORK RESEARCH METHODS AND DATA ANALYSIS

A Tool For Investigating Social Problems and Evidence-Based Practice

First Edition

Thanh V. Tran
Boston College

Siyon Y. Rhee
California State University, Los Angeles

Ce Shen
Boston College

cognella®
academic publishing

Bassim Hamadeh, CEO and Publisher
Michael Simpson, Vice President of Acquisitions
Jamie Giganti, Managing Editor
Jess Busch, Senior Graphic Designer
John Remington, Acquisitions Editor
Brian Fahey, Licensing Specialist
Mandy Licata, Interior Designer

Cover images copyright © 2012 by Depositphotos / malyuginphoto; © 2012 by Depositphotos / johan-jk; © 2014 by Depositphotos / elwynn.

First published in the United States of America in 2015 by Cognella, Inc.

Printed in the United States of America

ISBN: 978-1-62661-332-4 (pbk) / 978-1-62661-333-1 (br)

www.cognella.com   800-200-3908

CONTENTS

ACKNOWLEDGEMENTS

We owe our former professors, authors, researchers, and colleagues for the knowledge of research methods that we have learned throughout our academic career. Our students have inspired us to write this book. We thank our families and our universities for the support. Kaipeng Wang, a doctoral student of Social Work at Boston College, developed the PowerPoint lectures for this book.

MULTICULTURAL SOCIAL WORK RESEARCH METHODS AND DATA ANALYSIS: A TOOL FOR

Investigating Social Problems and Evidence-Based Practice

Overview

Purpose: The goals of this textbook are to introduce research methodology to social work students and practitioners interested in multicultural research, and to provide hands-on examples in conducting data analysis using SPSS, Stata, and Excel. This book will equip readers with the knowledge to become critical research consumers and the practical skills to engage in agency-based research and evaluation projects that may range from needs assessment to program evaluation. The book can also be useful to students and practitioners of allied disciplines in human services.

Scope: There have been other textbooks available on research methods written for both undergraduate and graduate social work students. There is no textbook, however, that integrates both methods and sensible approaches for data analysis that can be useful, practical, and fundamental to not only students, but also instructors, researchers, and practitioners. In previous social work research textbooks, most authors have addressed the methods, but not the statistical approaches, appropriate for the selected research design. Thus, it is difficult for students to truly comprehend various research designs including survey and experimental designs, and how to translate their theoretical understanding of these designs into research practice. Moreover, given the increasing diversity of the US population, students should learn to be culturally sensitive in their work and become competent research consumers and practitioners.

In this book, we will provide examples for each research design and demonstrate how to analyze data using appropriate statistical techniques. Our book differs from existing social work research textbooks in the following manners:

1. We address research methods from a multicultural perspective.
2. We inherently link research methods and data analysis to help students learn theoretical concepts and practice simultaneously.
3. We provide hands-on examples of statistical analysis for each selected research design, while avoiding the use of highly specified statistical jargons and terminologies.
4. We teach students to use statistical software packages for data analysis: SPSS (Statistical Package for Social Sciences), Stata, and Excel. We will present brief and relevant review questions at the end of each chapter, which can be used for individual or group exercises.

ONE

Introduction to Scientific Methods from Social Work and Human Service Perspectives

This chapter will discuss the purpose and characteristics of scientific methods in the context of social work and human service perspectives. You might argue that social workers are not scientists, and thus there is no need to use scientific methods in social work. This is an erroneous assumption held by many social workers, social work students, and even some who are teaching social work. What is science? Here is the nominal definition found in the Merriam-Webster dictionary:

"Knowledge about or study of the natural world based on facts learned through experiments and observation," or "Knowledge or a system of knowledge covering general truths or the operation of general laws especially as obtained and tested through scientific method" (http://www.merriam-webster.com/dictionary/science). As the definition implies, science is a process of empirically learning to know the nature of things that happen around us in a systematic way. Unlike knowledge obtained through everyday tradition and experience, science, as a body of knowledge and also as a method to describe the world more precisely, is characterized by its general agreement with the factual reality. In other words, the scientific body of knowledge is obtained by following the generally agreed-upon procedures that can be replicated by other scientists. As such, scientific knowledge produced by an array of systematic observation tends to more or less reflect the reality of the world—and, thus, make sense to many people in general. For example, there is a well-accepted theory of child abuse regarding why child maltreatment occurs within the family. An environmental theory posits that parental social stress arising from poverty, unemployment, and divorce, for example, is likely to contribute to child abuse and neglect (Justice, Calvert, and Justice, 1985; Straus, 1980). This theory was formulated by observing many abusive parents and perpetrators and conducting large-scale nationwide surveys. When this theory is presented to the general public, including social workers and researchers, it sounds logical and makes sense. Therefore, social workers, through scientific research, need to learn why our clients behave in different social circumstances as they do, how people cope with stress, why there are incidents of child abuse, what keeps people living in poverty, and so forth.

Scientific research methods are tools for social workers to describe, explore, test hypotheses, and evaluate social work practice. Scientific methods are systematic and replicable. The use of scientific method helps social workers collect reliable and valid data to find answers to various individual and societal problems. Historically, social work research has focused on various psychological and social problems that are often overlapped with research in psychology and sociology. And also historically, the academic discipline of social work has been rather action-oriented than knowledge testing and theory development. Generally agreed-upon theory can only be developed by reliable and valid observations and logical reasoning. Accurate theory helps social workers explain and predict human behaviors in the social environment. Similarly, good theory helps social workers select a more effective intervention or treatment strategy for specific human or social problems. To develop theories for practice, social workers should follow the basic steps of scientific method. The scientific methods provide a logical process to predict and explain what occurs in the environment by researching the outcome of an intervention, public opinion on a specific social issue, and social needs of a community on a regular basis.

INDUCTIVE AND DEDUCTIVE REASONING PROCESS

Scientific research uses both inductive and deductive reasoning processes in producing knowledge or general theories. In the process of generating theoretical propositions, inductive reasoning begins from individual observations with a few members of the group and then moves on to broader generalizations leading to theories. When published material on a chosen research topic is almost nonexistent, social work researchers may choose to begin with specific observations with limited numbers of research participants in their exploratory research about certain human behavior, psychological problem, or social phenomena without formulating research hypotheses. They can take notes of similarities and differences, explore tentative hypotheses evolved from their observations, collect systematic data or conduct experiments, and in the end arrive at some general conclusions or theories. This is sometimes called a "bottom up" approach.

On the other hand, in the deductive reasoning process, social work researchers work in the following reasoning processes: beginning with an existing general theory, identified through an extensive literature review; deriving hypotheses from this existing theory; testing hypotheses with observed or collected data; confirming the existing theory, by accepting the hypotheses or rejecting the hypotheses; and then drawing a conclusion. This process refers to deductive investigation or deductive reasoning. It is the "top down" approach of investigation. Although deductive reasoning is much more frequently practiced in scientific investigation historically, social work research today should use both inductive and deductive reasoning processes to more accurately describe social problems. For example, Durkheim's classic study of suicide is a great example of both inductive and deductive processes. Durkheim (1858–1917), a French sociologist, is considered one of the pioneers in modern social research. He began his study by examining the tables of official statistics on suicide rates in different areas, and discovered that the rate of suicide was consistently higher among Protestant than Catholic populations (Anderson and Taylor, 2009). From these initial observations Durkheim developed his theory of religion, social integration, anomie, and suicide. This is his inductive reasoning or inductive research method. Based on his theoretical interpretations of suicide he further developed more hypotheses and collected more observations to verify his theory. Durkheim is known as a researcher who promoted empirical positivism and the deductive model in social science; his study is based on a mixture of inductive and deductive reasoning processes.

BASIC STEPS OF SCIENTIFIC METHODS

There are a variety of research projects in terms of scope, design, population, and topic of interest. Some might be interested in investigating factors contributing to domestic violence in the Latino American community, while others undertake projects to examine whether behavior medication techniques are more effective in improving autistic children's attention span among Chinese American families. Despite this diversity, however, all research in general shares the following steps:

Step 1. Identification of Research Problem: Social workers need to observe the community to identify social problems or social needs. The observations should be objective and empirical. To present an example of *empirical*: a social worker reviews several cases of domestic violence, and finds the rate of alcohol consumption is consistently higher among the abusers.

Step 2. Development of Initial Assumption and Formal Hypothesis: For example, from the social worker's initial observations of alcohol consumption and domestic violence, he or she forms an assumption that alcohol addiction is likely to be associated with the occurrence of domestic violence. This type of reasoning is called **inductive reasoning** (deriving a tentative assumption about the topic area from specific details).

The social worker can now formally form a hypothesis about the association between alcohol consumption and domestic violence. From a multicultural perspective, the social worker can address the hypothesis that includes racial/ethnic differences in socioeconomic status (SES), family values, indigenous cultural practices, and disparity in health and mental health status, for instance. This formal hypothesis is derived from a general theory identified from literature review, clinical case observations, and extensive reviews of agency case files. This is the beginning of the deductive reasoning process. It should be noted that if you review the research articles published in social work journals or many other research journals, researchers seldom state their hypotheses explicitly. The use of advanced statistics to analyze several variables simultaneously could be the reason that formal research hypotheses are no longer a common practice in research journals.

A formal hypothesis should have the following characteristics:

- It should be a general statement about possible relationship or association.
- It should be a **tentative** statement.
- It should be congruent with available observations.
- It should be simple and clear.
- It should be testable and potentially refutable or falsifiable. In other words, there should be a way to disprove the hypothesis.

A research hypothesis is an alternative statement for a *null hypothesis*, which always assumes no relationship between variables, no association, or no effect.

Step 3. Selection and Refinement of Research Design: A research design pertains to a plan to implement a study in the chosen field of interest. The design addresses not only the type of research—e.g., survey, experimental study, program evaluation, ethnographic case study, participant observation—but also sampling research participants from whom data will be systematically collected. Different hypotheses require different types of data. There are hypotheses that require social workers to conduct a survey to collect appropriate data. It's impossible and unethical to make people become alcohol-dependent to learn an association between alcohol consumption and domestic violence. Thus, a survey is an appropriate method to collect data for this hypothesis. Other hypotheses require a manipulation or implementation of the independent variable for appropriate data collection. For example one would want to test the effectiveness of a psychotherapeutic treatment for social anxiety. An experiment can be designed to provide psychotherapeutic treatment for individuals who suffered from social anxiety and learn whether the treatment works. Therefore, there is no such thing as "the best design." How to select the most appropriate design depends on the area of research that a researcher pursues to investigate. Before collecting data from human subjects, the validity and reliability of measures should be assessed.

Step 4. Collection of Data: In survey, data are primarily collected by asking questions of respondents by constructing a research instrument, such as questionnaire and interview schedule, while the main source of participant observation, as part of qualitative research, is observing actual human behaviors occurring in the natural environment. A survey data collection technique is widely used in attitude studies; however, since what people say and do is inconsistent, data are often collected by participating in the activities of the particular community of interest.

Step 5. Analysis of Data and Hypothesis Testing: Once we have the data from a survey or an experiment, we can use appropriate statistical tests to assess the hypothesis. If the result of a statistical test provides significant evidence for the rejection of the "null hypothesis," we can conclude that our research hypothesis is supported by our data.

Step 6. Drawing a Conclusion: From our analysis of the experiment, for example, we have two possible outcomes: the results supports our prediction, or they fail to support our prediction.

Step 7. Presentation of the Results and Proposing New Hypotheses: Sharing the results or publishing the results is an important step in scientific investigation. This allows other researchers to verify our results or to replicate our research. If we are confident with our results, we can form further hypotheses based on what we learned.

SCIENTIFIC METHOD AND SOCIAL WORK EVALUATION

Social work evaluation is a deductive reasoning process. We have a strong theory of practice, or evidence-based service or treatment, for a specific psychological or social problem; we implement an evidence-based service and measure its outcome. Thus, the scientific method of social work evaluation has the following basic steps:

Step 1. Determine Psychological or Social Need: The first step in social work evaluation process is the identification of psychological or social problems that require intervention. This can be done by clinical observations or a formal need assessment. Sometimes, psychological or social problems arrive due to man-made crises or natural disasters.

Step 2. Select an Evidence-Based Service: Once a problem is identified and a need is assessed and documented, a proper intervention should be considered and selected. Any selected social work intervention should satisfy the requirements of cultural and linguistic diversity of the prospective clients.

Step 3. Set Practical, Measurable Goals, and Meaningful Intervention: It's important to know what goals and outcomes we want to achieve and how much the intervention would produce. This requires the selection and use of outcome measures that could capture the changes expected from the intervention. The selected outcome measures must also be relevant to diverse clients in cultural, generational, and linguistic backgrounds.

Step 4. Design and Implement the Service: The implementation of an intervention requires a careful program design so that correct data can be collected to assess the intervention outcomes. Different types of experimental designs should be considered before any service implantation. In this book we will address three practical designs that are feasible for social work evaluation.

Step 5. Collect Data: Once an evaluation design is selected, a plan for data collection must be determined. This requires valid and reliable outcome measures.

Step 6. Evaluate Changes: It is necessary to use appropriate statistical tests to evaluate the changes produced by the intervention. In Chapter 9, we will explore the experimental designs and statistical tests that can be used for each design.

Step 7. Draw Conclusions: Conclusions should be based on both statistical significance and clinical significance. Statistical significance is evident in the result of a statistical test, but clinical significance is based on clinical observations, experience, and practice wisdom.

Step 8. Disseminate the Results: The results from a social work evaluation should be shared with practitioners in the fields. This is an important step in advancing the theory of practice among social workers. It also opens the door for further implementations and evaluations of a selected social work intervention.

BASIC RESEARCH TERMINOLOGY

Social work research problems can arise from various situations. For example, during and after the major natural disaster caused by Hurricane Katrina, numerous psychological and social problems required a systematic investigation to provide answers to policy makers, health-care providers, and social-service providers to help the survivors confront and cope with their physical and psychological losses. Thus, a social work research problem can be defined as a situation involving individual, family, and community that requires solutions. In investigating multicultural social problems, researchers and students should have a clear understanding of various terminologies frequently used in research.

Theory: Theory can be defined as the systematic body of knowledge and statements developed and tested over time. Theory helps social workers understand why things happen in certain ways or to predict what could happen in a given situation. Thus, theory is the foundation of a research project. It helps social work researchers ask the right questions, explain the outcome, and predict the future.

Hypothesis: Social work research hypothesis is a testable statement suggesting a possible relationship between two or more variables. For example, we can hypothesize or assume that survivors of Hurricane Katrina would make a quick recovery from both physical and psychological losses if they had a strong support network. This hypothesis consists of two key variables: recovery and support network. To test this hypothesis, we have to measure them or quantify them.

Hypothesis Testing: Testing a hypothesis is a systematic procedure that compares two competing assumptions (the null hypothesis versus alternative or research hypothesis) about a particular association or relationship of at least two variables using observable data and appropriate statistical procedures.

Null Hypothesis: This hypothesis states there is no relationship between the two phenomena or two variables (i.e., alcohol consumption is not related to domestic violence).

Alternative Hypothesis: This hypothesis states there *is* a relationship between the two phenomena or two variables (i.e., alcohol consumption is related to domestic violence).

One-Tailed Hypothesis: A one-tailed hypothesis specifies a directional relationship between variables. For example, the hypothesis stating there is a *higher* rate of domestic violence among spouses who consume alcohol more frequently than those who do not consume alcohol assumes the direction in which the difference between the two groups of people will exist.

Two-Tailed Hypothesis: A two-tailed hypothesis does not specify a directional relationship. Instead, it aims to test that there is a difference between two variables. For example, the hypothesis "the rate of domestic violence is different between spouses who consume alcohol frequently and spouses who do not consume alcohol" would only predict a difference between the two groups.

In hypothesis testing, if we can reject one of the two hypotheses, the other hypothesis should always be accepted provisionally. We should never come to an absolute conclusion. Our findings are subjected to further replication and verification.

Concept, Variable, and Attribute. A concept in research is a building block of a theory, which is composed of interrelated concepts. In research, **concept** refers to a name or label we assign to persons, things, events, and thoughts that enables us to perceive their characteristics in common. In other words, a concept is a mental image about persons, things, and events. Some examples of social work concepts include immigrant, poverty, discrimination, social isolation, self-esteem, domestic violence, positive reinforcement, conflict, minority, homelessness, and so forth. The level of abstraction among these concepts varies widely. Some concepts (i.e., chair, money, hat, etc.) are relatively concrete and within the range of direct observation. Concepts such as self-esteem and positive reinforcement, however, are very abstract and therefore beyond the reach of our direct observation. Thus, we can state there are two types of concepts—concrete and abstract. To measure abstract concepts accurately in research, it is essential to operationally define the concept, meaning that we turn abstract concepts into something that can be observed or measured.

A **variable** is an operationally defined concept, and a property of a concept that contains at least two or more values or levels. For example, the concept "poverty" can be operationally defined as the lacking of adequate income to meet basic needs. Once it is operationally defined, the term "poverty" becomes a variable that has a wide range of income level, and we can measure levels of poverty based on the amount of income for an individual or family in a given year. Similarly, depression is a variable that can be measured by a standardized scale or clinical assessment. Individuals have different degrees or levels of depression based on their social and psychological status. There are two types of variables—independent and dependent. The **independent variable** is the causal variable that stands alone and has an influence on a change in the dependent variable. The **dependent variable** is the effect variable that is influenced by the independent variable.

An **intervening variable**, also called an **intermediary variable** or a **mediating variable**, provides an explanation between other variables as a causal link. For example, the relationship between income and health status needs a further explanation since income itself does not warrant good health. Other variables, such as health practice (including healthy diet and exercise), intervene between income and health status. Individuals with higher income are more likely to exercise on a regular basis. In this case, the variable "exercise" mediates the relationship between income and health status as an intervening variable.

There is a clear distinction between a mediating variable and a **moderating variable** (also known as a **moderator**). A moderator is a third variable that modifies the direction or strength of the relationship between the independent variable and the dependent variable. A moderation effect generally addresses "when" or "for whom" an independent variable most strongly or weakly causes a dependent variable (Baron and Kenny 1986; Wu and Zumbo 2008). The moderation effect is an interaction, meaning that the effect of an independent variable depends on the level of the third variable. For example, a statistical association between social support (independent variable) and psychological distress (dependent variable) may depend on gender (male and female). In this example, gender is a moderating variable since it alters the strength of the relationship between social support and psychological distress.

There is a distinction among the **categorical variable** (synonym for **nominal variable**), the **discrete variable,** and the **continuous variable**. A categorical variable is a group variable that contains a finite set of answer categories called values. Gender is a categorical variable as it has two response categories, namely male and female. It is useful to assign a numerical value to each answer category used as a label (1 = male; 2 = female). A discrete variable is a variable that takes on only integer values. For example, discrete variables include number of students in class; and responses to a 4-point rating scale (1 = rarely; 2 = sometimes; 3 = mostly; 4 = always). A continuous variable (synonym for interval variable), on the other hand, is a variable that takes on any value including decimals. Each value can be placed on a point (integer or decimal) along an infinite line segment. For example, income is a continuous variable since there are nearly infinite numbers of values we can imagine ($10,002.28; $24,005.00; $43,592.52, etc.). Table 1.1 provides additional types of variables frequently cited among researchers.

Attribute refers to categories within a variable. For example, the attributes of the variable "religion" include Catholic, Protestant, Muslim, Buddhism, other, and none. Research variables have to be measureable. In other words, we have to be able to categorize a variable into various attributes or characteristics and assign numerical values to each category.

Table 1.1: Types of Variables

TYPES OF VARIABLES	DEFINITION
Binomial variable (synonym for binary variable or dichotomous variable)	A type of categorical variable that has only two attributes or answer categories. For example, 1 = yes, 2 = no; 1 = pass; 2 = fail.
Categorical variable	A categorical variable is a group variable that contains a finite set of possible answer categories (or values). Gender is a categorical variable as it has two response categories, namely male and female. It is useful to assign a numerical value to each answer category used as a label (1 = male; 2 = female).
Confounding variable	An extraneous variable that affects the variables under investigation and obscures the effects of the independent variable on the dependent variable. For example, when a researcher examines a relationship between exercise and health status, diet can confound the influence of exercise on health status.
Continuous variable (synonym for interval variable)	A variable that takes on any value including decimals. Each value can be placed on a point of an infinite line segment. For example, income is a continuous variable since there are nearly an infinite number of responses we can imagine ($10,002.28; $43,592.52, etc.).
Control variable (synonym of covariate)	An extraneous variable whose value is held constant throughout the experiment. For example, when data are collected from all females, gender is a control variable.
Dependent variable	The effect variable that is influenced by the independent variable.
Discrete variable	A variable that takes on only integer values. For example, number of students in class; responses to a 4-point rating scale (1 = rarely; 2 = sometimes; 3 = mostly; 4 = always).

(continued)

Table 1.1: Types of Variables (continued)

Dummy variable	A variable that takes the value of only 0 or 1 in regression analysis. It is created by recoding categorical variables into two mutually exclusive categories (0 and 1) to examine group differences. For example, the gender variable whose original values were 1 = male and 2 = female can be recoded into 0 = male and 1 = female. If a variable has two answer categories, we create one dummy variable. If a variable has three values, we need to create two dummy variables. For example, the ethnicity variable could have three values: 1 = white; 2 = African American; 3 = Latino American. This variable is recoded into two dummy variables (i.e., D1 and D2). D1 variable has two values: 1 = African American; 0 = otherwise. D2 variable has two values: 1 = Latino American; 0 = otherwise. In this case, for a white respondent, his or her value of both D1 and D2 variables will be 0. In general, a categorical variable with k categories is recoded into $k - 1$ dummy variables.
Independent variable (synonym for manipulated variable and treatment variable)	A causal variable that stands alone and has an influence on a change in the dependent variable.
Intervening variable (synonym for intermediary variable and mediating variable)	A variable that provides an explanation between other variables as a causal link. For example, the relationship between income and health status needs a further explanation since income itself does not warrant good health. Other variables, such as health practice (including healthy diet and exercise), intervene between income and health status. Individuals with higher income are more likely to exercise on a regular basis. In this case, the variable "exercise" mediates the relationship between income and health status as an intervening variable.
Latent variable	A variable that cannot be observed directly but inferred from other variables that are within the scope of direct observation.
Manifest variable (synonym for indicator variable)	A variable that can be directly measured or observed, while a latent variable cannot be directly observed. A manifest variable generally indicates the exhibition of a latent variable. For example, personality is a latent variable because we cannot observe it directly. We can measure indicator variables, such as job success, popularity among peers, number of friends.
Mediating variable	Synonym for intervening variable. Example: social support could mediate the relationship between poverty and delinquency.
Moderating variable	A moderator is a third variable that modifies the direction or strength of the relationship between the independent variable and the dependent variable. The moderation effect is an interaction, meaning the effect of an independent variable depends on the level of the third variable.
Nominal variable	Synonym for categorical variable.
Ordinal variable	A[c] type of categorical variable that has a rank ordered set of possible values with respect to certain characteristics. An ordinal variable classifies research participants into a series of rank-ordered categories (i.e., strongly disagree to strongly agree).
Predictor variable	A variable that is presumed to cause the variation in a dependent variable in regression analysis.

Relationship: There are two key relationships between variables often discussed in a research project: *correlation* and *causality* (or causal relationship).

Correlation: The commonly used correlation is the *Pearson Product-Moment Correlation Coefficient. The letter "r" is used to denote the correlation coefficient that is a measure of the degree of linear relationship between two continuous variables, such as years in school and earned income.* The correlation coefficient "r" may take on any value between plus and minus one (+1 and −1). The sign of the correlation coefficient (+, −) defines the direction of the correlation. A positive correlation coefficient means that as the values of one variable increase, the values of the other variable also increase; or as the values of one decrease, the values of the other also decrease (e.g., more years in school, higher earned income; fewer years in school, lower earned income). A negative correlation coefficient indicates that as the values of one variable increase, the other decreases, and vice versa (e.g., more friends, less isolation). The absolute value of the correlation coefficient measures the strength of the relationship. For example, a correlation coefficient of $r = .70$ indicates a stronger degree of linear relationship than one of $r = .40$. Likewise, a correlation coefficient of $r = −.70$ indicates a stronger degree of relationship than one of $r = −.40$. A correlation coefficient of zero ($r = 0.0$) indicates the absence of a linear relationship. But correlation coefficients of $r = +1.0$ and $r = -1.0$ indicate a perfect linear relationship.

Causal Relationship: This is the association of a cause and an effect. For example, a social work intervention is the cause and the outcome of the intervention is the effect. A causal relationship must satisfy the following conditions:

   e. The cause must precede the effect.

   f. There must be a correlation between the cause and its effect.

   g. There must be no plausible alternative explanations.

SUMMARY

This chapter addressed the basic principles and steps of the scientific methods, which provide the objective and systematic guide for social work research and inquiry. The chapter also presented some basic concepts of social work research. We employ scientific methods in social work research because they are objective, systematic, and replicable. Its objectivity requires social work researchers to avoid biases in collecting data and interpreting the results. Its systematic characteristics require social work researchers to follow a logical process of investigation. Finally, scientific methods are replicable, suggesting that other researchers can replicate or study to further verify the results.

CLASS EXERCISE

Write three hypotheses relevant to social work practice. Explain your independent and dependent variables for each hypothesis. Why do you think these hypotheses are interesting? Discuss the implications of the possible results of these hypotheses.

REFERENCES

Anderson, M. L., & Taylor, H. F. (2009). *Sociology: The essentials*. Belmont, CA: Thomson Wadsworth.

Baron, R. M., & Kenny, D. A. (1986). The moderator-mediator variable distinction in social psychological research: conceptual, strategic, and statistical considerations. *Journal of Personality and Social Psychology, 51*(6), 1173–1182.

Justice, B., Calvert, A., & Justice, R. (1985). Factors mediating child abuse as a response to stress. *Child Abuse & Neglect, 9*, 359-363.

Straus, M. A. (1980). Stress and child abuse. In C. H. Kempe & R. E. Helfer (Eds.), *The battered child* (3rd ed.). Chicago: Chicago University Press.

Wu, A. D., & Zumbo, B. D. (2008). Understanding and using mediators and moderators. *Social Indicator Research, 87*(3), 367–392. DOI 10.1007/s11205-007-9143-1

TWO

Boundaries and Types of Social Work Research and Ethical Issues

This chapter will highlight the focus of social work research as an academic discipline. We will address the differences between social work research and other social science research. We will explain different types of research (i.e., need assessment, evidence-based, applied, clinical trial, translational, and program evaluation) and examine what types of research are relevant to social work. This chapter will address various issues of research ethics throughout the research and evaluation process.

THE BOUNDARY OF SOCIAL WORK RESEARCH

What is social work research? This sounds easy to answer but difficult to explain. Historically, social work research tends to be descriptive and encompassing a variety of social and psychological problems from poverty to mental illnesses. Although social work, by nature, is an intervention- and service-oriented profession, there has been a lack of research on evidence-based practice research.

TYPES OF RESEARCH

There has been confusion in the attempt to both define types of research and also research approaches. In this book, we intend to classify social work research according to its purposes and approaches. Generally, there are two major types: **basic research** and **applied research**. The boundary between the two is not always clear. Basic research is commonly referred to as pure research and often focuses on theory development and hypothesis testing. Although the results from basic research might not have any immediate implications for practice, they can further advance the knowledge base for practice. Given the nature of the profession, social work research tends to be more applied than basic. Applied research and social work research often focus on need assessments and intervention evaluations. The results of this type of research often have immediate implications. For example, findings from a need-assessment survey may help social workers design new services to meet the needs of a community and also help policy makers establish new policies. Results from a program evaluation help social workers modify, change, or improve services. Although selection of evidence-based services and treatments is a crucial aspect of social work research and practice, it's important for social workers to re-evaluate any "effectively proven service or treatment" before applying them to clients or the community.

Social science research can be also classified into two main types: **quantitative** and **qualitative research,** according to types of data and methods of data analysis. Quantitative research primarily collects numerical and mathematical data to describe social phenomena empirically relying on statistics, while qualitative research collects narrative data using in-depth interviewing or observational techniques. Both approaches can be used in basic and applied research. In this book, we explore the two approaches in detail in later chapters (seven, eight, nine and ten).

Research is often classified according to the main purpose of the study. Those include (1) **exploratory research**, (2) **descriptive research**, (3) **explanatory research**, and (4) **evaluation research**. As the term suggests, the primary purpose of **exploratory research** is to "explore" the chosen topic area when little or nothing is known in that particular area, with an aim to gain insights and ideas about what is occurring around us. Since the amount of published information and knowledge is limited, it is nearly impossible to formulate a hypothesis at the initial stage of the study. Many projects conducted with qualitative research designs are, in essence, exploratory. Exploratory research is least rigorous in terms of following the research protocols, including hypothesis testing, using valid and reliable instruments, and sampling methods. Findings gained from exploratory research can be used as hypotheses by future researchers. For example, "a study of care preferences among Puerto Rican families with older adults diagnosed with Alzheimer disease" can be well investigated with an exploratory research project since the amount of published findings is just a handful.

On the other hand, **descriptive research** aims to find facts and describe social phenomena concerning relevant variables, instead of attempting to show that one variable causes the other variable to vary. For example, in descriptive studies, an investigator may be interested in describing general attitudes, the level of psychological distress, self-esteem, and prevalence of violence within immigrant families. When the knowledge base about the chosen field is well established, and when a researcher is interested in furthering knowledge and understanding about the phenomena, descriptive research is appropriate. Compared with exploratory research, the process of descriptive research is more rigorous. This type of research generally has some hypotheses, and samples are drawn from the target population in a manner to assure "representativeness."

The intent of **explanatory research** is to establish a causal relationship between variables and explain why things are occurring in the way they are. If a researcher attempts to identify factors contributing to spousal abuse among some ethnic or racial American families and why the abuse is occurring, the study is beyond the scope of descriptive research, whose main interest is to understand how serious the problem of spousal abuse is in this population. Since "explanation" is the main purpose in explanatory research, the study design must reflect the stringent research process with respect to types of hypothesis, instrument, sampling, and statistical data analysis plan. One of the hypotheses to test in the study of spousal abuse is that "Males who adhere to traditional family values (i.e., machismo or male-dominance) are more likely to be involved in the practice of family violence compared to those with more Westernized values of gender equity."

Evaluation research monitors and evaluates practice among helping professionals in human services. Evaluation research focuses not only on evaluating the existing programs concerning strengths and weaknesses, but also on planning new programs step-by-step and monitoring the progress of human service programs implemented by practitioners. The majority of private nonprofit social service organizations operate with many different government funding sources, and it is required by government funding agencies to show that their services are effective and accountable. Therefore, evaluation of human services is an integral part of the most service programs today.

ETHICAL CONSIDERATIONS IN SOCIAL WORK RESEARCH

We might wonder what ethics is and why social work researchers need to consider ethics? Every publicly organized profession has its own code of ethics. These ethical standards across different disciplines often overlap but complement one another. This code of ethics spells out the standards of right and wrong that prescribe what members of a profession should follow. The National Association of Social Work (NASW) has prescribed an official Code of Ethics for professional social workers, and this code can be the guide for social work research (http://www.socialworkers.org/pubs/code/code.asp).

As stated in the NASW Code of Ethics, the core values of social work represent the foundation of what social workers should strive to do in carrying out their professional activities. This foundation includes "service, social justice, dignity and worth of the person, importance of human relationships, integrity, and competence." Based on these core values, social workers are required to promote the well-being of their clients, respect clients' self-determination, assure informed consent, possess, professional competence, being able to understand and embrace cultural competence and social diversity, avoid conflicts of interest, respect and protect clients' privacy and confidentiality, respect and ease clients' access to their records, avoid sexual relationships with clients under all circumstances, avoid physical contacts that could potentially be harmful to the clients, avoid verbal or physical sexual harassment against clients, avoid the use of derogatory language with clients, set reasonable and fair service/treatment fees, safeguard the interest and right of vulnerable clients who lack decision-making capacity, make an effort to ensure continuity of services, and terminate the services when they are no longer necessary. These are prescribed standards of conduct for all professional social workers and also applicable to social work researchers.

RESEARCH ETHICS

David B. Resnik (2011) wrote an insightful essay titled "What is Ethics in Research & Why is it Important?" and posted it on the website of the National Institute of Environmental Health Sciences, one of many research institutes of the National Institute of Health (NIH). In his essay Resnik defined research ethics and listed a set of ethical standards that must be abided by researchers (http://www.niehs.nih.gov/research/resources/bioethics/whatis/). Research ethics can be defined as "norms for conduct" that distinguish between acceptable and unacceptable behavior in the conduct of a research project or activities (Resnik, 2011; Shamoo and Resnik, 2009). These authors suggested the following five norms for researchers:

(a) Researchers should promote the seeking of knowledge and truth and avoiding errors as the aims of research.

(b) Researchers need to promote the values essential to collaborative work: trust, accountability, mutual respect, and fairness.

(c) Researchers must be accountable to the public. That is, avoid conflicts of interest, and follow the rules and regulations as required by government policies and laws.

(d) Researchers should build public support by gaining public trust, because people are the ultimate supporters of public-funded research projects.

(e) Researchers should promote and protect moral and social values including human rights, health safety, and animal welfare.

CODES AND POLICIES FOR RESEARCH ETHICS

Nearly all legally and publicly recognized professional associations and government research institutions have a code of research ethics or a set of policies and rules that require researchers' adherence. We selected thirteen research ethical conducts that are relevant to social work research from the list provided by Resnik (2011) in the following:

1. **Honesty.** Social wok researchers must always be honest in their report of data, results, methods and procedures, and publication status. We should avoid fabricating, falsifying, or misrepresenting data. Deceiving colleagues, granting agencies, or the public is unacceptable in any situation.

2. **Objectivity.** Social work researchers must do everything possible to avoid bias in experimental design, data analysis, data interpretation, peer review, personnel decisions, grant writing, expert testimony, and other aspects of research where objectivity is expected or required. We should attempt to avoid or minimize bias or self-deception and disclose personal or financial interests that may affect research.

3. **Integrity.** Social work researchers must fulfill their promises and agreements with the participants, community, and funding agencies, and act with sincerity and consistency.

4. **Carefulness**. Social work researchers should strive to avoid careless errors and negligence; should be careful and critical in examining and evaluating their own work and the work of their peers; and should maintain proper records of research activities, including data collection, research design, and correspondence with agencies or journals.

5. **Openness**. Social work researchers should share data and results for possible verification and replication, and be open to criticism and new ideas.

6. **Respect for Intellectual Property**. Social work researchers must not plagiarize others' work or ideas, and always acknowledge the source of information or provide proper citations.

7. **Confidentiality**. Social work researchers must always protect participants' confidentiality. Other research and professional communications must also be protected.

8. **Responsible Publication**. Social work researchers should be conscientious about the purposes of publications. The ultimate goal of research and publication should be the well-being of the clients and society.

9. **Social Responsibility**. As cited in No. 8, social work researchers conduct research and evaluation to advance not only professional knowledge, but also the well-being of the clients and the society as a whole.

10. **Nondiscrimination**. Throughout the process of research and evaluation, social work researchers should avoid all forms of discrimination against clients, colleagues, or students on the basis of sex, race, ethnicity, or other factors not related to their scientific competence and integrity.

11. **Competence**. Social work researchers should always try to improve their research skills, and update and expand their knowledge to better serve their clients and community.

12. **Legality**. Social work researchers should comply with relevant laws and institutional and governmental policies.

13. **Human Subjects Protection**. In all research and evaluation activities, social work researchers must maximize clients' benefits and minimize their harms and risks; respect human dignity, privacy, confidentiality, and autonomy; and take special precautions with vulnerable populations.

THE HISTORICAL DEVELOPMENT OF RESEARCH ETHICS INVOLVING HUMAN SUBJECTS

Severe violations of human rights and well-being in the past have led to the enactments of laws to protect individuals from potential abuse and the harmful effects of both biomedical and behavioral research. The well-known violation of human right and well-being of "The Tuskegee Study of Untreated Syphilis in the Negro Male," also known as the **Tuskegee Syphilis Study**, marked the beginning of the development of law and ethical conducts for research in the United States. For many of us, this story sounds unreal and impossible today, but it actually occurred in Macon County, Alabama, from 1932 to 1972. Here is a snapshot of the study as summarized in the Final Report of the Tuskegee Syphilis Study Legacy Committee: "*In 1932, the United States Public Health Service (USPHS) initiated the Tuskegee Syphilis Study to document the natural history of syphilis. The subjects of the investigation were 399 poor black sharecroppers from Macon County, Alabama, with latent syphilis and 201 men without the disease who served as controls. The physicians conducting the Study deceived the men, telling them that they were being treated for "bad blood." However, they deliberately denied treatment to the men with syphilis and they went to extreme lengths to ensure that they would not receive therapy from any other sources. In exchange for their participation, the men received free meals, free medical examinations, and burial insurance.*" As reported by *The New York Times* on July 26, 1972, the Tuskegee Syphilis Study was revealed as "the longest nontherapeutic experiment on human beings in medical history." You can read more about this story, "Bad Blood The Tuskegee Syphilis Study: Final Report of the Tuskegee Syphilis Study Legacy Committee," at http://exhibits.hsl.virginia.edu/badblood/report/.

The revelation of the Tuskegee study and other studies have made the US government take a closer look at research involving human beings and enacted laws and regulations to prevent what had occurred in Tuskegee from happening again. Subsequently, the **National Research Act** (Public Law 93–348) was signed into law on July12, 1974, creating the National Commission for the Protection of Human Subjects of Biomedical and Behavioral Research. One of the tasks assigned to the Commission was to identify the basic ethical principles that should guide the procedure of biomedical and behavioral research involving human subjects. The Belmont Report, written by the National Commission in 1979, identified three basic ethical principles for using human subjects in research and recommended how to ensure these principles. The three basic ethical principles are (1) **respect for persons,** (2) **beneficence,** and (3) **justice**.

(1) **Respect for Persons**: This means that individuals should be treated in an ethical manner by respecting their autonomy and protecting them from emotional and/or physical harm. According to the Belmont Report, "The principle of respect for persons thus divides into two separate moral requirements: the requirement to acknowledge autonomy and the requirement to protect those with diminished autonomy…. In most cases of research involving human subjects, respect for persons demands that subjects enter into

the research voluntarily and with adequate information" (http://www.hhs.gov/ohrp/humansubjects/guidance/belmont.html). As a vehicle to promote the principle of respect for persons, **voluntary informed consent** from all persons taking part in studies funded by the Department of Health, Education, and Welfare (DHEW) was highly emphasized in the Belmont Report. The Commission also required that all DHEW-supported studies using human subjects be reviewed by **institutional review boards**, charged with studying protocols and deciding whether they meet ethical standards (http://www.cdc.gov/tuskegee/after.htm).

(2) **Beneficence**: The term "beneficence" in the Belmont Report is composed of two complementary rules: (1) do not harm persons, and (2) maximize possible benefits and minimize possible harms and risks. To comply with the obligations of beneficence, each investigator is obliged to give careful thought to the reduction of distress and harm that his or her research project may bring to human subjects knowingly or unknowingly, and the maximization of benefits by conducting research and improving the knowledge base in such areas as bio-psycho-social well-being of children and adults and majority and minority group members (http://www.hhs.gov/ohrp/humansubjects/guidance/belmont.html).

(3) **Justice**: The principle of justice in the scientific investigation is concerned primarily with fairness in distribution, in the sense that everyone should receive the benefits of research equally. In reality, it is widely recognized that injustices do occur by denying benefits to which a person is entitled and imposing unjustifiable burdens. The 1979 Belmont Report recommends the following five formulations on which the distribution of benefits and burdens should be based:

   a. To each person an equal share
   b. To each person according to individual need
   c. To each person according to individual effort
   d. To each person according to societal contribution
   e. To each person according to merit (http://www.hhs.gov/ohrp/humansubjects/guidance/belmont.html)

STRATEGIES FOR HUMAN SUBJECT PROTECTIONS

(1) Voluntary Informed Consent

Protections of human subjects in compliance with the 1974 National Research Act and the subsequent Belmont Report can be promoted by implementing the following key strategies: (1) voluntary informed consent, (2) assurance of anonymity and confidentiality, and (3) no harm and distress to participants. These three strategies, among many, are particularly important for researchers who plan to recruit research participants from multicultural communities. The National Institute of Health (NIH) Office of Extramural Research has a free training course on human subjects (http://phrp.nihtraining.com/users/login.php). All you need to do is to register, sign in, read the materials, take the quiz, and get the certificate. If you apply for a federal grant to do research, you are required to take this course and obtain the certificate. The training is interesting and you will be able to get the certificate fairly easy.

It's reasonable to say that all social work research involves human subjects and, thus, requires researchers to carefully consider the safety and well-being on the part of both researchers and research participants. Researchers must provide prospective participants with adequate information concerning possible risks and the potential benefits of their involvement so that they can make informed decisions. It's important for the researchers to educate the participants about risks and benefits, obtain their consent before involving them in the research or evaluation projects, and keep them informed. This is the "informed consent process." Most research institutes, hospitals, and universities have their own institutional review board (IRB) to review and approve all research projects conducted by their employees.

If your research project involves direct data collection form participants or clients, you must have the participants sign an informed consent form before you can collect the data. The main idea of an informed consent form involves a person's understanding and willingness to participate in your study. Prospective participants in your research study must understand the purpose, procedures, potential risks, and benefits of their involvement, along with their alternatives to participation. You and your research team should always give prospective participants adequate time to think about their decision and to discuss it, if necessary, with family, friends, and/or religious advisors.

As cited briefly above, the moral foundation of informed consent involves the rules of autonomy related to respect for persons, beneficence, and justice. These principles are imbedded in the NASW Code of Ethics. The term "autonomy" means that social work researchers must provide the time and opportunity for their prospective research participants to make their own decisions. With respect to the vulnerable populations such as children, the elderly, the mentally ill, or prisoners, social work researchers must take careful consideration of their situation and needs. The principle of beneficence requires social work researchers to protect participants from harm, and to make sure the participants receive all benefits from their involvement in the research project. The principle of justice implies that social work researchers must be fair in every aspect of their research project. For example, you cannot select a participant based on his or her demographic characteristics or background. There must be a fair and right reason to select a participant or to screen out a person from being selected into our study.

You can easily find a template for an informed consent form at your institution if it has an IRB office. Following is a list of the items you must include on your IRB form:

- Name of your institution
- Title of the research project
- Name of the principal investigator (P.I.)
- Other investigators
- Participant's printed name
- The introductory paragraph
- Invite prospective participants to participate
- Provide address and contact information
- Explain the importance of signing the informed consent form to the participate
- Purpose of the research: You are required to explain to the prospective participants why they were asked to participate in the study and the purpose of the research study.
- Procedures: You are required to list the procedures of the study and explain exactly what will happen to the individual should he or her choose to take part in the study.

- Time ruration of the procedures and study: Explain the time commitment required for each prospective participant.
- Discomforts and risks: For some studies, such as a simple social service need-assessment survey, it may suffice to say there are no known risks associated with the research. In an intervention study, however, you must provide information related to possible or known discomforts and risks for participants.
- Possible benefits: Explain both short- and long-term benefits of the project to the participant and others.
- Statement of confidentiality: This section is very important, and you must have it on your informed consent form. You must explain how all confidential information and/or materials will be treated, stored, and maintained and for what lengths of time, as well as how materials will be disposed of at the end of the study period. In addition, you must provide an assurance for privacy and confidentiality for the participants.
- Costs for participation: Be clear if there are costs to the participant that may result from participation in the research. Explain how your institution will cover treatment and compensation for possible injury that could occur during the research or afterward.
- Compensation for participation: If your project offers incentive for participation, you must explain and provide the incentive amount.
- Research funding: Disclose funding sources.
- Voluntary participation: Explain that taking part in this research study is voluntary. You also need to explain that if the participants decide not to participate, or if they decide to stop taking part in the research at a later date, there will be no penalty or loss of benefits to which otherwise entitled.
- Signature of participant
- Signature of legal guardian (if necessary when minors are involved in the study)
- Signature of the person explaining the research

(2) Anonymity and Confidentiality

Some researchers and students use the terms "anonymity" and "confidentiality" interchangeably, but there is a clear difference between these two terminologies. **Anonymity** infers that a researcher does not collect any identifying information from research participants, and that the researcher is unable to link individual responses to participants' identities. If a study is conducted through an interview method, we cannot say this is an anonymous study because the research can in the future identify the person as a source of information. "**Confidentiality**" refers to the maintenance of information collected from research participants by a researcher or a research team. Only the researcher or the research team can identify participants' responses, and the responses from participants are not released to anyone outside the project. When research is conducted with members from multicultural minority communities, an investigator must make every effort to ensure both anonymity and confidentiality, since traditional family-oriented cultures emphasize the importance of "saving face" and family integrity. If there is a concern personal information might be released to outsiders, the researcher may have a hard time recruiting research participants, aside from facing the problem of violating the code of ethics.

(3) No Harm or Distress

Members of minority communities are susceptible to psychological distress or harm when sensitive questions, such as immigration status, income, illegal drug use, or history of misconduct (i.e., sexual abuse and battery against spouse), are asked in multicultural research projects. Some, especially potential participants with undocumented immigration status, may become anxious about being exposed to deportation and, thus, unfair treatment by the government. Although the risk of physical harm and distress in social science research is relatively lower compared with the risk imposed by biomedical research projects, participants in social research are exposed to a variety of serious harm and danger, as cited above. Researchers in human services must take extra precautions to shield research participants from any potential harm or distress, especially in conducting multicultural research projects.

SUMMARY

This chapter addressed a very important aspect of social work research. Social work researchers must always consider the well-being and dignity of their research participants or respondents. There should be no compromise in efforts to protect our participants' confidentiality, safety, autonomy, and dignity. If a social work researcher conducts a need assessment or a program evaluation at an agency with no clear policy for human subject protection, the researcher should take the extra effort to consult with peers and researchers at institutions that have well-established IRB processes.

CLASS EXERCISE

Visit *The National Institute of Health (NIH) Office of Extramural Research* (http://phrp.nihtraining.com/users/login.php), register, log in, and take its online training on human subject protection. Print a copy of the training certificate to your instructor.

REFERENCES

Heller, J. (1972). Syphilis victims in the U.S. study went untreated for 40 years, *New York Times*, 1, 8.

Historical Collections at the Claude Moore Health Sciences Library. "Bad Blood the Tuskegee Syphilis Study: Final Report of the Tuskegee Syphilis Study Legacy Committee." University of Virginia, Historical Collections at the Claude Moore Health Sciences Library. Retrieved November 11, 2013 from http://exhibits.hsl.virginia.edu/badblood/report

Resnik, D. (2011). What is ethics in research & why is it important? National Institute of Health Environmental Sciences. From http://www.niehs.nih.gov/research/resources/bioethics/whatis/.

Shamoo, A., & Resnik D. (2009). *Responsible conduct of research* (2nd ed.). New York: Oxford University Press.

THREE

Formulation of Research Problem, Research Questions, and Literature Review

This chapter focuses on four important tasks that must be completed in the initial stage of a research project. Those tasks: (1) how to select and formulate a research problem; (2) how to develop well-defined research questions; (3) how to refine specific aims for various research projects including evaluation research, and how to operationalize the specific aims into measureable hypotheses or research objectives; and (4) how to retrieve a body of literature or published information on the selected topic area. We will use current research literature and government documents to provide concrete examples to aid students' learning and skills in developing specific aims, hypotheses, and/or objectives. In addition, this chapter will emphasize the involvement of clients, community leaders, and relevant stakeholders in the process of identifying and defining research questions that are relevant to community needs.

RESEARCH PROBLEM FORMULATION

The very first task in any research is to select a topic of interest to the researcher. A selection of research topics is often influenced by the researcher's own personal interests. For example, a researcher with a Hispanic cultural background might be interested in investigating a difference in mental-health service utilization patterns between US-born Latino Americans and foreign-born Latino immigrants. Every society in the world faces social problems not yet well addressed, such as ethnic disparities in poverty, unemployment, underemployment, domestic violence, child maltreatment, drug abuse, crime, juvenile delinquency, teen pregnancy, mental disorders, to cite but a few. If we look around prudently, researchers and students can grasp research topic areas without excessive difficulty.

There are two general selection criteria on which all research should be based. First, a topic should be selected when a researcher is convinced that his or her research project can fill the existing knowledge gap by exploring the problem area (in many cases under-researched) and rigorously describing the topic area, explaining what factors contributed to the problem selected for investigation. In other words, a selection should be justified in a way that researching the chosen topic will contribute to the expansion of scientific knowledge so that findings can be readily applied to solving the particular social problem. Second, a researcher should be cautious in determining whether the chosen topic lies within the scope of scientific investigation, whether the researcher can recruit participants relatively easily, whether valid and reliable research instruments (i.e., survey questionnaire) are available, and whether the project can be completed within the limited time frame and funding. All of these feasibility issues should be considered carefully before a research topic is finally selected for investigation.

DEVELOPMENT OF APPROPRIATE RESEARCH QUESTIONS

A **research question** is a statement expressed in a question format that illustrates what will be investigated in the research project, and guides the researcher in the process of scientific inquiries. Haynes (2006) suggests that clinical research questions often arise out of a "perceived knowledge deficit within a subject area or field of study." It's important to know the gap in the current knowledge about what we hope to investigate or intervene. Social workers' in-depth knowledge about a subject can generate a number of meaningful questions. If research is the process of acquiring knowledge, we can state that all social work research projects begin with research questions. Asking a research question is a cognitive process encompassing acquiring knowledge from previous research, observations of current issues, or responding to clients' and community needs.

Sources of Research Questions

Your research questions can come from different sources. As a clinical social worker, your question can arise from your own clinical experience, or your daily encounter with clients. As a community organizer or policy advocate, your involvements with community leaders, organizations, and government institutions could lead you to raise important research questions. Your research questions can also arise from your own academic training or what you learn through professional workshops, conferences, and from the literature.

As social work researchers attempt to find answers for the problems or crises of clients and communities, we should always involve the client and community into our research and evaluation project. Most social work research is applied research. What we investigate will have influences on the lives of our clients and community, and therefore both must become involved from the inception of our research.

Criteria for Good Research Questions

Asking wrong questions or unnecessary questions can lead social workers to erroneous answers and misleading solutions. Asking good, meaningful questions is important for the process of acquiring correct and meaningful knowledge. The following criteria will help you develop proper research questions.

Preparation for Research Questions

There are a few steps you should prepare before stating your research questions:

1. Conduct a systematic literature review to give you a broad understanding what has been done in the past, and to understand the gap in the existing knowledge about your topic or your concern.

2. Seek information from clients and service providers to learn more about the topic you hope to investigate.
3. Seek careful advice from experts, colleagues, and collaborators to identify what needs to be done in the area of your interest.

Evaluation of Your Research Questions

Once you write down your research questions, you need to revise, refine, and make sure they are the correct and feasible questions to investigate. How can you determine whether your question is worth asking? There are a few criteria you can use to assess your research questions before you move to the next step of your research project:

4. Is your research question answerable?
5. Is it feasible to finding the answers?
6. Is it clinically relevant?
7. Is it a new question?
8. Is it culturally sensitive and relevant to your clients or community?
9. Is it approved by your agency or your peer?

RESEARCH AIMS AND HYPOTHESES

Once your research question is approved by your agency and the prospective clients or community, you need to translate your questions into specific aims, which should include your research goals and expected outcomes and effect. Your research goals and outcomes must be as concise and realistic as possible.

Once your aims are formulated, you need to translate them into hypotheses. Good hypotheses include measureable variables. In an intervention evaluation research, you need to state your independent variable and your dependent variable or outcome variable. Your hypotheses will determine what statistical approaches you need to test them or to determine the success or failure of your intervention.

We are fortunate to have a valid example of research aims and hypotheses from a successful researcher, Dr. Uyen-Sa Nguyen, an epidemiologist at the University of Massachusetts Medical School. She allows us to use the research aims and hypotheses of her research project, funded by the American College of Rheumatology and conducted as a post–doctoral fellow at Hebrew Senior Life Research Institute, affiliated with Harvard University.

We present three versions of her research aims and hypotheses to illustrate the process of developing, revising, and finalizing research aims and hypotheses. The format she used to present her specific aim is the standard format use for National Institute of Health (NIH) grant applications.

Version 1: Initial Version

Background

Falls increase with increasing age and can be detrimental to older adults. It is unclear how foot pain affects falls. We propose to examine the influence of foot pain on risk of falls and to evaluate how balance affects this association, using data from a prospective cohort of elderly men and women.

Purpose

The goal of this research is to examine the relation between foot pain and subsequent falls over the follow-up. Specifically, the three specific aims of this study were to examine the longitudinal relations between 1) foot pain and risk for falls, 2) whether change in overall foot pain over time may affect falls risk, and 3) how balance affects the relation between the site of foot pain and falls. We hypothesize that compared with older adults without foot pain, those with foot pain will have more falls over the follow-up, and further that this relation may be affected by change in foot pain over time and poor balance. The strength of this proposal is the wealth of information regarding foot pain, balance, and falls. If foot pain does increase risk for falls and is affected by impaired balance, there is potential for immense public health interventions.

A. Specific Aims

Specific Aim 1

To determine whether the presence of foot pain, regardless of the site of the pain, increases risk of falls over the two-year follow-up. Further, we will assess the possible effect of knee osteoarthritis on the relation between foot pain and falls, controlling for confounding by other risk factors for falls such as comorbidities, gender, age, and body mass index upon this association.

> **Hypothesis 1a:** The presence of any foot pain will be related to the risk of falls over the two-year follow-up, and whether knee osteoarthritis modifies the relation between foot pain and risk of falls.
>
> **Hypothesis 1b:** To determine whether forefoot pain will be related to the risk of falls over the two-year follow-up, and whether knee osteoarthritis modifies the relation between foot pain and risk of falls.
>
> **Hypothesis 1c:** To determine whether hind-foot pain will be related to the risk of falls over the two-year follow-up, and whether knee osteoarthritis modifies the relation between foot pain and risk of falls.

Specific Aim 2

To determine whether impaired balance (defined by static balance measures derived using a balance platform as well as clinical performance tests of balance) affects the relation between foot pain and falls in elderly men and women. Again, foot pain will be evaluated as defined in Specific Aim 1.

> **Hypothesis 2a:** Poor balance modifies the association between overall foot pain and risk of falls over the two-year follow-up.
>
> **Hypothesis 2b:** Poor balance modifies the association between forefoot pain and risk of falls over the two-year follow-up.
>
> **Hypothesis 2c:** Poor balance modifies the association between hind-pain and risk of falls over the two-year follow-up.

Specific Aim 3

To determine whether change in foot pain status at the eighteen-month follow-up will affect risk of falls over two years, and whether change in foot pain status affects change in balance sway.

Hypothesis 3a: There is a possible gradient effect in increased falls risk for those who: 1) remained without foot pain at the eighteen-month follow-up; 2) those no longer with foot pain after eighteen months; 3) those who acquired foot pain after eighteen months; and 4) those still with foot pain at the eighteen-month follow-up.

Hypothesis 3b: Those in groups 1 and 4 from Hypothesis 3a will have no change in balance sway, those with new foot pain will have increase in sway, and those no longer with foot pain will have decreased sway.

Hypothesis 3c: The gradient effect in increased falls risk according to change in foot pain status will remain even after accounting for changes in balance sway.

Version 2: Revised Version

The above version was revised after she received comments from her mentors and colleagues:

Specific Aims

The purpose of the proposed study is threefold: 1) to determine the relation between foot pain and risk for falls, and whether impaired balance mediates this relation; 2) to examine whether knee osteoarthritis (OA) further compounds the relation between foot pain and risk for falls; and 3) to determine whether a change in foot pain status over eighteen months affects the risk of subsequent falls in a cohort of community-dwelling older adults.

Specific Aim 1

To ascertain whether the presence of foot pain at baseline increases risk of falls over the two-year follow-up, and whether poor balance mediates this relation.

Hypothesis 1: Foot pain increases the risk of falls over the two-year follow-up after accounting for potential confounding variables, and this relation is mediated in part by poor balance.

Specific Aim 2

To compare the relation of foot pain and risk of falls in clinical subsets of those with and without knee osteoarthritis to determine whether the presence of knee osteoarthritis further compounds the association between foot pain and falls.

Hypothesis 2: The increased risk of falls over the two-year follow-up due to foot pain at baseline is stronger among those with knee osteoarthritis.

Specific Aim 3

To determine whether change in foot pain status at the eighteen-month follow-up will affect risk of subsequent falls (Figure 2) after the follow-up, and whether change in foot pain status affects change in balance sway.

Hypothesis 3a: There is a possible gradient effect in increased falls risk for those who: 1) remained without foot pain at the eighteen-month follow-up; 2) those no longer with foot pain after eighteen months; 3) those who acquired foot pain after eighteen months; and 4) those still with foot pain at the eighteen-month follow-up.

Hypothesis 3b: Those in groups 1 and 4 from Hypothesis 2a will have no change in balance, those with new foot pain will have poorer balance, and those no longer with foot pain will have improved balance.

Hypothesis 3c: The gradient effect in increased falls risk according to change in foot pain status will remain even after accounting for changes in balance sway.

Version 3: Final Version

A. Specific Aims and Hypotheses

Little research has been done to examine clinically assessed knee osteoarthritis (OA) and risk of falls, and no studies have been published regarding the relation between knee OA and falls occurring indoors or outdoors. Moreover, no one has investigated the association between knee OA and risk of falls in the presence of important factors (possible mediators), such as foot pain, physical activity, and poor mobility performance (balance, gait speed, chair stand). Using data from the MOBILIZE Boston prospective cohort of older men and women, we propose to examine the relation between knee OA and risk of indoor and outdoor falls, and whether the relation may be mediated in part by foot pain, physical activity, and poor mobility performance. The knowledge to be gained, especially with the consideration of the possible mediating effects of knee OA and risk of indoor and outdoor falls, may influence falls prevention in older populations with knee OA and more targeted prevention programs for indoor and outdoor environments. The specific aims are:

Specific Aim 1

To determine the association between baseline knee OA and the risk of falls occurring <u>indoors</u> and falls occurring outdoors over a two-year follow-up.

Hypothesis 1a: Knee OA is associated with increased risk of indoor falls over a two-year follow-up in older men and women, adjusting for potential confounders.

Hypothesis 1b: Knee OA is associated with deceased risk of <u>outdoor</u> falls over a two-year follow-up in older men and women, adjusting for potential confounders.

Specific Aim 2

To investigate the possible mediating effect of foot pain, physical activity, and poor mobility performance on the association between knee OA and risk of both indoor and outdoor falls.

Hypothesis 2a: Foot pain will act as a mediating variable affecting the relation between knee OA and <u>indoor</u> falls, controlling for major confounders.

Hypothesis 2b: Physical activity will act as a mediating variable affecting the relation between knee OA and <u>indoor</u> falls, controlling for major confounders.

Hypothesis 2c: Poor mobility performance will act as a mediating variable affecting the relation between knee OA and <u>indoor</u> falls, controlling for major confounders.

Hypothesis 2d: None of the possible mediators will affect the relation between knee OA and <u>outdoor</u> falls.

Note that in version 1 and version 2, the principal investigator (P.I.) had three specific aims. In her final version, there are two specific aims. Let's examine her hypotheses detailed in specific aim 2 in the

Figure 3.1: Model of Knee Osteoarthritis and Falls with Hypothesized Intervening Variables

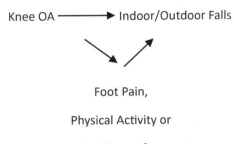

final version. In hypothesis 2a, the independent variable is knee pain or knee osteoarthritis (OA). This variable can be measured either by a dichotomous variable such as "1" for having knee OA and "0" for none. Alternatively, knee pain can be measured by the degree of knee pain using a discrete measure such as "1" for no pain, "2" for somewhat painful, "3" for fairly painful, and "4" for very painful. The dependent variable is indoor falls. The dependent variable could be measured by a dichotomous variable "1" for yes and "0" for no. The dependent variable can also be measured by the actual number of falls. As reviewed previously, the **mediating variables** (mediators) are those thought to intervene in the relationship between the independent and the dependent variables. Thus, the mediating variable is defined as a third variable that "represents the generative mechanism through which the focal independent variable is able to influence the dependent variable of interest" (Baron and Kenny 1986). In a simple causal model, the independent variable is considered to cause the mediator, and then the mediator causes the dependent variable (Wu and Zumbo 2008). In this case we can restate the hypothesis that individuals with knee OA are more likely to experience an indoor fall. At the same time, their knee pain could increase the likelihood of foot pain, and having foot pain could lead to indoor falls. It is hypothesized that "foot pain" is the mediator that was caused by knee OA, and then "foot pain" causes indoor and outdoor falls.

The nature of your hypothesis and the measurement of your independent, dependent, and control variables determine what research design you should use to collect the data and what statistical methods you can use to test your hypothesis. It's more likely you will need multivariable hypotheses rather than a simple hypothesis with only two variables. The reason is that you want to rule out possible confounding or extraneous factors that could confuse the direct association between your independent and dependent variables. For example, when you evaluate the outcome of a social service program, you want to make sure the causal relationship between the services and expected outcomes are not confounded (interfered) by factors such as age, sex, education, and income of the recipients. You need to control for these possible confounding factors by carefully selecting research participants who share similar characteristics or by including these variables in your statistical analysis.

In program evaluation, your hypothesis generally involves the effectiveness of the intervention. Your independent variable includes group membership, which determines receiving intervention or not receiving intervention. Your dependent variable is the expected outcome of the intervention. Your control variables are clients' demographic background, such as age, gender, education, income, ethnicity, and marital status as well as other relevant characteristics, such as availability of social support and intensity of psychological distress.

PROCESS OF LITERATURE REVIEW

A literature review is an integral part in furthering knowledge in the research world. Then, what is a literature review and what specific details are involved in this task of a research project? A **literature review** is a collection of published information pertaining to the chosen subject area. A careful review of a body of literature is very helpful in many aspects, including:

- A literature review is essential in identifying what has been found in the subject area, and whether there are gaps in knowledge that would justify why this particular research is important.

- A review process guides a researcher to integrate existing findings that often conflict with one another. For example, some findings indicate that depression is significantly less prevalent among acculturated US-born Americans compared with those who recently immigrated to the United States. Other findings, however, show that new immigrants are experiencing mental-health problems far less frequently because only emotionally stable individuals are more likely to come to America. In this event, a literature review can help a researcher develop accurate research questions that reflect many views of existing findings.

- A thorough literature review will guide a researcher to identify any agreement or consensus on the subject. For example, there is a general consensus that immigrants who brought their traditional values and customs consider corporal punishment as a child discipline, not as an act of child abuse. A researcher who is interested in multicultural child welfare research can develop cutting-edge research questions from this finding, such as "How do immigrant families who are reported to child protective services (CPS) agencies react to CPS workers, and what are their coping mechanisms when child abuse cases are substantiated?"

- Deductive quantitative research begins with an identification of the theoretical framework, from which research questions and testable hypotheses are derived. By reviewing a variety of literature sources, a researcher can identify a generally agreed upon theoretical perspective consisting of a series of well-measured variables. A theoretical framework not only provides an explanation about relationships between variables, but also guides a researcher to identify crucial variables and develop hypotheses to test his or her research.

Steps of Conducting a Literature Review

- **Identification of Literature Sources**: To formulate accurate research questions and hypotheses, it is necessary to review a wide range of known sources of information. Multilateral sources of literature review include scholarly journals, scholarly books, government databases (i.e., United States Bureau of Census documents), newspapers, magazines, films, audio/video tapes, and other authoritative databases (i.e., annual statistical information of human service organizations). Online scholarly databases are widely available at most university libraries. Before a literature search is initiated, a researcher should identify **key words** extracted from his or her research subject. For example, if the topic of a project is "Relationships between Family Type and Homelessness among African American Adolescents," four key words can be identified—family type, homeless, youth, and African Americans. There are many expansive scholarly databases that contain millions of abstracts, indexes, and full-text peer-reviewed journal articles in PDF form. And most libraries keep an enormously large collection of full-text electronic books. One of the largest databases in behavioral science and mental health is PsycINFO, which is managed by the American Psychological Association providing abstracts of peer-reviewed scholarly journal articles, books, book chapters, and dissertations. Social Work Abstracts, produced by the National Association of Social Workers (NASW), offers coverage of more than eight hundred fifty social work and human services journals. To retrieve scholarly articles and books online, you need to log onto your library databases remotely using your e-mail account user name and password.

- **Selecting, Organizing, and Reviewing Articles and Other Sources**: Once you identify abstracts and full-text articles available online, you need to organize them either by saving them on your removable USB (universal serial bus) flash drive or printing them. It is convenient to save retrieved data onto a flash drive. Storage capacities of flash drives are as large as 2 TB, and thousands of written information can be stored in a small portable device. If full-text articles are not available online, you can request the item through interlibrary loan, which is usually a part of library services. As shown in Table 3.1, if you decide to save only abstracts, you need to copy and paste the following information onto a file (such as Microsoft Word): title of the article, author(s), publication source, key words, and abstract.

Table 3.1: Example of Organizing Abstracts Retrieved from EBSCOHOST Online Database

Abstract #1

Title:
The relationship between Latino adolescents' perceptions of discrimination, neighborhood risk, and parenting on self-esteem and depressive symptoms.

Authors:
  (1) Behnke, Andrew O.
  (2) Plunkett, Scott W.
  (3) Sands, Tovah
  (4) Bámaca-Colbert, Mayra Y.

Source: Journal of Cross-Cultural Psychology, Vol 42(7), Oct, 2011. pp. 1179–1197.

Key Words:
Discrimination; Neighborhood Risk; Parenting; Self Esteem; Depressive Symptoms

Abstract:
Guided by Bronfenbrenner's bioecological framework, this study examined the roles of Latino adolescents' reports of discrimination, neighborhood risk, parent-child conflict over culture, and parental support in relation to their self-esteem and depression. Analysis of self-report data from 383 ninth grade, Latino students from one Los Angeles high school was used to validate a Multigroup Structural Equation Model of self-esteem and depressive symptoms for boys and girls. As expected, self-esteem was negatively and significantly related to depressive symptoms, yet the influence of other factors were less clear. Five paths marked the influence of mothers' and fathers' interactions on youths' outcomes, demonstrating a strong path from fathers' support to adolescent self-esteem and differing paths from cultural conflict with mother and father to youth outcomes. Neighborhood risks were significantly related to boys' and girls' self-esteem and depressive symptoms, especially for boys. Societal discrimination was significantly related to youths' reports of depressive symptoms yet not significantly related to self-esteem. Results are discussed in terms of applications for both practice and future research.

It is necessary to group together retrieved information and organize the findings into a table using a word processing software program (i.e., Microsoft Word, McIntosh, etc.). A table containing key findings of each article guides researchers in identifying consistencies and inconsistencies of main findings, general patterns portrayed in the subject area, and key concepts and variables emphasized among researchers that could be used to construct a conceptual framework for a proposed study. Table 3.2 guides you in organizing retrieved articles in a table.

Table 3.2: Overview of Literature Review on "Perception of Discrimination, Self-esteem and Depression among Minority American Adolescents"

AUTHOR	DATE	METHODS	RESULTS
Repress, et al.	2013	Used data from the Longitudinal Study for Adolescent Health (Add Health), Wave II, Public Use Data, and the Social Determinants of Adolescent Risk Behaviors (SDOARB) framework	The study found that GPA was a significant predictor of depressive symptoms across all three racial groups (black, white, and other minority). Teacher discrimination predicted depressive symptoms among white and other minority adolescents, but not black adolescents.
Tobler, et al.	2013	Regression analysis to examine associations between racial/ethnic discrimination and behavioral health outcomes (alcohol use, marijuana use, physical aggression, delinquency, victimization, depression, suicidal ideation, and sexual behaviors).	Adolescents who experienced any racial/ethnic discrimination were at increased risk for victimization and depression. Regardless of intensity, adolescents who experienced racial/ethnic discrimination at least occasionally were more likely to report greater physical aggression, delinquency, and suicidal ideation.
Behnke, et al.	2011	Used multigroup structural equation model of self-esteem and depressive symptoms.	Self-esteem was negatively and significantly related to depressive symptoms, yet the influence of other factors were less clear. Five paths marked the influence of mothers' and fathers' interactions on youths' outcomes, demonstrating a strong path from fathers' support to adolescent self-esteem and differing paths from cultural conflict with mother and father to youth outcomes.
Mitchell, et al.	2010	The study tests a conceptual model of the effects of community and contextual violence exposure on the mental health and parenting of young, African American mothers living in Washington, DC. A path analysis was used.	There were significant direct effects of witnessed and experienced violence on mothers' depressive symptoms and general aggression. Experiences of discrimination were also associated with increased depressive symptoms. Moreover, there were significant indirect effects of mothers' violence exposure on disciplinary practices through depression and aggression.
Borsato, G. N.	2008	Students were asked to complete an anonymous questionnaire assessing whether they had ever experienced stressful events that they interpreted as connected to their race or ethnicity.	The results obtained in this study also suggest that peer discrimination contributes to explain the difference in depression symptomatology found between whites and Latinos and between whites and Asian Americans. The results also lend support to a mediating role of adult discrimination relative to the academic achievement gap between whites and Latinos.
Chatman, J. D.	2007	The study investigated 172 tenth-grade adolescent boys and girls from an inner-city public senior high school in the Greater Los Angeles metropolitan area.	The results indicate a negative relationship between their environmental stress level and functioning. As stressors increased their functioning decreased, in particular in response to direct community violence, family stress, and peer discrimination.

SUMMARY

In this chapter we cited the importance of selecting a research topic that is feasible for investigation, formulating a clearly defined research problem, and developing appropriate and meaningful research questions. We also examined how you can formulate your research questions into specific aims and hypotheses. Good hypotheses may give the researcher clear guidance for selecting appropriate research designs and statistical tools for data analysis. Finally, we illustrated how to retrieve and organize a body of literature on a selected topic area.

CLASS EXERCISE

Select a social problem related to social work in a diverse community. Develop a research question and write two or more specific aims and hypotheses. Explain the importance of formulating research questions and the possible implications of the results generated from the specific aims and hypotheses.

REFERENCES

Baron, R. M., & Kenny, D. A. (1986). The moderator – mediator variable distinction in social psychological research: Conceptual, strategic, and statistical considerations. *Journal of Personality and Social Psychology, 51*(6), 1173-1182.

Behnke, A. O., Plunkett, S. W., Sands, T., & Bámaca-Colbert, M. Y. (2011). The relationship between Latino adolescents' perceptions of discrimination, neighborhood risk, and parenting on self-esteem and depressive symptoms." *Journal of Cross-Cultural Psychology, 42* (7), 1179-1197. doi:10.1177/0022022110383424

Borsato, G. (2008). Perceived discrimination, racial/ethnic identity, and adjustment among Asian American and Latino early adolescents. *Dissertation Abstracts International,* 69.

Chatman, J. (2007). Risk and resiliency among inner city minority adolescents: A study of coping and ethnic identity. *Dissertation Abstracts International,* 68.

Haynes, B. R. (2006). Forming research questions. *Journal of Clinical Epidemiology, 259,*881–886.

Mitchell, S. J., Lewin, A., Horn, I. B., Valentine, D., Sanders-Phillips, K., & Joseph, J. G. (2010). How does violence exposure affect the psychological health and parenting of young African-American mothers?. *Social Science & Medicine, 70*(4), 526-533. doi:10.1016/j.socscimed.2009.10.048

Respress, B. N., Morris, D. L., Gary, F. A., Lewin, L. C., & Francis, S. A. (2013). Social determinants of adolescent depression: An examination of racial differences. *Issues in Mental Health Nursing, 34*(7), 539-549. doi:10.3109/0 1612840.2012.758206

Tobler, A. L., Maldonado-Molina, M. M., Staras, S. S., O'Mara, R. J., Livingston, M. D., & Komro, K. A. (2013). Perceived racial/ethnic discrimination, problem behaviors, and mental health among minority urban youth. *Ethnicity & Health, 18*(4), 337-349. doi:10.1080/13557858.2012.730609

Wu, A. D., & Zumbo, B. D. (2008). Understanding and using mediators and moderators. *Social Indicator Research, 87*(3), 367-392. DOI 10.1007/s11205-007-9143-1

FOUR

Translation of Evidence-Based Practice Knowledge to Social Work Intervention

This chapter focuses on how social workers can translate the existing research knowledge into their practice with clients and communities. Students will learn how to conduct a systematic literature review for evidence-based practice (EBP) and select the appropriate intervention/treatment for multicultural and multiracial/ethnic communities.

What is evidence-based practice? Sackett (2002) posted the definition of EBP on the website of Duke University Medical Center as follows: "*EBP is the integration of clinical expertise, patient values, and the best research evidence into the decision making process for patient care. Clinical expertise refers to the clinician's cumulated experience, education and clinical skills. The patient brings to the encounter his or her own personal preferences and unique concerns, expectations, and values. The best research evidence is usually found in clinically relevant research that has been conducted using sound methodology*" (http://guides.mclibrary.duke.edu/content.php?pid=431451&sid=3529491). As Sackett's definition suggests, we can state the goal of social work EBP is to provide high-quality services reflecting the interests, values, needs, and choices of the clients we serve.

Social workers employ a variety of therapeutic intervention or treatment models in their practice. This is the process of translating results from previous empirical research into practice. Using the right intervention or treatment model is crucially important in social work practice. The question is how social workers know which one is the right intervention model to use. In recent decades, there has been a wealth of information on evidence-based practice. You can easily search for well-developed websites that provide useful guidance for EBP. At the end of this chapter, we will provide you with some important links that have been posted on well-established EBP educational sites.

Evidence-based social work practice is based on social workers' practice experiences, peer expertise, sound research findings, and clients' personal choices. Clients' choice of intervention could be influenced by their own experiences, knowledge, or peer advice. Evidence-based social work practice also means the ability of social workers to evaluate their own practice and reevaluate previous clinically proven intervention or treatment strategies. An example of EBPs is found in the practice goal adopted by the Family and Youth Services Bureau (FYSB), which is a runaway and homeless youth program. Its website states:

"FYSB has worked to create a framework that takes the best of what programs are doing individually to help all programs be successful. Based on the years of work by runaway and homeless youth providers and the best emerging evidence about what runaway and homeless youth need to succeed, FYSB believes the most critical outcomes for runaway and homeless youth are: safety, well-being, permanent connections, and self-sufficiency" (http://www.acf.hhs.gov/sites/default/files/fysb/evidencebasedpractice20120829.pdf).

SELECTING THE RIGHT INTERVENTION OR TREATMENT

The process of intervention or treatment selection includes the following evaluation steps:

1. Evaluate the purpose of the intervention: For what social or psychological problems was the intervention designed to address? This is to determine whether the selected intervention has the same or similar purpose with your prospective intervention. You can use peer consultation or expert opinion to make the decision. Your client can provide good information for the selection of a proper intervention. For a large-scale intervention, such as social intervention, focus group meetings are recommended.

2. Evaluate the client population: For whom was the intervention implemented? Knowing the characteristics of the targeted intervention population will help you in making comparisons with the characteristics of your clients. It's obvious the validity of the selected intervention could be challenged if the intervention was used for a population different from your population.

3. Evaluate the effectiveness of the intervention: This is achieved through a review process of the clinical and scientific evidence on the effectiveness of the selected intervention. You need to determine whether the intervention satisfies both clinical and statistical standards. Clinical evidence can be found in an agency's client records, from peer experiences and observations, and through your own practice experiences. Statistical evidence can be found in previous literature. You will need to know the research design used in previous research, and the size of the effect found in such research.

4. Evaluate the feasibility of the selected intervention: Both you and your agency need to determine whether you have the time and resources to implement the intervention.

5. Evaluate the cultural appropriateness of the intervention. This is an important decision to make, especially when you serve a particular racial, ethnic, or non-English–speaking client population. You can use professionals' expertise or focus group interviews with the prospective clients to determine the cultural appropriateness of the selected intervention.

SYSTEMATIC LITERATURE REVIEW OF PREVIOUS RESEARCH

When you review the literature to identify an appropriate intervention for your practice, there are four criteria that could help you determine both the interval validity (i.e., whether the intervention strategy actually produced a change in clients' psychological well-being) and external validity (i.e., whether findings can be generalized to a larger population) of the intervention.

1. The selection of the clients or participants: How did the study recruit and select clients or participants for the study? What are the characteristics of the selected sample?

2. The validity of the research design: Did the study use randomization to assign clients into intervention or control groups?

3. The reliability and validity of the outcome measure: Did the study use reliable and valid outcome measures to assess the effectiveness of the intervention?

4. The effect size of the intervention: How large was the effect of the intervention? This could be measured by the mean difference between the intervention and the control group. Was the difference statistically and clinically significant?

STRENGTHS AND WEAKNESS OF RESEARCH DESIGNS

In reviewing the research literature concerning health and mental health intervention strategies, you will very likely encounter the following research designs used in health services and epidemiological research. Many of these research designs are beyond the scope of this book. We briefly address these designs to help readers become familiar with the research terms that arise often in the literature of health services and epidemiological research.

Case series and case reports refer to results compiled from clients' records (from a group of clients or just a single client). Results from these reports are often not credible due to the lack of comparison and randomization.

Case control studies refer to studies that compare outcomes between clients who already have a specific condition with people who do not have the condition. The researchers can only identify the correlation between risk factors or protective factor and the outcome, not the causal relationship.

Cohort studies refer to studies on clients who are already participating in an intervention or have an exposure (i.e., clinical depression). Researchers follow them forward over time, and then compare their outcomes with a similar group that has not been affected by the treatment or exposure being studied. Results from cohort studies are not reliable since the outcome could be mediated by other variables rather than the intervention itself.

Randomized experimental designs, also called true experimental designs, refer to studies that randomly assign clients who suffer from the same health or mental-health condition into the treatment or the control group. The pretest and posttest design with an experimental group and a control group represents the strongest design. This design is also called "randomized clinical trial design."

Quasi experimental designs, also called "field experiments," refer to studies that compare the outcome of the experimental group with that of the control group, especially when experiments take place in community or practice settings. Quasi experimental studies are reasonable alternatives to true experimental studies, because it is extremely difficult to make the experiment and control groups equivalent by randomly assigning subjects to these two groups. Although the two groups have the same pretest condition, due to the lack of randomization, the results are not as reliable and valid as those from the randomized experimental studies.

Systematic reviews refer to published research that is based solely on the summary of the previous research. The quality of the summary often depends on the quality of the studies selected for the review. You should evaluate the selection criteria that authors used in choosing the previously published studies for their systematic review.

A **meta-analysis** refers to a subset of "systematic reviews" that combine qualitative or quantitative statistical data selected from several previous studies to summarize their results and present a statistically more powerful conclusion. Findings from a meta-analysis are stronger than those of the systematic reviews of the literature, but the reliability and validity of the results are also dependent on the reliability and validity of the selected studies.

Cross-sectional studies refer to the studies that collect data at one point in time. These studies can only identify the association or correlation between intervention and outcome. The results provide no information on the causal effect between the intervention and the outcome.

Qualitative studies can shed light on the subjective dimension of the effects of the intervention on the possible outcome. Nevertheless, the results are neither reliable nor generalizable.

Following is the list of EBP resources:

- http://nrepp.samhsa.gov/Index.aspx. The Substance Abuse and Mental Health Services Administration's (SAMHSA) National Registry of Evidence-based Programs and Practices (NREPP). This is a searchable online registry of several hundred interventions supporting mental-health promotion, substance-abuse prevention, and mental-health and substance-abuse treatment.
- http://www.samhsa.gov/ebpwebguide/index.asp. SAMHSA's Guide to Evidence-Based Practices (EBP) on the web. This guide provides a list of websites with information about specific EBPs or reviews of research findings.
- Relation to evidence-based programs and practices (no website). Their website contains the most current review of the literature on implementing evidence-based practices.The Technical Assistance Partnership for Child and Family Mental Health: More information about evidence-based practices and practice-based evidence.
- Choosing the Right Treatment- What Families Need to Know about Evidence-Based Practices (for children): This guide was designed by the National Alliance on Mental Illness (NAMI) to inform families on evidence-based practice (EBPs) in children's mental health and to share information on an array of treatment and support options.

SUMMARY

This chapter addressed the process of translating existing research results into social work practice. Evidence-based social work practice requires social workers to select interventions or services that have proven effective. Moreover, social workers must ascertain the cross-cultural reliability and validity of the selected intervention or services before implementing them in a diverse community.

CLASS EXERCISE

Select a therapeutic treatment that you have learned or been exposed to and discuss its cross-cultural reliability, validity, and cultural appropriateness for a special client population that you have worked with or have knowledge of.

REFERENCES

Family & Youth Services Bureau (2014). *What is evidence-based practice?* Retrieved from http://www.acf.hhs.gov/sites/default/files/fysb/evidencebasedpractice20120829.pdf

Sackett, D. L., Strauss, S. E., Richardson, W. S., Rosenberg, W., & Haynes, R. B. (2000). *Evidence-based medicine: How to practice and teach evidence-based medicine* (2nd ed.). Edinburgh (UK): Churchill Livingstone.

FIVE

Measurement in Multicultural Research

This chapter addresses basic concepts and issues in measurement, including the four levels of measurement in addition to instrument development and the validity and reliability of multicultural research instruments. We will explain the process of questionnaire development and questionnaire translation for multicultural and multi-linguistic research. Examples from previous research and real data will be presented to illustrate the definition of validity and reliability. Students will be introduced to common statistical approaches for assessing internal consistency (alpha coefficient) and factorial structure (exploratory and confirmatory factor analysis). The chapter will explain and illustrate possible biases of using research/evaluation measures that have poor multicultural validity and reliability.

LEVELS OF MEASUREMENT

In conducting research, it is critical to formulate the types of methodology that will answer research questions formulated by a researcher at the initial stage of the study. For example, if a researcher is interested in examining the influence of child maltreatment on self-esteem among minor victims in the immigrant Vietnamese community, one of the main research questions includes "Will child abuse perpetrated by care takers negatively influence children's self-esteem?" To answer this question in examining the research problem, the researcher needs to measure the variable "self-esteem." Many students might then ask what "measuring the variable" means. Bollen (1989) specifically defines measurement as "the process by which a concept is linked to one or more latent variables, and these are linked to observed variables" (p. 180). In a research study, the term **measures** are generally question items (i.e., survey inquiries in a questionnaire and interview questions) designed to examine research questions that consist of variables. Research participants are to respond to these measures when they are finalized. Thus, **measurement** is the process of observing and recording research participants' behaviors (i.e., attention span, discrimination, substance abuse, violent acts), attitudes (i.e., agreeing or disagreeing on abortion, same-sex marriage, affirmative action), and demographic characteristics (sex, age, ethnicity, education, income, occupation, religion). There are four main levels of measurement—**nominal, ordinal, interval,** and **ratio**—in measuring variables.

Nominal Level of Measurement

The nominal level of measurement is a way to measure categorical variables or nominal variables in which observations are classified into several answer categories or attributes. Researchers generally assign values to each of the attributes just for a labeling purpose. For example, ethnicity can be measured with the nominal measure by classifying respondents to one of the following categories: (1) African American; (2) Asian American; (3) Hispanic American; (4) Native American; (5) Non-Hispanic White; and (6) Other. Other variables, such as gender, religious preference, citizenship status, and political party affiliation, can be measured by nominal measures. The nominal level of measurement has the following distinctive characteristics:

- Observations are classified into **mutually exclusive answer categories,** meaning that those answer categories do not overlap with one another. For example, a person cannot be classified into both African American and Asian American groups.
- Answer categories (attributes of a variable) should be exhaustive, meaning that every case can be classified into one of the attributes.
- The distance between answer categories is unmeasurable and meaningless.
- There is no hierarchy or ranking to a value assigned to each attribute (i.e., 1 = male; 2 = female). We can assign number 1 to female and number 2 to male.
- Therefore, no arithmetic operation (addition, subtraction, multiplication, division) is possible when a variable is measured at the nominal level of measurement.

Ordinal Level of Measurement

Responses of certain variables, such as socioeconomic status (SES) and college standing (freshman, sophomore, junior, senior), are inherently rank-ordered. SES is an ordinal variable because it has three response groups—lower, middle, and upper class—and it is reasonable to state that those who belong

---

Table 5.1: Example of Commonly Used Nominal Measures

Your gender is:
   1. Male_____ 2. Female_____

What is your ethnic background?
   1. African American_____ 2. Asian American_____ 3. Hispanic American_____
   4. Native American _____ 5. Non-Hispanic White_____ 6. Other_____

What is your marital status?
   1. Single_____ 2. Married_____ 3. Separated_____ 4. Divorced_____ 5. Widowed_____
   6. Other_____

What is your religious preference?
   1. Catholic_____ 2. Protestant_____ 3. Buddhist_____ 4. Other_____ 5. None_____

What is your citizenship status?
   1. US-born Citizen_____ 2. Naturalized Citizen_____ 3. Foreign-born Resident_____

to middle-class groups are at a higher rank than those who take lower-class positions. Thus, the numbers assigned to answer responses represent the order or rank, and we can classify each case into one of these ranks that can be distinguished in terms of their magnitude. The ordinal level of measurement retains some of the characteristics displayed in nominal measures. For example, the values (or answer responses) of an ordinal variable are mutually exclusive and exhaustive, and the distance between the values cannot be measured (i.e., it is not mathematically and/or metaphysically possible to measure the gap between lower and middle class, between middle and upper class, between lower and upper class, and so forth). The difference between the two levels of measurement is that responses in ordinal measures are hierarchical in nature.

In addition to the variables cited in this section (i.e., SES and college standing), many of the standardized attitude scales (i.e., life satisfaction, self-esteem, and psychometric scales measuring psychological well-being) are ordinal measures. Particularly, a Likert scale, which is widely employed in survey questionnaires, is an example of ordinal measures. Psychologist Rensis Likert invented this scale (1932), and the scale was named after him in recognition of his contribution to psychometric attitude studies. In a Likert scale, responses are grouped together and scored along a scale range. For example, in a five-point Likert-type scale, respondents are asked to choose one of the following five points in response to a question item: 1. Strongly Disagree; 2. Disagree; 3. Neutral; 4. Agree; 5. Strongly Agree. The Beck Anxiety Scale shown in Table 5.2 is an example of Likert-type scales.

Interval Level of Measurement

Responses obtained from variables measured at the interval level of measurement are both mutually exclusive and exhaustive, and there is a rank order among the responses; however, responses of an interval level variable are expressed in numbers, rather than one of the answer categories, and has some mathematical magnitude. For example, in response to the question "What is the room temperature now?" possible responses can be 40 degrees Fahrenheit or 80 degrees, and so forth. These responses are mutually exclusive and exhaustive, and 80 degrees are higher than 70 degrees. But at the interval level of measurement, zero (0) is not absolute, meaning there are some numbers below zero, and that zero means something rather than nothing. If zero is absolute, there should not be any number below zero. And since zero degree does not mean there is no temperature or heat, we cannot state 80 degrees is twice as hot as 40 degrees, suggesting the distance between 40 degrees and 80 degrees is meaningless.

In social research, the number of variables that can be measured by interval level measures is very limited. Some of the few interval level variables include age and temperature variables. It's important to note that many social researchers combine scores obtained from Likert-type scales and use them as interval measures. For example, there are ten items in the Rosenberg Self-Esteem Scale that were measured on four points. After recoding the item numbers 2, 5, 6, 8, 9 to unify the direction of the items (the negative items are reverse-recoded into the positive items), scores are combined for each case. The resulting composite scores range from 10 to 40, and these scores are treated as an interval level measure among social researchers today. In other words, for example, a respondent's self-esteem level can be 20, and another person's composite score can be 40. Yet it's hard to agree that the score 40 is twice as high in self-esteem as the score 20.

Table 5.2: Beck Anxiety Scale

Beck Anxiety Inventory

Below is a list of common symptoms of anxiety. Please carefully read each item in the list. Indicate how much you have been bothered by that symptom during the past month, including today, by circling the number in the corresponding space in the column next to each symptom. The following includes the list of symptoms of anxiety asked in the Beck inventory. Review them individually and choose one of the answers:

(0) being "Not at all"; (1) "Mildly"; (2) "Moderately"; (3) "Severely"

1. Feeling hot.	0	1	2	3
2. Muscle numbness or tingling.	0	1	2	3
3. Feeling unable to relax.	0	1	2	3
4. Dizzy or light-headed.	0	1	2	3
5. Feeling wobbly in the legs.	0	1	2	3
6. Feeling unsteady.	0	1	2	3
7. Heart racing or pounding.	0	1	2	3
8. Nervousness.	0	1	2	3
9. Choking feeling.	0	1	2	3
10. Trembling hands.	0	1	2	3
11. Unsteadiness.	0	1	2	3
12. Terror or fear.	0	1	2	3
13. Afraid of losing control.	0	1	2	3
14. Indigestion.	0	1	2	3
15. Flushed face.	0	1	2	3
16. Hot or cold sweats.	0	1	2	3
17. Feeling scared.	0	1	2	3
18. Having laborious breathing.	0	1	2	3
19. Feeling the fear of dying.	0	1	2	3
20. Feeling like the worst is happening.	0	1	2	3
21. Feeling faint.	0	1	2	3

Column Sum

A grand sum between 0–21 indicates very low anxiety; grand sum between 22–35 indicates moderate anxiety; and a grand sum that exceeds 36 is a potential cause for concern.

Ratio Level of Measurement

The ratio and interval levels of measurement are similar in many ways. Ratio level variables, however, have absolute zero, meaning the value zero is nothing, and that there is no number below zero. For example, income can be measured by a ratio level measure. In response to the question "What was your total family income last year?" there are an infinite number of responses, including $0, $20,000, $40,000, $60,000, and so forth. From this example, we can detect there are equal units among responses. Since there are equal units in quantity among numbers on a number line, we can state $40,000 is exactly twice as much as $20,000, and that a ratio or a fraction can be calculated by dividing responses. Unlike nominal and ordinal measures,

Table 5.3: Example of Common Ratio Level Measures*

What was your total family income last year? $_____/Year

What is the total number of years of education _____Years

How many cigarettes do your smoke a day? _____Cigarettes/Day

How many children do you have? _____Children
(If you have no children, please enter 0)

How many times do you attend religious services a year? _____Times/Year
(If none, please enter 0)

How many times do you exercise a week? _____Times/Week
(If none, please enter 0)

*It should be noted that no answer categories are provided in ratio level measures.

a full range of mathematical operations is possible when variables are measured with ratio level measures including additions, subtractions, multiplications, and divisions.

THE PROCESS OF CROSS-CULTURAL INSTRUMENT DEVELOPMENT

Among the focuses of this chapter are the foundation of measurement and the process of cross-cultural instrument development. The foundation of measurement involves some fundamental elements such as "concept," "indicators," "latent variables," "reflective or effect indicators," "causal or formative indicators," and "theoretical framework." These terms will be illustrated by using examples relevant to social work. Once the research concepts and indicators are identified and defined, researchers need to transform them into a research instrument such as a survey questionnaire or a standardized scale. In cross-cultural research or evaluation, the selected concepts, indicators, and latent variables must be culturally relevant and appropriate among the target populations or communities (Tran, 2009).

FOUNDATION OF MEASUREMENT

As Tran (2009) suggested, the main goal of scientific social work inquiry is to investigate the relationships among variables and determine whether they are correlational or causal. As we know, many human behaviors, attitudes, and social and psychological conditions, or phenomena, are abstract. Therefore, researchers need to develop measures to quantify the variables of interest, such as perceived quality of services or client satisfaction. To measure the abstract concepts, researchers have to identify their observable and measurable indicators. In measurement development, researchers focus on the relationships between the constructs and their respective observable indicators (Edwards and Bagozzi, 2000).

DEFINING & MEASURING CONCEPTS

To measure an abstract variable, you first need to define it concisely. Then you have to provide the clients with an opportunity to express their assessments of the variable. And to compare different levels of an abstract, you will need to create a standardized instrument or questionnaire. This is what we researchers often call a scale. As reviewed previously, you can construct a set of questions using the Likert format in which each question or statement of the scale has a range of standardized responses, such as very satisfied, satisfied, somewhat satisfied, and dissatisfied. These responses are measured on an ordinal level of measurement, but you could assign numerical values to the responses and treat them as interval measures (very satisfied = 4, satisfied = 3, somewhat satisfied = 2, dissatisfied = 1, and very dissatisfied = 0). This is what most social science researchers have used. For example, if your client-perceived quality of services scale has ten questions or items, the scale can have a range of values from 0 to 40. The greater the score, the greater the perceived quality of services. Since these questions or items manifest the clients' reflection on the services they received, we refer to them as the reflective items of service satisfaction, or the reflective indicators of service satisfaction (Edwards and Bagozzi 2000).

TIPS TO DEVELOP MEANINGFUL QUESTIONNAIRES

Survey methodologists have suggested several standardized techniques for questionnaire development (Converse and Pressner, 1986; Schaeffer and Pressner, 2003). An effective survey instrument must satisfy some basic conditions as suggested by Fowler and Cannell (1996). Followings are six criteria for a good survey questionnaire design as recommended by Tran (2009):

1. The questions must be culturally relevant to respondents of diverse cultural backgrounds.
2. Respondents must understand the questions the researchers intend to ask.
3. Researchers must avoid asking for information not available to the respondents.
4. Respondents must be able to recall or retrieve information relevant to the questions.
5. Respondents can translate the information they have into the standardized forms of the questions.
6. Respondents' responses to the questions must be truthful and accurate.

These six basic principles do not offer a perfect solution for instrument development. The questions or scale items must be written in a clear and precise language for the clients or respondents to understand their true meaning. Tran (2009) emphasized that the language of a research instrument must be free from gender, age, educational, racial, and religious biases. Moreover, questions or items that require information not readily available, or information respondents are not accustomed to remember, must be avoided.

ASSESSMENT OF VALIDITY AND RELIABILITY OF MEASURES

The **validity** of measures refers to its ability to measure what it was intended to accurately and appropriately measure. If the scale was designed to measure client satisfaction of social services, it must be able to measure and capture the clients' true sense of satisfaction with the services they received. **Reliability** of a scale refers to its ability to measure what it was designed to measure consistently. How do we know whether an instrument has validity? It is difficult and complicated to present evidence of the validity and reliability of a measure. Nonetheless, researchers must demonstrate the measures they employed in examining their research questions are both valid and reliable before they are administered to research participants. There are several ways to assess the validity of measures: **face validity**, **content validity**, **criterion validity (concurrent and predictive)**, and **construct validity**.

VALIDITY

Face Validity

The first question that must be answered in establishing face validity of a measure is "Does the measure that I adopted in my measurement have face validity?" **Face validity** is one of the simplest forms of validity, in which the measure appears to measure what it intended to actually measure. You can present your scale to your peers, clients, and experts to help you ascertain the face validity of your measure. If those with expertise in the subject area take the validity of a scale at face value, then face validity is established. Since face validity only means the measure *appears* to measure variables, it does not mean it is actually proven to measure variables precisely. In this sense, face validity is a weak form of validity, and it is often necessary to move forward to establish additional forms of validity of measures.

Content Validity

The term "content validity" is often used interchangeably with the term "face validity." There is a clear distinction, however, between these two types of validity. While face validity refers to what the measure appears to measure, not to what it actually measures, **content validity** (or logical validity) refers to the extent to which a measurement instrument covers and represents all facets of a given concept that is intended to measure accurately. Content validity has been highly emphasized in psychometrics (or psychological measurements including knowledge, attitudes, personality traits, depression, anxiety, and educational achievement tests). Many measurement scales widely employed in survey and experimental research are multidimensional. For example, current depression scales attempt to measure a full range of depressive symptoms, including (1) depressed mood, (2) feelings of guilt, (3) suicidal ideation, (4) insomnia, (5) psycho-motor retardation, (6) work or daily activities, (7) agitation, (8) anxiety, (9) somatic symptoms, (10) sexuality, (11) hypochondriasis, (12) change in weight and appetite, (13) change in sleep patterns, and (14) reduction in insight (Cousin, Yang, and Yeung 2010). Lawshe (1975) emphasized the importance of rigorous statistical tests in assessing the content validity of a measure. He developed a widely used method to evaluate content validity by calculating the content validity ratio (CVR) that considered the level of agreement on test item essentials among the subject matter experts (SMEs) as shown in Table 5.4.

The possible CVR scores generated from this formula range between −1 and +1 (−1 < CVR Scores < +1). Specifically, negative CVR scores indicate that fewer than half of the SMEs rated an item as "essential," zero CVR score indicates that exactly half rated "essential" and the other half "not essential." Positive CVR scores indicate that more than half rated an item as "essential," while the CVR score that equals +1 indicates that all rated an item as "essential."

Table 5.4: Content Validity Ratio (CVR) Formulated by C. H. Lawshe (1975)

$CVR = (ne - N/2) / (N/2)$

Where:

CVR = Content validity ratio

Ne = Number of SME raters who indicated the test items as "essential"

N = Total number of SME raters

SME = Subject matter expert

Lawshe, C. H. 1975. "A quantitative approach to content validity." *Personnel Psychology,* 28: 563–575.

Criterion Validity

Criterion validity (also known as concrete validity) refers to the extent to which the results of a given measurement instrument under consideration are correlated to those of another well-established standard device as a criterion known to be valid in measuring a variable. Criterion validity is also assessed by examining the strength of the relationship between a variable measured in a given device to other well-tested criterion variable (see the example shown in Table 5.5). There are two subtypes of criterion validity—**concurrent criterion validity** and **predictive criterion validity. Concurrent criterion validity** is assessed by examining the relationship between the results of a given measurement instrument (or my device) and another device proven to be valid at the same time (concurrently). The other measurement device selected by a researcher is used as a criterion to which his or her instrument is compared. The correlation coefficient (r) between the two sets of measurements obtained from the same target population establishes the criterion validity. For example, a researcher has developed a new depression scale for immigrant Latino families residing in urban areas. The researcher administers both his or her instrument and the Radloff's Center for Epidemiologic Studies Depression (CES-D) scale (Radloff 1977) to one hundred immigrant Latino respondents, resulting in two sets of data—one from the researcher's measure and the other from the CES-D scale (Radloff 1977). If the correlation coefficient is high enough (usually r > 0.8), it can be stated that concurrent criterion validity is found. On the other hand, **predictive criterion validity** is concerned about how well a given device under consideration can predict the outcomes that will occur in the future. For example, a researcher constructs a new instrument intended to measure human service workers' aptitude and success in their job

Table 5.5: Correlation between Composite Psychological Distress Score and Self-Rated Health [Result from the 2011–2012 California Health Interview Survey-Adult Data (N = 42,935)]

PEARSON CORRELATION	SRH	PSY. DISTRESS
SRH	1.000	
Psy. Distress	.340***	1.000
Sig. (2-tailed)	.000	
N	42935	

*** Correlation is significant at the 0.01 level (two-tailed).

performance. The test was given to newly employed social workers, and the results are compared with their performance evaluation results obtained six months later. If the score of the correlation coefficient between the two sets of results is high, predictive criterion validity is established.

Let's evaluate the criterion validity of Kessler's six-item Psychological Distress Scale that used the five-point Likert format (0 = little of the time through 4 = all of the time) in the 2011–2012 California Health Interview Survey (CHIS)-Adult Data (Kessler et al. 2002). The CHIS study is known to be one of the largest public health surveys ever conducted in the United States, and the most current data were collected from 42,935 Californian households by the UCLA Center for Health Policy Research in 2011 and 2012. The CHIS study used a dual frame random-digital-dial (RDD) technique in collecting data. The Kessler six-item Psychological Distress Scale has been widely used worldwide. You can download this data set from the UCLA Center for Health Research (http://healthpolicy.ucla.edu/chis/data/Pages/public-use-data.aspx). The specific steps taken to assess the criterion validity of the CHIS Psychological Distress Scale are as follows:

Step 1.   We need to create a summative composite score by adding those six items together for each case. The resulting composite scores range from 0 to 24.

Step 2.   We run a correlation between this summative score and a criterion variable. Since there has been evidence in the literature that psychological distress relates to poor health status, we can run a simple correlation between the six-item scale of psychological distress and a measure of self-rated health status. In the CHIS survey, there is a question that asked the respondents to rate their general health status as excellent (1), very good (2), good (3), fair (4), and poor (5).

Step 3:   As shown in Table 5.5, the correlation coefficient (r) between psychological distress (stress) and self-rated health status (SRH) is 0.35 and has a statistical significance at $p < 0.000$. The result indicates respondents who had higher scores on the six-item Psychological Distress Scale tended to rate their health as poorer. Our result is consistent with the literature and with what we expected. Although the correlation is relatively weak, we can conclude that this six-item psychological distress scale has an acceptable criterion-related validity.

Construct Validity

To understand construct validity, it is necessary to address the definition of a construct. A construct is a theorized concept developed to symbolize certain abstract phenomena, such as love, hatred, aggression, intelligence, ability, abuse, fear, motivation, and so forth. Construct validity refers to the degree to which a variable measured by your instrument is related other concepts as demonstrated in theories. According to Messick (1989), who argued for a unified view of construct validity and consequential evidence of test interpretation, construct validity is "an integrated evaluative judgment of the degree to which empirical evidence and theoretical rationales support the adequacy and appropriateness of interpretations and actions based on test scores or other modes of assessment" (p. 13). As this definition indicates, construct validity emphasizes the importance of theoretical support behind a given measure under consideration. In other words, in establishing construct validity, researchers are concerned about whether the operationally defined variable in a given measure actually reflects the true definition of the concept specified in a theory. For example, various theories of depression uniformly point out that depressive symptoms are multidimensional, as cited previously. We can collect data using the CES-D scale from two groups—one group with the diagnosis of persistent clinical depression and the other with no depression. If the group with the diagnosis of depression scores higher on the CES-D compared with those without depression, the construct validity of the CES-D is established, as it measures the theoretically widely agreed upon construct of depression.

One way to assess the construct validity of a scale is to perform a **factor analysis**. This is a method of data reduction that can help you group variables or scale questions and items into meaningful dimensions or factors. As we've stated, many of the constructs or variables that we try to measure are multidimensional. For example, depression can be a combination of depressed or negative feelings, somatic symptoms or physical reactions, social isolation, and lack of a positive outlook toward life. One of the well-known measures of depression is the Radloff's CES-D scale, as already cited briefly in this chapter. This scale measures four dimensions or factors: somatic and retarded activity, depressed affect, positive affect, and interpersonal relationship. Factor analysis will help you determine which items of the scale represent which respective factors. It should be noted that each factor or dimension of a scale must have at least two items or questions. There are two common methods of factor analysis: exploratory factor analysis (EFA) and confirmatory factor analysis (CFA). If you use EFA, you do not specify the dimensions of the scale items since all items load on all factors, and the statistical software program will do this for you. If you use CFA, you need to specify in advance the dimensions of the scale and the items or questions that represent those dimensions or factors.

Let's use the 2011–2012 CHIS data to examine the construct validity of Kessler's six-item Psychological Distress Scale by applying the exploratory factor analysis technique (See Table 5.6 and 5.7).

As viewed previously, each item has possible scores from 0 to 4. The higher the scores, the more the psychological distress. We label these six items as *nervous, hopeless, restless, depressed, effort, and worthless*. Here is an example of principle factor analysis using the California Health Survey Interview data set to evaluate the construct validity of six items of psychological distress. Most, if not all, statistical software packages have the factor analysis application. There are different "options" for exploratory factor analysis, but the principle factor analysis option is more appropriate for construct validity assessment. This method assumes that the

Table 5.6: Kessler's Six-Item Psychological Distress Scale

Six Items of Psychological Distress
    0 = None of the Time
    1 = A little of the Time
    2 = Some of the Time
    3 = Most of the Time
    4 = All of the Time

(1) Feel nervous for the past 30 days
(2) Feel hopeless for the past 30 days
(3) Feel restless for the past 30 days
(4) Feel depressed for the past 30 days
(5) Feel everything an effort for the past 30 days
(6) Feel worthless for the past 30 days

UCLA Center for Health Policy Research
10960 Wilshire Blvd, Suite 1550
Los Angeles, CA 90024
CHIS 2011-2012
Website for Public Use Data Files: http://healthpolicy.ucla.edu/chis/data/Pages/overview.aspx

Table 5.7: Assessing Construct Validity of Kessler's Six-Item Psychological Distress Scale Using the Stata Statistics Software Program

Stata Syntax:
factor nervous hopeless restless depressed effort worthless
(obs = 42714)

Factor analysis/correlation   Number of obs   = 42714
   Method: principal factors   Retained factors = 2
   Rotation: (unrotated)   Number of params = 11

FACTOR	EIGENVALUE	DIFFERENCE	PROPORTION	CUMULATIVE
Factor1	2.71933	2.54418	1.1226	1.1226
Factor2	0.17515	0.24146	0.0723	1.1949
Factor3	−0.06631	0.04953	−0.0274	1.1675
Factor4	−0.11584	0.00726	−0.0478	1.1197
Factor5	−0.12311	0.04370	−0.0508	1.0689
Factor6	−0.16681	.	−0.0689	1.0000

LR test: independent vs. saturated: chi2(15) = 8.8e + 04 Prob > chi2 = 0.0000

questions or items of any scale always have certain degrees of errors. This is true because we would never be able to design a perfect scale.

The results displayed in Table 5.7 present a variety of statistical information, but all you need to know is: number of **obs**, which is the sample size; and the **eigenvalue**, which is the value that tells you how many factors the items of a sale would form. Each factor must have a minimum eigenvalue of 1. Eigenvalue is the total variance of the items that represent a respective factor. Our analysis indicates there was only one eigenvalue greater than 1, i.e., 2.719. Thus, you can conclude that these six items will very likely measure one factor or dimension of psychological distress.

Table 5.8 presents factor loading and error measurement of each factor loading. You can think of the factor loadings as the numerical values representing the relationship between each item of a scale and the overall construct. In this case, the factor loadings represent the relationship between six items and the construct of psychological distress. The value of a factor loading should be at least .30 or higher. This value can be either negative or positive. We want to see the factor loading of an item on its respective factor to be

Table 5.8: Factor Loadings (or Pattern Matrix) and Unique Variances

VARIABLE	FACTOR 1	FACTOR 2	UNIQUENESS
nervous	0.6236	0.2153	0.5647
hopeless	0.7586	−0.1227	0.4094
restless	0.5874	0.2372	0.5987
depressed	0.7376	−0.1418	0.4359
effort	0.6054	0.0799	0.6271
worthless	0.7066	−0.1760	0.4697

positive and ranges from .30 to 1.00. When an item that has similar factor loadings on two more factors, you should drop this item from your scale or you need to revise it to make it more clear and precise.

The factor loadings under the Factor 1 column in Table 5.8 have values from .5874 to .7586. These are acceptable factor loadings. All factor loadings under the Factor 2 column are lower than .30. Thus, the eigenvalue reported in the table indicated that these six items can only measure one factor. The information under the Uniqueness column represents the measurement errors. Each item has a measurement error. This can be understood as the amount of information about psychological distress that was not accounted for by each item. An item with a greater factor landing has a lower "uniqueness," or errors, accordingly. Given the information we generated from this exploratory factor analysis, especially the eigenvalue and factor loadings, we can conclude that this six-item scale of psychological distress appears to have acceptable construct validity. The six items were found to measure what they were expected to measure.

RELIABILITY

Reliability of a measurement instrument refers to the extent that the device produces consistent results. It should be noted that a valid instrument does not necessarily produce consistent results. Likewise, a reliable instrument does not always measure variables as accurately and appropriately as intended. How do you know your scale has reliability? You can assess the reliability of your scale by using the following methods: **test-retest reliability**, **inter-rater reliability**, and **internal consistency reliability**.

Table 5.9: Self-Esteem among Children of Immigrants Longitudinal Study (CILS), 1991–2006

ICPSR 20520
Alejandro Portes, Princeton University
Rubén G. Rumbaut, University of California, Irvine

Among other variables, this study collected data on self-esteem using the following ten items. Each item has scores ranging from 1 to 4, with a higher score indicating a higher sense of self-esteem. We coded all ten items to have the same score range.

1. I believe I am a person of worth, at least on an equal basis with others.
2. I believe I have a number of good qualities.
3. All in all, I am inclined to think I am a failure.
4. I am able to do things as well as most other people.
5. I believe I do not have much to be proud about.
6. I take a positive attitude toward myself.
7. On the whole, I am satisfied with myself.
8. I wish I could have more respect for myself.
9. I certainly feel useless at times.
10. At times I think I am no good at all.

http://www.icpsr.umich.edu/icpsrweb/ICPSR/studies/20520

Table 5.10: Test-Retest Reliability of the Rosenberg Self-Esteem Scale Used in the Children of Immigrants Longitudinal Study (CILS), 1991–2006

Stata Syntax: pwcorr SELF-ESTEEM_T1 SELF-ESTEEM_T2

PWCORR	SELF-ESTEEM_T1	SELF-ESTEEM_T2
Self-Esteem_T1	1.0000	
Self-Esteem_T2	0.4439	1.0000
Sig.		0.0000**

** Significant at the 0.01 level.

Test-Retest Reliability

Test-retest reliability is a measure of reliability obtained by administering the same test twice over a period of time to a group of individuals. The scores from Time 1 and Time 2 can then be correlated to evaluate the test for stability over time. We use an example drawn from the Children of Immigrants Longitudinal Study conducted by Portes and Rumbaut, as cited in Table 5.9.

To evaluate the test-reliability of this scale, we simply added the scores of the ten items to create a summative scale of self-esteem and performed a correlation analysis between the total scores of self-esteem between Time 1 and Time 2 using Stata, as shown in Table 5.10.

As indicated in Table 5.10, the correlation of Time 1 self-esteem and Time 2 self-esteem is 0.4439, and it is statically significant ($p = .000$). Does this ten-item scale of self-esteem have adequate test-retest reliability even if the correlation is not that great? Given a relatively long time interval between Time 1 and Time 2 data collection, we would say yes. If self-esteem were measured within a few weeks or months apart, the test-retest correlation would definitely be greater.

Inter-Rater Reliability

We use this measure of reliability to assess the degree to which different judges or raters agree in their assessment decisions. The following fictitious data (Table 5.11) are from two raters who rated the quality of ten questions developed to measure client satisfaction. Each rater was asked to rate whether each client satisfaction scale question is: very easy to understand (1), easy (2), fairly easy (3), difficult (4), or very difficult (5).

We can run a correlation between the rating scores of rater A and rater B to determine the inter-rater reliability. The results from a Stata "pwcorr" analysis reported below indicate the two raters agreed with each other fairly well (Table 5.12). We would like to see a correlation from .70 or higher. This is not the ideal way to evaluate the inter-rater reliability, but a useful and simple way. You can also calculate the percentage of agreement between the two raters by taking 8 divide by 10 (8/10=0.8 or 80%) since they agreed on 8 questions out of 10 questions; however, if you want to revise the questions, you should revise questions 3, 4, 8, and 9. Question 4 definitely needs to be revised as both raters judged this as the most difficult question. We should always avoid difficult questions in the development of a scale or measure.

Table 5.11: Ratings of Two Raters on the Quality of Ten Items of Client Satisfaction

QUESTIONS	RATE A	RATER B
Q #1	1	1
Q #2	3	3
Q #3	4	3
Q #4	5	5
Q #5	1	1
Q #6	1	1
Q #7	2	2
Q #8	4	4
Q #9	5	1
Q #10	1	1

Internal Consistency Reliability

We use this measure of reliability to evaluate the degree to which different test items that measure the same construct produce similar results. A construct is generally known to be a well-defined concept or variable that can be measured for a specific purpose. We can also think of internal consistency as a measure of how well the scale items "hang together" under a specific construct. We use the 2011–2012 data from the California Health Interview Survey (CHIS) to demonstrate the assessment of internal consistency of Kessler's six-item scale designed to measure psychological distress. The statistical approach used to assess internal consistency using Stata is "alpha." This approach estimates the Cronbach's alpha coefficient, which assesses how well the items relate to one another in measuring the overall concept or construct of psychological distress. The alpha coefficient ranges from 0 to 1.00, and coefficient values from 0.70 and higher suggest acceptable or strong reliability.

In Table 5.13, we only report three statistical results that are important to review when you run an "alpha" analysis. The second column refers the correlation of each item with the remaining items of the scale. This statistic is important when you compare the reliability of a scale between two groups, such as race, ethnicity, or gender. The statistics in the third column suggest that if you remove a particular item from the scale, you will have such alpha coefficient. Comparing the total scale alpha or the overall alpha of the six items of .8205, we would not remove any item from the scale.

Table 5.12: Correlation Analysis of Inter-Rater Reliability Using Stata

Stata Syntax: pwcorr Rater_A Rater_B

PWCORR	RATER_A	RATER_B
Rater_A	1.0000	
Rater_B	0.6897	1.0000
Sig.	0.0000**	

** Significant at the 0.01 level.

Table 5.13: Cronbach's Alpha Internal Consistency Reliability Test with Kessler's Six-Item Psychological Distress Scale Used in the 2011–2012 CHIS Study

Stata Syntax:

alpha nervous, hopeless, restless, depress, effort, worthless, detail item

ITEM (1)	ITEM-REST CORRELATION (2)	ALPHA (3)
nervous	0.5794	0.7941
hopeless	0.6678	0.7781
restless	0.5478	0.8025
depress	0.6482	0.7843
effort	0.5573	0.8048
worthless	0.6158	0.7906
Test scale		0.8205

LINGUISTIC TRANSLATION OF RESEARCH INSTRUMENTS

Because many prospective research participants or clients do not speak English, some research instruments have to be translated into other languages. There are a variety of methods of translation, but no one approach has become a universal one. Tran (2009) discussed three common approaches of cross-cultural translation that have used in the past: (1) **forward only translation approach** is a one-way translation from the source language to a target language. This approach suffers from poor reliability and validity; (2) **forward translation with testing approach** is stronger than the previous one; and (3) **back translation approach** appears to be stronger than the previous two approaches, but it tends to emphasize the literal translation or linguistic equivalence. These three approaches do not warrant cross-cultural equivalence.

Harkness (2003) offers a stronger questionnaire translation approach, called **TRAPD**, referring to translation, review, adjudication, pre-testing, and documentation. This is a committee-based approach including translators, reviewers, and adjudicator. Committee or team translation approach is a more effective compared with other approaches (Guillemin, Bombardier, and Beaton, 1993; Harkness, Pennell, and Schoua-Glusber, 2004). The committee approach, however, does not require **gender representatives** in either the translation or evaluation processes. It's important to use skilled translators who have adequate knowledge of the research topic and understand the culture of the research population in order to perform valid translation. Using team translation with translators from diverse backgrounds will help the team determine the best translation outcomes (Guillemin, Bombardier, and Beaton 1993).

RECOMMENDATIONS FOR APPROPRIATE CROSS-CULTURAL TRANSLATION

Tran (2009) recommended that meaningful cross-cultural translation of research instruments requires the involvement of different stakeholders, including clients or prospective research participants; prospective consumers of research outcomes such as practitioners and policy makers; and the use of multi-method cross-cultural translation (e.g., back translation, group translation, cognitive interviews, focus group, expert evaluation, and pilot testing) to warrant the original validity and the comparability of the translated instrument. Good cross-cultural translation is beyond language translation. The translators must be able to translate the meanings of a concept from one culture to another. Participants from different cultures must be able to understand a selected concept in a similar manner even though they do not speak the same language.

SUMMARY

This chapter covered four levels of measurement, issues involved in examining the validity and reliability of a given research instrument, and a few critical considerations in translating measurement instruments into other languages. The four levels of measurement are nominal, ordinal, interval and ratio. There are a few approaches to assessing validity—face, content, criterion, and construct validity. Reliability is assessed by examining the test-retest reliability, inter-rater reliability, and internal consistency reliability (Cronbach's alpha). There are a few critical points that researchers should avoid including using a single translator, translating word by word from a source language to a target one, assuming cross-cultural reliability and validity without verification. The chapter also provided a few best practices in dealing with cross-cultural instrument development. Due to the high costs of cross-cultural research and evaluation, researchers might be tempted to cut costs by avoiding use of a multi-translation method, excluding prospective subjects and consumers throughout the research process. Finally, in every aspect of instrument development, one should always include equal numbers of female and male representatives.

CLASS EXERCISE

1. Select a scale or an index that was designed to measure psychological status or social behaviors. Discuss its validity and reliability in the context of diversity.
1. Develop a Likert format scale to measure a concept related to social work that you think would be useful to social work research and practice. Explain why you chose this concept.

REFERENCES

Converse, J. M., & Pressner, S. (1986). *Survey questions: Handcrafting the standardized questionnaire (quantitative applications in the social sciences)*. Thousand Oaks, CA: Sage Publications.

Cousin, C., Yang, H., Yeung, A., & Fava, M. (2010). Rating scales for depression. In L. Baer & M. A. Blais (Eds.), *Handbook of clinical rating scales and assessment in psychiatry and mental health* (7–36). New York, NY: Humana Press, Springer.

Edwards, J. R., & Bagozzi, R. B. (2000). On the nature and direction of the relationship between constructs and measures. *Psychological Methods, 5*, 155–174.

Fowler, F. J., & Cannell, C. F. (1996). Using behavioral coding to identify cognitive problems with survey questions. In N. Schwarz & S. Sudman (Eds.), *Answering questions: Methodology for determining cognitive and communicative processes in survey research* (15–36). San Francisco, CA: Jossey-Bass.

Guillemin, F., Bombardier, C., & Beaton, D. (1993). Cross-cultural adaption of health-related quality of life measures: Literature review and proposed guidelines. *Journal of clinical Epidemiology, 46(12), 1417-1432.*

Harkness, J. A., Van de Vijver, F. J. R., & Mohler, P. (2003). *Cross-cultural survey methods,* Hoboken, NJ: Wiley.

Harkness, J. A., Pennell, B. E., & Schoua-Glusberg, A. (2004). Survey questionnaire translation and assessment. In S. Presser, J. M. Rothgeb, M. P. Couper, J. T. Lessler, E. Martin, J. Martin, & E. Singer (Eds.), *Methods for testing and evaluating survey questionnaires.* New York, NY: Wiley.

Kessler R. C., Andrews, G., Colpe, L. J., Hiripi, E., Mroczek, D. K., Normand, S. L. T., Walters, E. E., & Zaslavsky, A. (2002). Short screening scales to monitor population prevalences and trends in nonspecific psychological distress. *Psychological Medicine, 32,* 959–976.

Lawshe, C. H. (1975). A quantitative approach to content validity. *Personnel Psychology, 28,* 563-575.

Likert, R. (1932). A technique for the measurement of attitudes. *Archives of Psychology, 140,* 1–55.

Messick, S. (1989). Validity. In R. L. Linn (Ed.), *Educational measurement* (3rd ed.) (13-103). New York, NY: Macmillan.

Radloff, L. S. (1977). The CES-D scale: A self-report depression scale for research in the general population. *Applied Psychological Measurement, 1(3),* 385-401.

Schaeffer, N. C., & Presser, S. (2003). The science of asking questions. *Annual Review of Sociology, 29,* 65–88.

Tran, T. V. (2009). *Developing cross-cultural measurement.* Oxford University Press.Zimmerman, T., Haddock, S. A., & McGeorge, C. R. (2003). Mars and Venus. In *Points & counterpoints: Controversial relationship and family issues in the 21st century (an anthology)* (17-24). Los Angeles, CA: Roxbury Publishing Co.

SIX

Sampling, Data Collection, and Data Management

This chapter introduces the basic concept and process of obtaining probability and non-probability samples. Students will be exposed to surveys that employ different types of probability samples drawn from national archives of social science. We will examine common data collection methods and compare and contrast the selected data collection methods that are relevant and meaningful for social work research. Finally, we will discuss the best practices of data collection and how to enter data into SPSS and Stata and modify existing variables prior to data analysis.

SAMPLING

For a quantitative study, after we have developed meaningful research questions and chosen an instrument (i.e., survey questionnaire or interview schedule) to measure relevant variables, we need to decide how to select a sample of research participants that will provide data to answer our research questions and test our hypothesis. It is usually impossible or infeasible to obtain data from all cases in a population under investigation. The absolute majority of studies are conducted with samples chosen from populations of research interest. Before we address various sampling techniques, it's necessary to define and scrutinize a few sampling vocabularies. The terms frequently used in sampling methods include sampling, population, sample, sampling element, sampling unit, and sampling frame.

Sampling is a process of selecting sample elements or cases from a population. If the selection of cases is carried out in accordance with the requirements of rigorous sampling theory, the data obtained from the sample should be representative of the entire population from which the sample was taken. **Population** (denoted by N) refers to the aggregation of entire elements from which a sample is drawn, and the elements of a population share certain distinctive characteristics in common. A **sample** (denoted by n) is defined as a subset of a population consisting of elements or cases selected from the larger population. A **unit of analysis** refers to the basic entity about which a study aims to describe. Common units of analysis in most social science research include individuals, households, human service agencies, business entities (i.e., corporations), religious groups, and formal and informal self-help organizations. A **sampling element** generally refers to the unit of analysis. A **sampling frame** is a list of all possible elements or cases from which a sample is actually selected.

Let's suppose a researcher plans to examine the prevalence of depression among one thousand Latino American college students residing in Los Angeles County. In this research project, the population is the list of all Latino American students currently living in Los Angeles County. The common characteristic of this population that differentiates them from other populations is that all of the elements in the target population are attending college in Los Angeles County, and that they are Latino Americans. The unit of analysis is individual Latino American college students. In conducting this research, we may say it would be ideal to study the entire Latino American college students in Los Angeles County, and it is possible to obtain the list of all Latino American students in college as a sampling frame. In reality, however, complete lists of a population rarely exist. Due to various reasons, the sampling frame and the population are not identical, although it is desirable that the sampling frame approximates the population as closely as possible. Since our sample is drawn from our sampling frame in practice, the representativeness of our sample is limited by how closely our sampling frame approximates the population of interest. The sample consists of one thousand Latino American college students living in Los Angeles County drawn from the sampling frame. If the researcher does not have a sampling frame, there are other ways to select the sample, as will be examined in the later section.

TYPES OF SAMPLING

Probability sampling is one in which every element or unit in the population has an equal and known chance (greater than zero) of being selected, and this probability can be accurately determined by a researcher. The combination of these traits makes it possible to produce unbiased estimates of population totals, by weighting sampled units according to their probability of selection. Probability sampling strategies include one-stage probability sampling and multistage probability sampling. For one-stage probability sampling, the selection is completed in one process. It includes three sampling methods.

<u>**Simple Random Sampling**</u>: In a simple random sample of a given size n, everyone in the sampling frame has an equal probability of being selected. The selection of a simple random sample is the simplest of all probability sampling techniques, and an unbiased random sample simplifies statistical analyses of collected data. To select a simple random sample, it is necessary to first develop a complete sampling frame, put a serial number next to each element listed in the sampling frame $(1, 2, 3, 4, \ldots)$, and then select elements randomly until a simple random sample of size n is obtained. The selection of numbers listed in the sampling frame can be carried out with the aid of a computer. For example, the Random Number Generator, a computer program, creates a list of random numbers, which are randomly arranged sets of digits (see Table 6.1). All that is needed to create a table of random numbers is to enter into the computer any specifications of the range within which selections are to be made, and the quantity of random numbers required. The computer then generates a list of the required quantity of numbers. As shown in Table 6.1, this table was created by entering "00000" as the minimum value into the Random Number Generator, a maximum value of "99999," and a random number quantity of "100." Alternatively, a published table of random numbers can be used to select the sample manually.

Table 6.1: Partial Table of Random Numbers

53127	62740	33901	20419	34305	92648	17620	16147	47123	54195	59536	43514	91580
20824	06534	75962	41118	45650	85171	40050	48855	75558	95448	35778	61672	37105
10806	63145	06129	03734	57804	22151	55668	28560	36441	86239	36846	58468	46718
81967	76221	20015	62077	09334	94121	86644	09074	41782	70217	11470	87712	05870
51395	41378	97989	01598	64213	02925	13347	28964	08670	69554	86903	87971	84767
94380	38982	52059	65945	24287	49259	47786	78762	85835	91175	75153	23219	52463
38173	07602	72758	77290	16811	71690	80494	07197	00529	67417	93312	42187	42446
94784	11211	35373	89444	27233	87307	33642	68081	17879				

Retrieved on February 6, 2014, from:

http://stattrek.com/statistics/random-number-generator.aspx#randomnum.

Simple random sampling can be vulnerable to sampling error because the randomness of the selection may result in a sample that does not reflect the makeup of the population. For instance, any given trial of a simple random sample of one hundred people from a given neighborhood would very likely overrepresent one ethnicity and underrepresent the other. Simple random sampling may also be cumbersome and tedious when sampling from an unusually large target population.

Systematic Random Sampling: Although simple random sampling sounds relatively simple and straight-forward, such a process is rarely used, particularly when the population from which a sample is to be selected is fairly large. As cited earlier, the procedure can be quite tedious and time-consuming. A more practical alternative is systematic random sampling, which relies on arranging the study population according to some ordering scheme and numbering each element listed in the sampling frame, and then selecting elements at regular intervals from the ordered list of the sampling frame. Systematic random sampling involves a random start and proceeds from then onward with the selection of every kth element. In this case, k = population size/ sample size = N/n. It's important that the starting point is not automatically the first number on the list, but is selected at random to minimize any personal bias. This process is called a **systematic sample with a random start**. For example, if a researcher plans to conduct a study with one hundred individuals selected from a list of one thousand elements, the sampling interval is 10 (k = 100/10 = 10), and the researcher needs to choose every tenth name from the list (an "every 10th" sample is also referred to as "sampling with a skip of 10"). The researcher can start selecting from a random number 17, and the final sample will be made up from those with the following numbers on the list: 17, 27, 37, 47, 57,… 997. Since the starting point is randomized, systematic random sampling is a type of probability sampling in which every element has an equal chance of being selected, and tends to overcome the limitation of simple random sampling.

Stratified Random Sampling: Simple random sampling and systematic sampling techniques are based on the assumption the population from which a sample will be drawn is relatively homogeneous with respect to certain characteristics, such as ethnicity and socioeconomic status. Therefore, a sample selected using these techniques often cannot accommodate specific needs of researchers, who are interested in examining subgroup differences in a given heterogeneous population, because the process cannot provide subsamples of the population. For example, a simple random sample selected from a geographic area populated largely by Latino immigrants may not allow a researcher to pursue his or her research interest— comparing the difference between Hispanic and Asian American immigrants in life satisfaction—because of the lack of Asian immigrants selected for the sample. In this case, "stratified random sampling" is a strong alternative to simple random sampling or systematic sampling techniques. Very often, a population embraces a number of distinct subgroup categories (i.e., first generation immigrant Japanese, second generation, third generation, etc.). In this case, we need to divide the overall population into more homogeneous subpopulations, called "strata," before sampling. Each stratum is considered an independent subpopulation, from which a simple random sample or systematic sample is selected. For example, a comparative study of health practices among African, Asian, and Latino Americans may require three separate sampling strata obtained by stratifying the population into three ethnic subgroups. The researcher then draws three separate samples from each stratum by applying simple random or systematic sampling techniques. This method has several potential benefits:

a. Dividing the population into distinct independent strata can enable researchers to draw inferences about specific subgroups that may be lost in simple random and systematic random sampling methods.

b. Utilizing a stratified sampling method can lead to more efficient statistical estimates, provided that each stratum is proportional to the group's size in the population.

c. Since each stratum is treated as an independent population, different sampling approaches can be applied to different strata, potentially enabling researchers to use the approach best suited (or most cost-effective) for each identified subgroup within the population under study.

There are, however, some potential drawbacks to using stratified sampling. First, identifying strata and implementing such an approach can increase the cost and complexity of sample selection, as well as lead to increased complexity of population estimates. Second, when examining multiple criteria, stratifying variables may be related to some, but not to others, further complicating the design, and potentially reducing the utility of the strata. Finally, in some cases (such as designs with a large number of strata, or those with a specified minimum sample size per group), stratified sampling can potentially require a larger sample than would other methods, although in most cases the required sample size would be no larger than would be required for simple random sampling. A stratified sampling approach is most effective when the following three conditions are met:

a. Variability within a stratum is minimized.

b. Variability among strata (subgroups) is maximized.

c. The variables upon which the population is stratified are strongly correlated with the desired dependent variable.

Stratified sampling techniques have both advantages and disadvantages. Some of the most notable advantages are that researchers can compare various subgroup differences quite clearly, and can employ various probability sampling techniques in drawing subsamples from different strata. For example, a simple random sample can be obtained from one stratum, while a systematic random sample can be drawn from a different subgroup. Sometimes, however, it is not easy to grasp on what variable the population should be stratified (i.e., ethnicity, SES, gender, etc.).

There are two subtypes of stratified random sampling methods: **proportionate stratified sampling** and **disproportionate stratified sampling**. Proportionate stratified random sampling is a sampling technique in which the sample size of a stratum is precisely proportional to the population size of that stratum. For example, let's say the ratio between male and female residents of a psychiatric hospital is 54 to 46. If a mental health researcher intends to examine gender differences in responding to group treatment, the researcher needs to construct two sampling frames, one consisting of male residents and the other consisting of female residents. If the researcher plans to draw a proportionate stratified random sample of size 100, he or she needs to obtain a sample consisting of 54 males and 46 females selected respectively from these lists. It seems apparent the male and female sample sizes are proportional to the relative population sizes of male and female. On the other hand, disproportionate stratified random sampling is a method in which the sample size of a stratum is not proportional to the population size of that stratum, disregarding the original population subgroup ratio. This technique is generally adopted when sample elements in the population are not evenly allocated throughout the strata, and, therefore, a researcher needs to allot different sampling ratios to different strata. Let's say that the population subgroup ratio is 9 to 1 between male and female residents of a forensic locked mental-health facility. This ratio, for example, means that in a facility of 1,000 residents, there are 900 male residents and 100 female residents. For a comparative study with a proportionate stratified sample of size 100, we need to draw 90 male and 10 female residents. But a study with only 10 female participants may not produce precise and meaningful results if a researcher intends to compare these two groups on certain variables. In this case, it is more reasonable to allot a different ratio of 1 : 1 (a sample consisting of 50 male and 50 female residents) instead of the original ratio of 9 : 1. When we employ a disproportionate stratified random sampling technique, a researcher should be careful not to make mistakes of overrepresentation or underrepresentation of a stratum, which may lead to skewed results.

Multistage Probability Sampling: Multistage probability sampling is a sampling technique in which samples are selected at multiple stages from two or more levels of clusters, rather than drawing a sample at a single stage from a cluster consisting of all possible sampling units. The most commonly used multistage probability sampling procedure is cluster sampling, which is more complicated than single-stage sampling strategies. In cluster sampling, the first stage involves selecting clusters (large groups) using a simple random sampling or a systematic random sampling strategy. In the second stage, a sample of primary units is randomly selected from each cluster. In following stages, in each of those selected clusters, additional samples of units are selected, and so on. All ultimate units (i.e., individuals, households, or organizations) selected at the last stage of this procedure are then surveyed.

For instance, if surveying households within a city, we might select one hundred city blocks and then interview every household within the selected blocks only. It means that one does not need a sampling frame listing all elements in the target population. Instead, clusters can be chosen from a cluster-level frame, and then an element-level frame can be created only for the selected clusters. In the example above, the sample only requires a block-level city map for initial selections, and then a household-level map of the one hundred selected blocks, rather than a household-level map of the entire city. Thus, clustering can reduce travel and administrative costs. In the example above, an interviewer can make a single trip to visit several households in one block, rather than having to drive to a different block for each household. Compared with traditional cluster sampling, multistage sampling can reduce the large amount of work because the work involved in describing unselected clusters is omitted.

Non-probability Sampling: This is a sampling technique in which the elements in the population are not given equal chances of being selected; some may have *no* chance, while others may have a full probability of being selected. Thus, the probability of selection of each element into the sample cannot be accurately estimated. It involves the selection of elements based on the investigators' knowledge, purpose, and assumptions regarding the population of interest, which form the criteria for selection. Because the selection of elements is nonrandom, non-probability sampling does not allow the estimation of sampling errors. These conditions give rise to various sources of bias due to the exclusion of many sampling elements. Information about the relationship between the sample and the population is limited, making it difficult to extrapolate from the sample to the population. Several sampling methods fall into this type of sampling strategies: convenience, judgment, purposive, quota, and snowball sampling techniques. In social research, a sampling frame from which a random sample is drawn is unavailable in many cases. If a researcher is unable to obtain a random sample, non-probability sampling strategies are the only feasible alternative. In this case, however, the researcher cannot generalize his or her findings to the whole population due to a possible sample bias stemming from the exclusion of some segments of the population.

Convenience Sampling: Convenience sampling, also known as accidental or availability sampling, relies on selecting the most available subjects to constitute the sample. Convenience sampling is generally used in exploratory research where the researcher is interested in getting an approximation of the reality within a short period of time. The researcher using such a sampling technique cannot make generalizations about the total population from this sample because it would not represent the population of interest. This type of sampling is most useful for pilot testing.

Purposive Sampling: Purposive sampling, also called judgment sampling, is a common non-probability method in which a researcher selects a sample based on his or her knowledge of a population and the purpose of the study. Especially when it is difficult and time-consuming to find appropriate research participants in a given location, and/or when it is better to collect data from members in the population who fit a specific purpose of the study, it is far more convenient to use the researcher's own knowledge and judgment about the population in the sampling process. In this regard, we can state that this method is an extension of convenience sampling. For example, a researcher familiar with social service agencies for victims of domestic violence may decide to draw a sample entirely from a domestic violence shelter even though all domestic violence shelters, as well as hidden victims who never utilized shelter services, constitute the population. When using this method, the researcher must try to ensure that the chosen sample is a close approximation of the entire population.

Quota Sampling: Quota sampling is generally regarded as the non-probability counterpart of stratified sampling. As in stratified sampling, the researcher first divides the population into several subgroups (strata) and identifies their proportions as they are represented in the population. Then, unlike stratified sampling that relies on random samples selected from two or more subgroups, convenience or judgment nonrandom sampling is used in quota sampling to select the required number of subjects from each stratum.

Snowball Sampling: Snowball sampling is a special type of non-probability sampling methods used when the desired sample characteristic is rarely visible (i.e., bisexual individuals, children diagnosed with AIDS, transgender among Vietnamese families, etc.). It may be extremely difficult for researchers to locate research subjects sharing these characteristics. Snowball sampling relies on referrals from initial subjects to generate additional subjects. Usually the sample size is small. Obviously, this sampling method is susceptible to sampling bias because the technique itself reduces the likelihood that the sample will represent a good cross section of the population.

Table 6.2: Types of Sampling Techniques

PROBABILITY SAMPLING	NON-PROBABILITY SAMPLING
(1) Simple Random Sampling (SRS)	(1) Convenience Sampling (Availability Sampling, Accidental Sampling)
(2) Systematic Random Sampling	(2) Purposive Sampling (Judgmental Sampling)

(3) Stratified Random Sampling
   a. Proportionate Stratified Random Sampling
   b. Disproportionate Stratified Random Sampling
	(3) Quota Sampling

(4) Cluster Sampling (Multistage Sampling, Area Sampling)	(4) Snowball Sampling

DATA COLLECTION

Data collection is an important aspect of any type of research. Inaccurate data collection can influence the results of a study and ultimately lead to invalid results. Data collection methods vary along a continuum. At the one end of this continuum are quantitative methods and at the other end are qualitative methods for data collection.

QUANTITATIVE SURVEY DATA COLLECTION METHODS

Quantitative survey data collection methods rely on random sampling and structured research instruments, such as a questionnaire that distributes diverse responses collected from research participants into predetermined response categories. Quantitative data produce results that are easy to summarize, compare, analyze and generalize. Quantitative research is concerned with testing hypotheses derived from theory and/or previous empirical research. Depending on the research question, participants may be randomly assigned to different treatment groups in experimental research. If this is not feasible, the researcher may collect data on participant and situational characteristics to statistically control for their influence on the dependent or outcome variable. If the intent is to generalize from the research participants to a larger population, the researcher will employ probability sampling to select participants and analyze the data using inferential statistical tests.

Quantitative data are typically collected through administering **surveys** with mostly closed-ended questions using the following data collection methods: (1) questionnaire methods that include two subtypes of the paper-pencil-questionnaire and web-based online questionnaire; and (2) interview methods with three subtypes of face-to-face interviews, telephone interviews, and computer-assisted personal interviewing (CAPI). Other data collection strategies used in quantitative research include experiments/clinical trials, documenting well-defined events, and obtaining relevant data from existing information systems.

Questionnaires

A **paper-pencil-questionnaire** is a research instrument designed for research participants to answer questions on their own without relying on any help from researchers. Questionnaires can be mailed to a large number of people or administered in public and private places (i.e., social service agencies, hospital lobbies, classrooms, cafeterias, etc.). Among the advantages of a questionnaire as a method of data collection is that it's less expensive and time consuming compared with other methods. And people are more truthful while responding to questionnaires regarding controversial and sensitive issues because their responses are anonymous. But they also have drawbacks. Many people who receive questionnaires do not return them, which makes the response rate quite low.

Web-based online questionnaires are a new and inevitably growing methodology based on use of the Internet. Participants receive an e-mail and are instructed to click on an address that will take them to a secure website to fill in a questionnaire. This type of research is often quicker and less complicated. Some disadvantages of this method include the exclusion of people who do not have a computer (i.e., older adults and uneducated or undereducated people) or are unable to access a computer. Also, the validity of such surveys is in question as people may be in a hurry to complete them and therefore not give accurate responses.

Questionnaires often make use of checklist and rating scales. These devices help simplify and quantify participants' behaviors and attitudes. A **checklist** is a list of behaviors, characteristics, or other entities that the researcher is seeking, with either the researcher or survey participant simply checking whether each item on the list is observed, present, true, or vice versa. A **rating scale** is more useful when a behavior needs to be evaluated on a continuum. They are also known as Likert scales.

Interviews

Both quantitative and qualitative studies utilize interviews extensively in collecting data. In quantitative research (i.e., survey research), however, interviews are more structured than in qualitative research. In a structured interview, the researcher asks a standard set of questions, including closed-ended questions. There are three general types of interviews commonly used in survey research: face-to-face interviews, telephone interviews, and computer-assisted personal interviewing (CAPI).

A **face-to-face interview** is a reliable data collection method in which an interviewer asks questions face-to-face and records the answers. The interview method has a distinct advantage of enabling the researcher to establish rapport with potential participants, gain their cooperation, and generate accurate and rich responses. And interviews tend to yield high response rates in survey research. They also allow the researcher to clarify ambiguous answers and, when appropriate, seek follow-up information. Informants can also ask questions when question items are unclear. Conversely, some of the disadvantages of interviews include: (a) this method is impractical when the sample size is relatively large and, as such, would prove too costly and time consuming; (b) respondents are reluctant to provide accurate responses when questions are too personal and sensitive (i.e., questions on sexual behavior, experience of child abuse, history of delinquency, etc.); (c) interview surveys do not assure anonymity of research participants; and (d) interviewers can contaminate data by influencing the respondents' responses.

Telephone interviews are less expensive and time consuming compared with face-to-face interviews. Researchers have ready access to anyone who has a telephone. One of the main disadvantages is that the response rate is not as high as the face-to-face interview, but considerably higher than the mailed questionnaire. The sample may be biased to the extent that people without phones are part of the targeted population.

Computer-Assisted Personal Interviewing (CAPI) is a form of personal interviewing, but instead of completing a questionnaire, the interviewer brings along a laptop or handheld computer to enter the information directly into the database. This method saves time in processing the data as well as preventing the interviewer from carrying around hundreds of questionnaires. This type of data collection method, however, can be quite expensive to set up and requires that interviewers have a computer and good typing skills.

In survey research, interviews are conducted by using one of the following three levels of interviews: (1) **unstructured interview**, (2) **semi-structured interview**, and (3) **structured interview**. An unstructured interview refers to the least-structured data collection method that does not rely on structured sets of written questions and only covers a limited number of subject areas (one or two subjects at the most). This type of interview covers only a couple of subject areas and is largely conducted based on the interviewer's judgment as to what questions are appropriate for the respondent in exploring the subject. A semi-structured interview refers to an interview structure relying on loosely structured, open-ended questions from which an interviewer often breaks away in pursuing detailed responses. A structured interview is the most rigid form of interview conducted with a series of fixed questions, which are mostly closed-ended. An interviewer should follow the specific instructions and the order of questions, ask questions as written in the interview schedule, and record responses precisely.

LIMITATIONS OF QUANTITATIVE DATA COLLECTION METHODS: REACTIVITY

One of the main limitations of survey research is the occurrence of reactivity among researchers and research participants during the research process. **Reactivity** primarily refers to the degree to which people alter their natural behavior in reaction to the study. Generally speaking, people tend to change their usual behavior to satisfy others' expectations (called "social desirability") whenever they are aware they are being watched. The **Hawthorne effect** was first described by Landsberger (1954) in his landmark study of the relationship between work conditions and productivity in the Hawthorne works of the Western Electric Company in Chicago. Ironically, it was found in this study that productivity increased although the amount of light at the plant decreased. Landsberger defined this improvement as the Hawthorne effect, or reactivity, showing that the amount of attention given to the workers, not improvement of the work environment, could improve productivity for a short period. Undoubtedly, research should describe the true nature of human behavior, but the phenomenon of reactivity contaminates data by serving as a significant threat to the study's internal validity. Therefore, for certain research topics and problems, it's necessary to conduct blind research, especially when a researcher is convinced that participants will not behave naturally during the study. For example, research on discriminatory behaviors among middle-class people may not be able to accurately describe the nature of social reality when the research is conducted with a survey design. It is highly unlikely interviewees will readily admit during interviews that they are engaged in discriminatory acts against racial minorities. Then, what methods will yield more accurate data? An answer to this question may include qualitative data collection methods, especially observation methods.

QUALITATIVE DATA COLLECTION METHODS

Qualitative data collection methods play an important role in impact evaluation by providing information useful in understanding the processes behind observed results and assess changes in people's perceptions of their well-being. Also, qualitative methods can be used to improve the quality of survey-based quantitative evaluations by helping generate evaluation hypothesis; strengthening the design of survey questionnaires and expanding or clarifying quantitative evaluation findings. Qualitative data collection methods are characterized by the following characteristics:

- Questions tend to be open-ended and have less structured protocols (i.e., researchers may change the data collection strategy by adding, refining, or dropping techniques).
- Qualitative methods rely more heavily on interactive interviews; respondents may be interviewed several times to follow up on a particular issue, clarify concepts, or check the reliability of data.
- Qualitative data collection methods use triangulation to increase the credibility of their findings (i.e., researchers use multiple data sources, including, for instance, individuals, family members, and community organizations, to check the authenticity and the validity of their results).
- Generally their findings are not generalizable to any specific population. Each case study produces a single piece of evidence that can be used to seek general patterns among different studies of the same issue.

Regardless of the kinds of data involved, data collection in a qualitative study takes a great deal of time. The researcher needs to record any potentially useful data thoroughly, accurately, and systematically, using field notes, sketches, audiotapes, photographs, and other suitable means. The data collection methods must observe the ethical principles of research.

There are two types of qualitative data collection methods most frequently used in social research: in-depth interviews and observation methods.

In-Depth Interviews

An in-depth interview is a useful qualitative data collection technique that can be used for a variety of purposes including needs assessment, program refinement, issue identification, and strategic planning. In-depth interviews are most appropriate for situations in which you want to ask open-ended questions that elicit depth of information from relatively few people (as contrasted with surveys, which tend to be more quantitative and are conducted with larger numbers of people).

Interviewing is typically conducted face-to-face, but can also be done via telephone. It allows the interviewer to deeply explore the respondent's feelings and perspectives on a subject. Many open-ended questions begin with "why" or "how," which gives respondents freedom to answer questions in their own words. This results in rich background information that can shape further questions relevant to the topic. Qualitative in-depth interviews are different from quantitative survey interviews in terms of the level of interview structure. In contrast with quantitative survey interviews in which questions are rigidly structured, in-depth qualitative interviews are much more flexible. They are not locked in stone, and specific interview questions are often not prepared in advance. The interviewer has a general plan of inquiry, but no specific set of questions that must be asked with particular words and in a particular order. The interviewer must, however, be fully familiar with the subject, potential questions, and plan so that things proceed smoothly and naturally. Ideally, the respondent does most of the talking while the interviewer listens, takes notes, and guides the conversation in the direction it needs to go. It is the respondent's answers to the initial questions that should shape the subsequent questions. The interviewer needs to be able to listen, think, and talk almost simultaneously.

An in-depth interview usually takes place in a private home, where the respondent is in his or her natural surroundings. In this way, the respondent is relaxed and therefore open and willing to reply to the exhaustive questions. An in-depth interview typically varies between ninety minutes and two hours and is recorded on tape or video and complemented with written notes (i.e., field notes) by the interviewer. Written notes include observations of both verbal and nonverbal behaviors as they occur and immediate personal reflections about the interview. In sum, in-depth interviews involve asking questions, systematically recording and documenting the responses to probe for deeper meaning and understanding.

Observation Methods

Observation methods (also called **participant observation or field research**) refer to a type of data collection typically adopted in qualitative research in which researchers immerse into the group or community setting and collect data, not through asking questions as in survey research, but through observing something to answer their research questions. Participant observation helps researchers gain a familiarity with the physical, cultural, economic, historical, social, and religious contexts where their target population is located. Through direct contact with study subjects and experience interacting with them, researchers acquire a factual understanding of the motivations and ideas underlying the subjects' explicit behaviors that is inherently lacking in survey data. Qualitative data include written field notes and audio and video recordings. Participation observation researchers take field notes during activities or shortly afterward while their memory is still clear. Taking field notes is an important aspect of qualitative data documentation. Audio and video recordings are permitted only when informed consent is signed by the research participants. If a researcher's identification remains hidden during participant observation, data collections using audio and video devices are not recommended due to several ethical considerations. There are two types of observation methods in qualitative research: (1) participant observation, and (2) nonparticipant observation (also called unobtrusive observation).

Participant observation refers to a data collection method in which the researcher becomes an active member of the subjects' group activities with or without revealing his or her identity. If access to the group of interest is denied or the study becomes too reactive when the researcher's status is revealed, it may be necessary to conceal the researcher's role as observer. There are a number of famous studies conducted using participant observation techniques with the hidden status of researchers. One of them is Rosenhan's study on labeling mental illness in psychiatric institutions (Rosenhan, 1973). The researcher, in his article, "On Being Sane in Insane Places," reports that eight sane researchers were admitted to psychiatric hospitals for seven to fifty-two days as pseudo patients who pretended to hear voices, and that all of their behaviors were interpreted as pathological in different psychiatric wards although they acted normally. The study aimed to test the hypotheses that psychiatrists cannot tell who is sane and who is insane, and that every patient's behavior is interpreted in accordance with psychiatric labels attached by mental-health professionals. If those researchers had not participated in the activities of psychiatric hospitals as complete participant observers, they would not have gained knowledge in how mental-health professionals diagnose and label patients, and how they treat people according to their labels.

Nonparticipant observation (unobtrusive observation) is another data collection method in which the researcher as observer does not directly participate in the activities of those who are observed. For example, the nonparticipant observer may watch and record toddlers' plays behind a one-way mirror without making any interaction with them. In **overt nonparticipant observation**, it is revealed to participants that they are being observed. On the other hand, in **covert nonparticipant observation**, it is generally unknown to research participants that the observer is watching them.

With regard to participant observer roles, the typology described by Raymond Gold (1958) is widely used. He classified participant observers into four types based on the roles they play. Those four types: (1) the **complete participant,** referring to the one who takes an insider role and fully participates in a wide range of activities, mostly without revealing his or her status as observer; (2) the **participant as observer**, who participates in the activities of those who are being studied and with his or her status known to the study subjects; (3) the **observer as participant,** who maintains a minimal level of involvement in the setting being studied and with his or her status as observer revealed; and (4) the **complete observer,** referring to the one who does not take part in any of research subjects' activities and observes their behaviors behind a two-way mirror.

One of the great strengths of observation methods is the depth of knowledge that the researcher can obtain. This type of research has been an outstanding source of some of the most striking and valuable studies in the social sciences. There are also several weaknesses, however, in using observation methods as a data collection technique. First, it is very time consuming. Researchers typically spend months or years living in the place of study. Second, the researchers have to screen their own data and select some of them from vast amounts of notes for research purposes. Third, since such studies usually focus on fairly small groups, it is hard to make any generalizations from the findings. Finally, researchers may lose their sense of objectivity by overly identifying with the study group, as exemplified in Zimbardo's famous Stanford Prison experiment, a simulation study of imprisonment (Haney, Banks, and Zimbardo, 1973). In this study, Zimbardo himself acted as the prison warden and eventually lost objectivity in pursuing his study goal despite his role as the principal investigator.

DATA MANAGEMENT

In this section, we'll examine how to prepare data for entry into SPSS and Stata, create variable names, labels, value categories, recode variables, and create new variables. The data set we will use for this session is from the Children of Immigrants Longitudinal Study (CILS), 1991-2006.

Data are usually collected by preconstructed instruments such as a questionnaire or an interview schedule. Participants in a study are asked either to circle their choices for closed-ended questions or write their answers for open-ended questions. Chapter 12 will address data analysis and reporting for qualitative data based on open-ended questions. Here we will focus on data management for responses from close-ended questions. Each question included in the questionnaire represents a variable that will be entered in a statistical software package such as SPSS or Stata. Before data entry, we need to create an instrumentation key. The following is an example of the instrumentation key, which can be used as a codebook, based on a small number of selected variables from the Children of Immigrants data.

As shown in Table 6.3, each case has a case ID, each question is given a variable name and a variable label, and each categorical value for categorical variables (such as sex and health condition) must be given a numerical value (such as male = 1 and female = 2). All questions, items, and categories included in any questionnaire must be given a code prior to data entry into a statistical software package. The first step in preparing data for entry is creating an instrumentation code book such as the one in Table 6.3. Guided by the codebook, data can be entered as numerical values so that statistical analysis will be conducted.

Table 6.3: Codebook on Selected Variables from Children Immigrant Data

QUESTION/LABEL	VARIABLE NAME	VALUE CATEGORIES, IF ANY
ID number	CASEID	
Student's grade	V5	1=7th 2=8th
		3=9th 4=10th
R's sex	V18	1=Male 2=Female
R's age	V19	
R's birth year	V20	
R's US citizen	V23	1=Yes 2=No
R's ability speak English	V24-V27	1=Not at all
R's ability understand English	... ...	2=Not well
R's ability read English	... ...	3=Well
R's ability write English	... ...	4=Very well
		(These values apply for all four items)
Felt sad past week	V114-V117	1=Rarely
Could not get going past week	... ...	2=Some of the time
Did not feel like eating past week	... ...	3=Occasionally
I felt depressed past week	... ...	4=Most of the time
		(These values apply for all four items)
Grade point average	V139	
Parent SES index	V1348	
Education respondent wants	V260	1=Less than high school
		2=Finish high school
		3=Finish some college
		4=Finish college
		5=Finish a graduate degree
Self-reported race	V323A	1=White 2=Black
		3=Asian 4=Multiracial
		5=Hispanic 6=Nationality
		7=Other
Respondent health	V449	1=Excellent
		2=Very good
		3=Good
		4=Fair
		5=Poor

DATA ENTRY, RECODE, AND COMPUTE USING SPSS

The SPSS main toolbar provides access to various buttons and functions available in the SPSS program. Use the mouse to scroll up and down, or click on the appropriate button to complete the analysis or employ any other function. The *File* menu allows users to open a new data file or SPSS syntax file, an existing data file or SPSS syntax file, save files in different data format such as Stata, and many other functions.

Data Entry

Once you have your data (i.e., completed questionnaires) ready to enter and a codebook at hand, you may open a new data file for data entry. To open a new data file:

(1) Click on *File.*
(2) Click on *New.*
(3) Click on *Data.* A new SPSS *Data Editor* screen will then open.

Defining Variables: Before entering data into the SPSS spreadsheet, you need to first define the variables contained in your research instrument (i.e., questionnaire). This means that you must create a variable name in correspondence with each question in your questionnaire and define the variable type (numeric, comma, dot, scientific notation, date, string, etc.), width, decimals, label, values, missing, columns, and measures. If you already have an instrumentation codebook, you can transfer the information created in your codebook to the *Variable View* screen by clicking on the *Variable View* tab, located on the left bottom of the spreadsheet. Each row in the *Variable View* screen represents a variable; each column represents a variable property, which allows you to define and edit all variables in the study according to their type, width, decimals, label, values (for categorical variables), missing values, column width, alignment, and the level of measurement. The next step is to enter all data collected from your research participants. When you create a new variable name, you need to follow certain rules set by IBM SPSS. Those basic rules are:

1. Variable names must be unique. The program does not allow you to have duplicate names.
2. The first character must be a letter (A through Z, lowercase or uppercase) or one of the following special characters: @, #, $. But a variable name beginning with a # sign is defined as a scratch variable, which cannot be saved in a data file. Therefore, unless you have a special purpose, try not to use this character in the first position of a variable. A variable name beginning with a $ sign indicates a system variable that cannot be modified. As such, avoid a dollar sign as the first character of a variable when you define variables.
3. Spaces are not allowed within variable names.
4. Certain reserved keywords (ALL, AND, BY, EQ, GE, GT, LE, LT, NE, NOT, OR, TO, and WITH) cannot be used as variable names.
5. A variable name can be formed with any mixture of lowercase and uppercase characters.

Click on the *Data View* tab at the lower left corner in the main SPSS screen. A new spreadsheet with all the variable names will appear on the top row. You may enter the data case by case according to the instruction of the codebook. To open an existing SPSS data set, you need to take the following steps:

(1) Click on *File*.
(2) Click on *Open*.
(3) Click on *Data*. A new *Open File* dialogue box will open.
(4) Choose the directory where the data set is located, click on the file name.
(5) Click on *Open*.

The *Analyze* menu allows you to run descriptive statistics including frequency tables, and run compare means, correlations, regression analysis (linear and nonlinear), reliability (Cronbach's alpha), factor analysis, various nonparametric tests, and many other functions.

The SPSS main tool bar is the main method used to run various descriptive and inferential statistics and other analyses. Another way to run statistical analysis in SPSS is through use of the SPSS syntax file. It is the SPSS programming language, a text file composed of statistical commands, that instructs the SPSS to run a specific requested analysis. Click on *File*, then click *New*, and then *Syntax*. A syntax screen will then open. The SPSS syntax commands for each function appear throughout the book. We will illustrate how to type syntax commands and run them for specific analyses.

Data Cleaning

Everyone may make errors in data entry, especially with a large sample. Errors will significantly affect analysis results, and therefore it is necessary to check the data and correct errors. For example, the codebook in Table 6.3 defines the value for male as 1 and female as 2. Due to carelessness, you might enter 3 instead of 2 for female. Therefore, before conducting any statistical analyses, we need to clean and screen the data. Running frequencies for all variables in the study may help us locate possible errors. For example, let's run frequency for V323A (self-reported race) in Children Immigrant data.

To run frequency in SPSS, follow the following steps:

a. Open the *Children Immigrant* data file.
b. Click on *Analyze* in the SPSS main toolbar.
c. Click on *Descriptive Statistics*.
d. Click on *Frequencies*. A new dialog box called *Frequencies* will open.
e. Scroll down in the variables list and click on V323A.
f. Click on the arrow button between the two boxes to move V323A in the *Variable(s)* box.
g. Click *OK*.

You'll get the following output table as presented in Table 6.4.

According to the codebook of Children Immigrant data (Table 6.2), the variable "self-reported race" has seven values, and the number 1 (value) was assigned to White (value label); 2 to Black; 3 to Asian; 4 to Multiracial; 5 to Hispanic; 6 to Nationality; and 7 to other. From the frequency table of self-reported race shown in Table 6.4, we do not see any cases with a value out of the valid range of 1 through 7, but we see 974 cases with missing value. It means that 974 cases did not answer this question. If you find cases with a value out of the range, you must correct them first before running any command.

Table 6.4: Frequency Table of Self-reported Race (Variable Name V323A)

Statistics

Self-reported race

N	Valid	4288
	Missing	974

Self-reported race

		FREQUENCY	PERCENT	VALID PERCENT	CUMULATIVE PERCENT
Valid	1.White	612	11.6	14.3	14.3
	2.Black	281	5.3	6.6	20.8
	3.Asian	1106	21.0	25.8	46.6
	4.Multiracial	487	9.3	11.4	58.0
	5.Hispanic	1008	19.2	23.5	81.5
	6.Nationality	639	12.1	14.9	96.4
	7.Other	155	2.9	3.6	100.0
	Total	4288	81.5	100.0	
Missing	System	974	18.5		
Total		5262	100.0		

SPSS may help you locate the source of the error. Suppose you find a case whose value for sex is 3, you may open *Data View* and click on the variable Sex. This will highlight all data for this variable. Then you click on *Edit* in the SPSS main toolbar and select *Find*. A new dialogue box called *"Find and Replace—Data View"* will open. Then type "3" on the *Find* field, and then click *Find Next*. The number 3 under Sex will be highlighted. You will find the CASEID (case ID) whose Sex is 3, and then correct it.

Recoding Value(s) for a Variable

As shown in the codebook table on selected variables from Children Immigrant data (Table 6.3), the value labels for the variable V449 (Respondent Health) are 1=Excellent, 2=Very good, 3=Good, 4=Fair, and 5=Poor. You may want to recode the values with the high value referring to Excellent=5 and the low value as Poor=1.

Recode into Same Variables: We can use the SPSS main toolbar or SPSS syntax file to do the job. When you use the SPSS main toolbar to recode values of this variable, you can recode this variable into the same variable or a different variable. To recode a variable into the same variable, you need to take the following steps:

(1) Click on *Transform,* and then
(2) Click on *Recode into Same Variables.*

Figure 6.1: Recoding a Variable into the Same Variable Using SPSS

OLD VALUE	NEW VALUE
1 →	5
2 →	4
3 →	3
4 →	2
5 →	1

Then, a new dialog box called "*Recode into Same Variables*" will open. From the variables list in the left box, scroll down and click on V449, then click on the arrow button to move it into the *Numeric Variables* box. Then click on *Old and New Values*. A new dialogue box called "*Recode Into Same Variables: Old and New Values*" will open. Type 1 in the *Value* box under *Old Value*. Type 5 in the *Value* box under *New Value*. Click on *Add* to confirm this recode. Repeat this until you finish recoding 5 to 1 as shown in Figure 6.1, click on *Continue*, and then click on *OK*.

You can also use "syntax" to do the same job. In the SPSS syntax window, type:

---

(1) RECODE V449 (1=5) (2=4) (3=3) (4=2) (5=1) (SYSMIS=SYSMIS).
(2) EXECUTE.

In the syntax, "SYSMIS=SYSMIS" means that if there is system missing for any cases, after recoding, these cases will still have system missing. After you highlight this syntax, click on the arrow button on the toolbar to run it. You may want to save this file in a new file.

Recode into Different Variables: You can create a new variable by recoding the values for an existing variable. The steps are as follows:

---

(1) Click on *Transform*.
(2) Click on *Recode into Different Variables*, and a new dialogue box will then open.
(3) Highlight the variable V449 from the left side, and move it to "Input Variables ⟶ Output Variables" box.
(4) Type a new variable name (i.e., RecV449) under "Output Variable Name."
(5) Type a new label under "Output Variable Label" (i.e., recoded V449).
(6) Click on "*Old and New Values*."
(7) Follow the same steps as specified in "*Recode into Same Variables*."

Recode to Combine Groups: You can use the *Recode* function to regroup by combining answer categories. By combining groups, you create a new variable. For example, in Children Immigrant data, self-reported race (variable name V323A) has seven categories: 1=White, 2=Black, 3=Asian, 4=Multiracial, 5=Hispanic, 6=Nationality, and 8=Other. We may want to regroup them into four categories for analysis convenience:

1=White, 2=Black, 3=Asian, 4=Hispanic, and 5=Other including Multiracial, Nationality, and Other. The following syntax can do the job:

---

(1) RECODE V323A (1=1) (2=2) (3=3) (4=5) (5=4) (6=5) (8=5) (SYSMIS=SYSMIS) INTO newrace.
(2) EXECUTE.

After you highlight this syntax, click on the arrow button on the toolbar to run it. You need to define a new value label for 5=Other. Now your data has a new variable named "newrace" (with five categories). You can also use the main toolbar to do the job. Whenever you recode or compute a new variable, it's a good habit to verify that you did it correctly. We can run a cross tab to verify the recoding job. The SPSS syntax is:

```
CROSSTABS
/TABLES=V323A BY newrace
/FORMAT=AVALUE TABLES
/CELLS=COUNT
/COUNT ROUND CELL.
```

The output table is presented in Table 6.5.

We see that the number of children with V323A (self-reported race) as *White, Black, Asian,* and *Hispanic* matches the numbers in the new variable *newrace,* but the value label for *Hispanic* changes from 5 to 4. That is what we wanted. Also, we see that children with self-reported race as *Multiracial, Nationality,* and *Other* now fall into category 5 with the value label as *Other* in the new variable—*newrace.* System missing cases were excluded from the cross tab analysis. Now we can see that we did the recoding correctly.

Table 6.5: Cross Tabulation of Self-reported Race (V323A) and Newrace (Recoded Variable)

		NEWRACE					TOTAL
		1	2	3	4	5	
V323A Self-reported race	1 White	612	0	0	0	0	612
	2 Black	0	281	0	0	0	281
	3 Asian	0	0	1106	0	0	1106
	4 Multiracial	0	0	0	0	487	487
	5 Hispanic	0	0	0	1008	0	1008
	6 Nationality	0	0	0	0	639	639
	8 Other	0	0	0	0	155	155
Total		612	281	1106	1008	1281	4288

Creating a New Variable Using the Compute Command in SPSS

From time to time it is necessary to create a new variable by adding a set of scale items or questions. For example, as shown on the codebook listed earlier, the researcher collected information on four items to measure children's English proficiency. The variable names of these items are V24, V25, V26, and V27, representing the respondent's ability of speaking, understanding, reading, and writing English. The response categories are four-point Likert scale: 1=Not at all, 2=Not well, 3=Well, and 4=Very well. The potential total score will have a range from 4 to 16. We are definitely most interested in the total score of the scale, because the scale has a higher reliability and greater variance than individual items. To add these four items using the main toolbar in SPSS, we need to take the following steps:

(1) Click on *Transform.*
(2) Click on *Compute Variable.* A dialogue box called *Compute New Variable* will open.
(3) Type a new variable name you want to create in the *Target Variable* box in the upper left corner of the *Compute Variable* dialogue box. You can select the name "English" in this case.
(4) Scroll down under *Function Group* and select *Statistical.*
(5) Under *Functions and Special Variables,* click on *SUM.*
(6) Click on the upward arrow button ( ) next to *Functions and Special Variables.* You will now see SUM (?,?) in the *Numeric Expression* box.
(7) Click on the variable V24 listed in the variable box on the left side under *Type & Label* and replace the first "?" in the *Numeric Expression* box.
(8) Type "to" and then highlight V27 to replace the second "?" The expression appears as: SUM(V24 to V27). Alternatively, you may move all four variables from V24 to V27 to the *Numeric Expression* box. In this case, make sure that you type a comma (,) between each item: SUM(V24,V25,V26,V27).

There is a short-cut to run the Compute command in SPSS that adds designated scale items. The steps are as follows: (Note that the first three steps are identical.)

(1) Click on *Transform.*
(2) Click on *Compute Variable.* A dialogue box called *Compute New Variable* will open.
(3) Type a new variable name you want to create in the *Target Variable* box in the upper left corner of the *Compute Variable* dialogue box. You can use the name "English" in this case.
(4) Highlight V24 in the variable list box on the left, move it to the *Numeric Expression* box, and then click on " + "; highlight V25, move it to the *Numeric Expression* box, and then click on " +." Repeat this until you move all four variables to the *Numeric Expression* box. The expression appears as: [V24 + V25 + V26 + V27], and then click on OK.

In adding scale items, you can also use syntax to do the same job. You need to click on *File, New,* and *Syntax,* and then type the following syntax:

COMPUTE English=SUM(V24 to V27).
EXECUTE.

After you highlight this syntax, click on the arrow button on the toolbar to run it. Both methods will create and add a new variable called "English" to the data file. The new variable can be found in the last column in the *Data View* screen.

DATA ENTRY, RECODE, AND COMPUTE USING STATA

Stata is the most popular program for statistical analysis in many fields, as it is extremely powerful and relatively easy to learn. Its straightforward but flexible syntax makes it a good choice for data management and various statistical analyses. There are two approaches one can take to use Stata. One is to use it as an interactive tool: you start Stata, load your data, and start typing or clicking on commands. But interactive work cannot be easily or reliably replicated, or modified if you change your mind. It is also very difficult to recover from mistakes because there is no "undo" command in Stata.

The other approach is to treat Stata as a programming language and use syntax to do the job. In this approach you write your own programs, called "do files," and run them when they are complete. Since they are written in a permanent file, they can be debugged or modified and then rerun at will. They also serve as an exact record of how you obtained your results—a lab notebook for the researcher. Any work you intend to publish or present should be done using "do files." This book will teach you how to use Stata commands and prepare you to write "do files" for data analysis.

Stata's User Interface

When you start up Stata, the first thing you will see is the main user interface window.

The Command window is where you type commands that are executed when you press Enter. **Command**— What do you want to do?

The Results window contains output from the commands. The Results window also echoes the command that generated the output.

The Review window lists the commands that have been entered.

The Variables window lists the names of variables that are in memory. If you click on a name, it is pasted into the Command window.

The Properties window lists variable names, labels, and data set information (number of variables and number of cases).

Finding and Opening Data

To open a data file in the command window, click: .use *filename.dta*, clear.

Descriptive Statistics for Individual Variables

Let us run simple descriptive statistics for the two variables from the Children Immigrant data. But first, we use Codebook command for the two variables.

Stata syntax: . codebook V19 V139.

Table 6.6: Codebook for Age (V19) and GPA (V139)

V19	RESPONDENT AGE
type: numeric (double)	
range: [12,18]	units: 1
unique values: 7	missing: 1/5262
tabulation: Freq. Value	
24 12	
1005 13	
2329 14	
1541 15	
342 16	
18 17	
2 18	
1 .	

V139				GRADE POINT AVERAGE
type: numeric (double)				
range: [0,4.96]			units: .01	
unique values: 285			missing: 108/5262	
mean: 2.52155				
std. dev: .911147				

percentiles:	10%	25%	50%	75%	90%
		1.3	1.9	2.58	3.2	3.7

Table 6.7: Summary of Two Variables (V19 and V139)

Stata syntax: sum V19 V139

VARIABLE	OBS	MEAN	STD. DEV.	MIN	MAX
V19	5261	14.23456	.8626775	12	18
V139	5154	2.521548	.9111471	0	4.96

As shown in Table 6.6 and Table 6.7, both variables are numeric rather than string variables. In string variables, letter data are often used for open-ended questions. V19 (age) is a discrete variable, and V139 (GPA) is a continuous variable. Therefore, codebook output for V19 provides the age range (from 12 to 18), unique values (7), missing cases (1 out of 5,262), as well as a frequency table for children in the data set with different ages. The codebook for V139 (GPA) provides mean score (2.52), standard deviation (.91), missing cases (108 out of 5,262), and percentiles from 10% to 90%. Stata Command Summarize (or sum) provides basic descriptive statistics including mean, standard deviation, minimum and maximum value, in addition to valid N for the two variables:

Run frequency tables using command tabulate (or tab). For example, we want to know the distribution of variable V323A—self-reported race:

Stata syntax: tab V323A, missing.

After command tab V323A, followed by a comma "missing." Stata allows users to add various options for additional or conditional requests from the user. As in this example, after the comma, "missing" means that in addition to the frequency of valid responses, we want to know how many cases have a missing value for this variable. As shown in the output, out of 5,262 children, 974 did not report their race.

Stata can produce various visually handy graphs, such as Figure 6.2. Here are two examples. First, we will request a dot plot for a categorical variable V449—self-reported health status with 1 as "Excellent" and 5 as "Poor."

Stata syntax: dotplot V449.

Table 6.8: Frequency Table for Self-reported Race (V323A)

SELF-REPORT ED RACE	FREQ.	PERCENT	CUM.
White	612	11.63	11.63
Black	281	5.34	16.97
Asian	1,106	21.02	37.99
Multiracial	487	9.26	47.24
Hispanic	1,008	19.16	66.40
Nationality	639	12.14	78.54
Other	155	2.95	81.49
.	974	18.51	100.00
Total	5,262	100.00	

Figure 6.2: Dot Plot of Self-Reported Health (SRH)

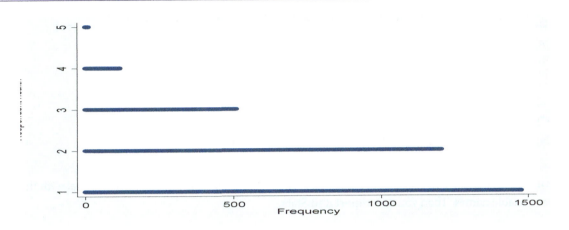

The second graph is a histogram for a standardized continuous variable V148 scale for a parent socioeconomic status (SES) index (See Figure 6.3).

Stata syntax: . histogram V148, normal
(bin=37, start=−1.66, width=.10135135).

Reading Data and Data Entry

If you have data in a different software package, you can use the StatTransfer program to convert the file to Stata format. If your data is in SPSS, you can also save it directly into Stata format. If your data are in a

Figure 6.3: Histogram of Parent's Socioeconomic Status (SES) Index

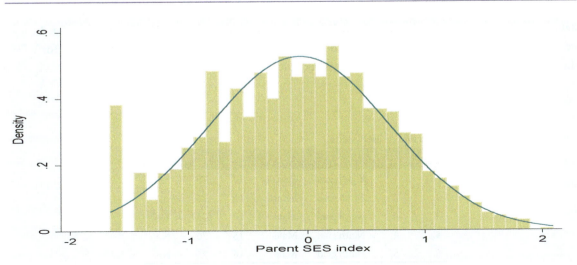

spreadsheet, such as Excel, you can use the specific import command available for that in Stata: "import Excel." Entire worksheets can be read, or custom cell ranges can be read. You can also transfer files from Excel using StatTransfer. For example, if you have data in Excel, in your Stata command window you can type:

import excel *filename*.xls, clear firstrow.

The firstrow option reads in the variable names from the first row.

If you have new data, you may enter your data directly into the Stata Editor window.

---

(1) Click on Data button on the top toolbar.
(2) Next click on Data Editor (Editor), at File, select new, and then you may enter your data.

Alternatively, you may enter your data at Excel spreadsheet to establish a spreadsheet data file, with the first row as variable names. Then you can import it to Stata.

Data Screening

No matter what analysis methods or procedures you use, before you conduct the analysis you will need to perform a thorough data examination or data screening. A number of Stata commands provide us with good tools to do so, such as the codebook and summarize tabs previously cited. You can also use the **list** command to list all or some of the observations. For example, below we "list" the first five observations for selected variables in the Children Immigrant data.

list CASEID V5 V18 V19 V20 V23 in 1/5

Recoding into New Variables

When you recode data into a new variable, you need to check your recoded version against the original to make sure you did it correctly. Let's suppose we want to recode V139 - children's GPA (range from 0 to 4.96) into a dummy variable with values of only 0 and 1.

gen GPA2 = (V139>=2.5) if V139<.

(108 missing values generated)

GPA2 is the recoded new variable name. We use 2.5 as a cut point. If the original value is 2.5 or higher, Stata will assign a value of 1, otherwise it is 0. We added a condition as long as V139 is not missing. A missing value is labeled as "." (dot) in Stata. As the output in Table 6.10 shows, 108 cases have missing for V139. These cases are still missing for the recoded new variable.

Table 6.9. Listing Cases with Selected Variables

Stata syntax: list CASEID.

	CASEID	V5	V18	V19	V20	V23
1.	1	Eighth grad	Female	14	77	.
2.	2	Ninth grad	Female	15	76	.
3.	3	Ninth grad	Male	16	75	Yes
4.	4	Ninth grad	Male	15	76	No
5.	5	Ninth grad	Male	16	75	No

Table 6.10: Frequency Distribution of GPA2 (Recoded Variable)

GPA2	FREQ.	PERCENT	CUM.
0	2,338	44.43	44.43
1	2,816	53.52	97.95
.	108	2.05	100.00
Total	5,262	100.00	

Alternatively, we may use the following approach to accomplish this:

gen GPA2=.

(5,262 missing values generated)

For the new variable, we initially assign missing for everyone. So 5,262 is the sample size.

replace GPA2 = 0 if V139<2.5

(2,338 real changes made)

Then we use the "replace" command to assign value 0 for those whose GPA (V139) is less than 2.5. As the output reveals in Table 6.10, 2,338 children have value 0 for this new variable.

replace GPA2 = 1 if V139>=2.5 & V139<.

(2,816 real changes made)

Finally, we assign value 1 to those whose GPA (V139) is 2.5 or higher, excluding a missing value. As shown in Table 6.10, 2,816 cases have value 1 for GPA2. We need to check whether we got what we expected.

tab GPA2, missing

You can also run a cross tabulation to check the recoding.

tabstat V139, by(GPA2) statistics(min max)

A display table of selected summary statistics is presented in Table 6.11.

After creating a new variable, we need to label the new variable and also assign value labels. The steps are as follows:

```
. *labeling variables and values
. label variable GPA2 "1=High GPA"
. label define GPA2lb 0 "LowGPA" 1 "HighGPA"     //(creating a label name)//
. label values GPA2 GPA2lb                       //linking variable to label name//
. tab GPA2
```

Table 6.11: Summary for Variable: V139

by categories of: GPA2		
GPA2	MIN	MAX
0	0	2.49
1	2.5	4.96
Total	0	4.96

Table 6.12: Frequency for a Dichotomous Variable (GPA)

1=HIGH GPA	FREQ.	PERCENT	CUM.
LowGPA	2,338	45.36	45.36
HighGPA	2,816	54.64	100.00
Total	5,154	100.00	

Creating a New Variable by Summing Items in Stata

Sometimes we need to create a new variable from a series of scale items by combining them. For example, in Children Immigrant data, four items asked children their English ability (speaking, understanding, reading, and writing). Each item is a four-point Likert scale question. By summing them together, we create a new variable, which is considered as an interval variable. The Stata commands are as follows:

gen English = V24 + V25 + V26 + V27
label variable English "English Ability Scale"
sum V24 V25 V26 V27 English

As shown in Table 6.13, the mean score of the newly created variable (English) is 14.83779 with the minimum score of 4 and the maximum score of 16.

Table 6.13: Summary Statistics

VARIABLE	OBS	MEAN	STD. DEV.	MIN	MAX
V24	5247	3.732609	.5371893	1	4
V25	5246	3.778117	.4842078	1	4
V26	5246	3.679565	.5571871	1	4
V27	5247	3.644368	.591977	1	4
English	5240	14.83779	1.943373	4	16

SUMMARY

In this chapter we introduced the basic concept of probability and non-probability sampling techniques. Students learned surveys that employ different types of probability sampling drawing from national archives of social science. We discussed common data collection methods and compared and contrasted the selected data collection methods that are relevant and meaningful for social work research. We also examined the best practices of data collection and data entry into SPSS and Stata. Also, data modification techniques, such as recoding and computing to create new variables based on old variables, were introduced for advanced statistical data analyses.

CLASS EXERCISE

- Select a research topic and discuss what type(s) of sampling is (are) the most appropriate.
- If a sampling technique is chosen, discuss how to sample research participants, and what might be the right sample size.
- Select a questionnaire or a scale from this book, complete it as a fictitious respondent, define variable names and values, and enter data into SPSS or Stata.

REFERENCES

Engel, R. J., & Schutt, R. K. (2010). *Fundamentals of social work research*. Thousand Oaks, CA: Sage Publications.

Gold, R. (1958). Roles in sociological field observation. *Social Forces, 36,* 217-213.

Haney, C., Banks, W. C., & Zimbardo, P. G. (1973). A study of prisoners and guards in a simulated prison. *Naval Research Review, 30,* 4-17.

Landsberger, H. A. (1958). *Hawthorne revisited*. Ithaca, NY: Cornell University Press.

Levy, S. P., & Lemeschow, S. (1999). *Sampling of populations: Methods and applications* (3rd ed.). New York, NY: John Wiley & Sons, Inc.

Portes, A., & Rumbaut, R. G. "The Children of Immigrants Longitudinal Study (CILS), 1991-2006." Inter-University Consortium for Political and Social Research. From http://www.icpsr.umich.edu/icpsrweb/landing.jsp.

Rosenhan, D. L. (1973). On being sane in insane places. *Science, 179*(4070), 250-258. doi:10.1126/science.179.4070.250

Royse, D. (2011). *Research methods in social work* (6th ed.). Belmont, CA: Brooks/Cole, Cengage Learning.

SEVEN

Descriptive Statistics

In this chapter, we will introduce specific descriptive statistics and demonstrate how they are used by researchers in describing sampling characteristics using SPSS and Stata. **Descriptive statistics** are the procedures for quantitatively describing and summarizing the main features of sample data. Descriptive statistics are distinguished from inferential statistics in many ways. Descriptive statistics aim to summarize a sample, rather than use the data to infer about the population from which a sample is drawn. For example, means and standard deviations calculated to describe a sample property are **statistics**, not population parameters. On the other hand, **inferential statistics** are techniques used to make generalizations about the population beyond the sample data. Inferential statistics aim to estimate population parameters and test statistical hypotheses. The term **univariate analysis** refers to the description of a single variable at a time. Single variables can be described in three major ways in descriptive statistics: (1) frequency distributions, (2) measures of central tendency, and (3) measures of dispersion (variability). Frequency distributions are used when variables are measured by nominal or ordinal levels of measurement in univariate analysis. For interval and ratio levels of variables (i.e., income and years of residence in the United States), measures of central tendency and dispersion are mostly used to describe the variables, although frequency distributions can be used technically. Table 7.1 lists a number of sample questions that can be described using one of these descriptive statistical tools.

FREQUENCY DISTRIBUTIONS

Frequency distributions are used if researchers collect data using nominal or ordinal levels of measures. Frequency distributions classify cases into mutually exclusive response categories. Typical frequency tables include frequencies, indicating how many cases belong to that answer category, percentages, valid percentages, and cumulative percentages. The SPSS frequencies command is as follows:

(1) Click on *Analyze.*
(2) Click on *Descriptive Statistics.*
(3) Click on *Frequencies.*

Table 7.1: Univariate Descriptive Statistics by Variable Type

SAMPLE QUESTIONS	VARIABLE TYPE	METHODS OF UNIVARITE ANALYSIS
1. How old are you? AGE:_____ Years Old	Continuous Variable	Mean and Standard Deviation & Frequency Distribution
What is your gender? 1. Male___ 2. Female____	Categorical Variable	Frequency Distribution Only
What was your family's annual income last year? $_____	Continuous Variable	Mean and Standard Deviation & Frequency Distribution

What is your religious preference?
  1. Catholic
  2. Protestant
  3. Buddhist
  4. Other
  5. None (Atheist)
	Categorical Variable	Frequency Distribution Only

What is your ethnic background?
  1. African American
  2. Asian American
  3. Latino American
  4. Native American
  5. White American
  6. Other
	Categorical Variable	Frequency Distribution

The output of frequency distribution calculated for the gender variable (variable name: SRSEX) of 2011–2012 CHIS (California Health Interview Survey) is presented in Table 7.2.

MEASURES OF CENTRAL TENDENCY

A useful way to describe a group as a whole is to find a single number that represents what is average of that set of data. In social research, such a value is known as a measure of **central tendency**, because it is generally located toward the middle or the center of a distribution where most of the data tend to be concentrated. There are three kinds of averages, and we will describe these three measures of central tendency that provide information about the point around which values are clustered: the **mode, median, and mean**.

Mode

The **mode** is the value with the greatest frequency. In other words, it is the most commonly occurring value in a distribution. For example, consider the values of 2, 5, 3, 4, 7, 6, 4. Perhaps these values represent the number of clients served by seven social workers. The mode is 4 because it occurs twice, more than any other value. The mode is simple to figure out and easy to compute. It is usually not affected by extreme

Table 7.2: Frequency Distribution of Sex, 2011–2012 CHIS

SRSEX GENDER					
	RESPONSE CATEGORY	FREQUENCY	PERCENT	VALID PERCENT	CUMULATIVE PERCENT
Valid	1 MALE	17848	41.6	41.6	41.6
	2 FEMALE	25087	58.4	58.4	100.0
	Total	42935	100.0	100.0	

UCLA Center for Health Policy Research
10960 Wilshire Blvd, Suite 1550
Los Angeles, CA 90024
CHIS 2011-2012
Website for Public Use Data Files: http://healthpolicy.ucla.edu/chis/data/Pages/overview.aspx

values (outliers). Unlike other measures of central tendency (mean and median), one disadvantage of the mode is that a given distribution may include more than one mode. A distribution with one mode, which is desired, is called **unimodal**. A distribution with two modes is called **bimodal**, and a distribution with three or more modes is called **multimodal**. Another disadvantage of the mode is that it does not provide any information about the variation of scores.

Median

The **median** is the middle value when values are listed in order; there is the same number of values higher than and lower than it. The median divides an array of values into two equal groups. Like the mode, the median is not affected by outlier scores. To determine the median, first arrange raw data in an array. If the data are not in order from low to high (or high to low), you need to put them in order first. The position of the median value can be located by inspection or by the formula:

$$\text{Position of the median} = \frac{N+1}{2}$$

If the distribution has an odd number of cases, the median will be the middle value of the distribution. For the scores of 7, 9, 10, 12, 15, 16, 17, the median is 12 because there are three scores on either side of it. According to the above formula, $(7 + 1)/2 = 4$, 12 is the fourth number. If the distribution has an even number of cases, the median will be the sum of the two middle scores divided by two. For example, for the following data, 7, 9, 10, 12, 14, 15, 16, 17, there are eight numbers, and according to the above formula $(8 + 1)/2 = 4.5$, the median falls between the fourth and fifth cases. Therefore, the median is the number between 12 and 14 or $(12 + 14)/2$. That is 13.

Mean

The **mean** is the sum of the values of all cases divided by the number of cases. It is by far the most commonly used measure of central tendency. The formula is:

$$\overline{} = \frac{\Sigma}{N}$$

where

$\overline{X}$ = mean (read as X bar)

Σ = sum (expressed as the Greek capital letter sigma)

X = raw score in a set of scores

N = total number of scores in a set

For the data set of 2, 5, 3, 4, 7, 6, 4, we can calculate the mean as follows:

$$\overline{X} = \frac{2+5+3+4+7+6+4}{7} = 4.43 \quad \text{or}$$

$$\overline{X} = \frac{(2\times1)+(5\times1)+(3\times1)+(4\times2)+(7\times1)+(6\times1)}{7} = 4.43$$

Unlike the mode, the mean is not always the score that occurs most often. The main difference between median and mean is that the mean is not necessarily the middlemost point in a distribution.

In the three measures of central tendency, each provides different information about the distribution of a variable; however, the type of data, their levels of measurement, and their distribution will determine what is most appropriate to report. Table 7.3 summarizes the required level of measurement for the three measures of central tendency. An x indicates the measure may be appropriately used at a given level of measurement. Note that the mode may be used with variables at all levels of measurement. The median may be used when the level of measurement is ordinal or interval/ratio. Finally, from a formal perspective, the use of means requires interval/ratio level of measures.

For nominal variables, the **mode** is the only measure of central tendency to report. For example, the variable Gender is classified as male = 1 and female = 2. It is meaningless to report the median or the mean. If we found that most are female in a study, then we can safely report that the mode is female, or 2, the value associated with it.

For ordinal data, both the **mode** and the **median** could be reported. For example, we asked forty clients to rate their perceived satisfaction with the services they received on a four-point Likert scale (1 = very dissatisfied, 2 = dissatisfied, 3 = satisfied, 4 = very satisfied). Five clients rated their satisfaction as 1, eight as 2, twelve as 3, and fifteen as 4. Here, the mode is 4 because 4 is the most frequent score (fifteen subjects chose 4); the median is 3, because according to the formula for computing median, the middle point position is 20.5, located with the score of 3.

Table 7.3: Measures of Central Tendency Appropriate at Different Levels of Measurement

	MEASURES		
LEVEL OF MEASUREMENT	MODE	MEDIAN	MEAN
Nominal	x		
Ordinal	x	x	
Interval/ratio	x	x	x

Why can't we report the mean for ordinal data? With the same example, these responses were then entered into a computerized data file. If the response was "very satisfied," the number 4 was entered; for "satisfied," 3 was entered; for "dissatisfied," 2 was entered; and for "very dissatisfied" 1 was entered. With the numbers entered, a software program can indeed calculate a mean. Totaling the numbers for all the responses and dividing by sample size (N = 40), SPSS for Windows and Stata would calculate the mean to be 2.925. This value is between 2 (dissatisfied) and 3 (satisfied), though it is much closer to 3. Can we conclude the mean is 2.925 and that this represents an "average" response for this specific question? The answer is no. The numbers 1, 2, 3, and 4 were basically selected at the researcher's choice. They are codes for keeping track of responses and have little meaning beyond that. Therefore, the mean of 2.925 is "meaningless," although numbers 1, 2, 3, and 4 seem to be sensible and straightforward choices. Since the measurement is at the ordinal level, one cannot determine whether the interval from "dissatisfied" to "satisfied" represents the same difference as the interval from "satisfied" to "very satisfied." Although the calculated mean of 2.925 is close to the median of 3, given that we do not know whether the numbers represent responses accurately, the validity of the mean is questionable.

Thus, formally, ordinal-level measures do not permit the calculation of the mean. As a matter of practice, however, we still see some researchers report means for ordinal-level variables cautiously with appropriate recognition of limitations. While many researchers recommend against calculating the mean for ordinal-level data, nearly all concur that one may indeed use the mean for almost-interval-level data, such as multi-item attitudinal scales.

As shown in Table 7.3, with quantitative data, either discrete or continuous including interval or ratio data, the mean could be reported along with the mode and median. However, the mean is very sensitive to outlying cases. For example, if we want to report the average age of a class and found that majority of students were between 18 and 22 but one was 40, with this student included, the mean age would be much higher than without the older student. We may want to treat this case as missing and report the mean based on other students.

MEASURES OF DISPERSION (VARIABILITY)

As cited earlier, measures commonly used to describe a data set are frequency distributions, measures of central tendency and measures of dispersion or variability. We saw that the mode, median, and mean could be used to summarize in a single number what is typical of a distribution; however, measures of central tendency only provide a point estimate of the data and yield only an incomplete picture of a set of data. If used alone, it can be misleading because any measure of central tendency does not tell us how the scores are scattered around the center of the distribution. We need a measure of what is commonly referred to as *dispersion* (also known as *variability*). If most values are tightly clustered together, the dispersion is low. If values are widely dispersed, variability is high. Three measures of variability describe the dispersion of each value or score from the mean: **range, variance**, and **standard deviation**.

Range

The **range** is the simplest measure of dispersion. It is the difference between the highest and lowest scores in a distribution. For example, a class of students aged from 18 to 22 with a range of 4, and another class aged from 18 to 30 with a range of 12. With the exception of one student who is 30 in the second class, the two classes are actually similar in the age distribution. We see that the range is clearly influenced or even distorted by just one case. Therefore, the range provides only a preliminary or very rough measure of dispersion.

Variance

The second measure of dispersion is **variance**. To understand the concept of variance, we need first to understand deviation, which is the distance of any given raw score from its mean: $(X - \overline{X})$. We might be tempted to sum all mean deviation to get an overall variance, $\Sigma(X - \overline{X})$. But this summation is zero. To get the variance, we need to square the actual deviations from the mean and add them together, $\Sigma(X - \overline{X})^2$. Mathematically, the variance is defined as the average (mean) of the sum of squared deviations around the mean. The symbol for the variance in a population is σ^2 (sigma squared), and in a sample it is s^2.

$$s^2 = \frac{\Sigma(X - \overline{X})^2}{N-1}$$

where $s^2 = $ variance

$\Sigma(X - \overline{X})^2 = $ sum of the squared deviations from the mean

$N = $ total number of scores

It is a statistic that measures how spread out a distribution of scores is from the mean. The more dispersed a distribution, the greater the deviation is from the mean, and so is its variance.

Standard deviation

Although variance is an important measure of dispersion, it is difficult to interpret. The variance is expressed as the square of whatever unit expresses the data. If the data were age, the variance would be expressed in years squared. To put the measure of dispersion into the original unit of measurement, we take the square root of the variance. This gives us the **standard deviation**, which is the most frequently used measure of variability. We obtain it by summing the squared deviations from the mean, dividing by N, and then taking the square root.

$$s = \sqrt{\frac{\Sigma(X - \overline{X})^2}{N-1}}$$

where
$s = $ standard deviation

$\Sigma(X - \overline{X})^2 = $ sum of the squared deviations from the mean

$N = $ total number of scores

The Meaning of Standard Deviation: The standard deviation has a very important meaning for interpreting scores in what we call the normal distribution. As shown in the figure below, for a roughly normal distribution, 68% of its scores fall within one standard deviation above and below the mean, and 95% of its scores fall within two standard deviations above and below the mean. Thus, if for a given class, the mean test score is 500 with a standard deviation of 100, then the normal range may be defined as 400–600, and approximately two-thirds of students' test scores lie within the normal range.

PERCENTILES AND QUARTILES

A **percentile** is a point or score in a distribution, at or below which a given percentage of scores is found. The 50th percentile (P_{50}) is the score that about half of the cases fall at or below. This is also called the median (median = 50th percentile). For example, a student's score on a test was at the 75th percentile, meaning 75% of all students who took the test scored at or below his score, and 25% scored higher than this student.

Quartiles denote the 25th, 50th (median), and 75th percentiles, symbolized by Q1, Q2, and Q3, respectively. Quartiles divide a distribution of scores into four equal parts. To find a quartile, first find the median, or 50th percentile, which divides a distribution into two equal groups. We need to treat each half as a separate distribution. For all scores below the median, find the middle point. This will be the 25th percentile. Now locate the middle point for all scores above the median. This is the 75th percentile. The interquartile range is the distance between the 75th percentile (Q3) and the 25th percentile (Q1), symbolized by IQR, and computed by subtracting the 25th percentile from the 75th percentile.

Formula: IQR = Q3 − Q1

where

IQR = interquartile range
Q3 = 75th percentile
Q1 = 25th percentile

Figure 7.1: Normal Distribution of Class Test Scores

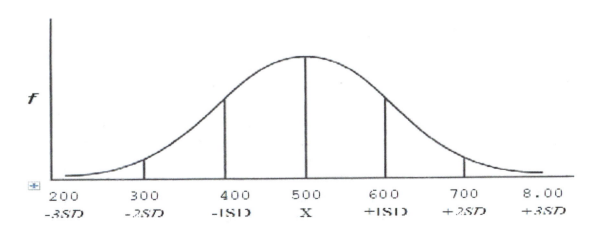

| 200 | 300 | 400 | 500 | 600 | 700 | 8.00 |
| -3SD | -2SD | -1SD | X | +1SD | +2SD | +3SD |

CENTRAL TENDENCY AND VARIABILITY USING SPSS AND STATA

SPSS

To illustrate this, we will use the variable Stanford Math Achievement score from the SPSS Children Immigrant data file. To run measures of central tendency and variability in SPSS, take the following steps:

(1) Open the Children Immigrant data file.

(2) Click on *Analyze* in the SPSS main toolbar.

(3) Click on *Descriptive Statistics*.

(4) Click on *Frequencies*. A new dialogue box called *Frequencies* will open.

(5) Scroll down in the variables list and click on Stanford Math Achievement.

(6) Click on the arrow button between the two boxes to move the Stanford Math Achievement in the *Variable(s)* box.

(7) Click on *Statistics* in the *Frequencies* dialogue box. A new dialogue box called *Frequencies: Statistics* will open.

(8) Check the *Mean, Median,* and *Mode* under *Central Tendency*.

(9) Click on *Quartiles* under *Percentile Values* to get the 25th, 50th, and 75th percentiles. You can also click on *Percentile(s)* to request a specific percentile. Let us request the 10th, 50th, and 90th percentiles. After you check the *Percentiles,* type 10 in the *Percentile(s)* box and click on *Add,* type 90, and click on *Add*.

(10) Click on *Std. Deviation, Variance, Range, Minimum,* and *Maximum* under *Dispersion*.

(11) Click on *Continue* to return to *Frequencies* dialogue box.

(12) You can also click on *Charts* to request a chart. A new dialogue box called *Frequencies: Charts* will open. You may request a histogram. Check *Histogram* and check *With normal curve*.

(13) Click on *Continue*.

(14) Click on *OK*.

SPSS syntax file

```
DATASET ACTIVATE DataSet1.
FREQUENCIES VARIABLES=V133
  /NTILES=4
  /PERCENTILES=10 90
  /STATISTICS=STDDEV VARIANCE RANGE MINIMUM MAXIMUM MEAN MEDIAN MODE
  /HISTOGRAM NORMAL
SPSS output file:
```

The statistics table in Table 7.4 reports the number of valid and missing cases, measures of central tendency (mean, median, mode), measures of dispersion (standard deviation, variance, range, minimum, and maximum), and percentiles.

The last part of the output displays a histogram (below) with a normal curve for Stanford Math Achievement score. This figure also reports the standard deviation, mean, and number of cases (N).

Table 7.4: Descriptive Statistics for Stanford Math Achievement Score Using Frequencies Command

Stanford Math Achievement Score

		Statistics
Valid		4431
Missing		831
Mean		696.34
Median		693.00
Mode		713
Std. Deviation		
Variance		47.167
Range		2224.758
Minimum		291
Maximum		
		566
		857
Percentiles	10	637.00
	25	661.00
	50	693.00
	75	728.00
	90	757.00

Figure 7.2: Histogram for Variable (V133) Stanford Math Achievement Score

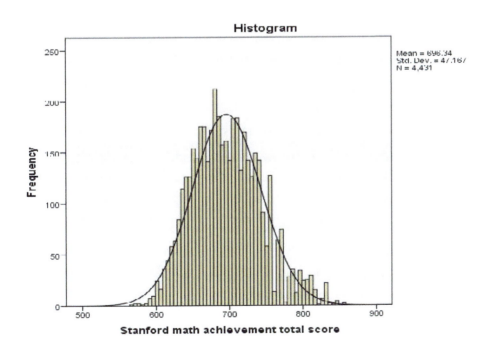

Mean = 696.34
Std. Dev. = 47.167
N = 4,431

We may also obtain measures of central tendency and dispersion using SPSS through *Descriptives*, rather than *Frequencies*. The SPSS command steps are as follows:

---

(1) Open the Children Immigrant data file.

(2) Click on *Analyze* in the SPSS main toolbar.

(3) Click on *Descriptive Statistics*.

(4) Click on *Descriptives*.

(5) Scroll down in the variables list and click on Stanford Math Achievement.

(6) Click on the arrow button between the two boxes to move the Stanford Math Achievement in the *Variable(s)* box.

(7) Click on the Options button. A new dialogue box called *Descriptives: Options* will open.

(8) Check *Std. Deviation, Variance, Range, Minimum,* and *Maximum* under *Dispersion*.

(9) Click on *Continue* to return to *Descriptives* dialogue box.

(10) Click on *OK*.

SPSS syntax

DESCRIPTIVES VARIABLES=V133
 /STATISTICS=MEAN STDDEV VARIANCE RANGE MIN MAX.
SPSS output file:

The output results are presented in Table 7.5.

As shown in the output Table 7.5, measures of central tendency and variance are reported, including mean, range, standard deviation, and variance of Stanford Math Achievement score.

Table 7.5: Descriptive Statistics for Stanford Math Achievement Score Using Descriptives Command

				DESCRIPTIVE STATISTICS			
	N	RANGE	MINIMUM	MAXIMUM	MEAN	STD. DEVIATION	VARIANCE
Stanford Math Achievement total score	4431	291	566	857	696.34	47.167	2224.758
Valid N (listwise)	431						

Stata

After opening the Children Immigrant data file, in the syntax window, type codebook followed by the variable name of Stanford Math Achievement score, V133:

.codebook V133

Stata output file:

The Stata output file in Table 7.6 reports the number of valid and missing cases, measures of central tendency (mean), measures of variability (standard deviation, range, minimum, and maximum), and percentiles.

Table 7.6: Codebook for Stanford Math Achievement Score

V133	STANFORD MATH ACHIEVEMENT TOTAL SCORE
range: [566,857]	units: 1
unique values: 202	missing .: 831/5262
mean: 696.341	
std. dev: 47.1673	
percentiles: 10% 25% 50% 75% 90%	
637 661 693 728 757	

Table 7.7: Summary Table for Stanford Math Achievement Score

VARIABLE	OBS	MEAN	STD. DEV.	MIN	MAX
V133	4431	696.3408	47.16734	566	857

Table 7.8: Selected Measures of Central Tendency and Variance for Stanford Math Achievement Score

VARIABLE	MEAN	P50	RANGE	SD	VARIANCE
V133	696.3408	693	291	47.16734	2224.758

Stata *summarize* command requests descriptive statistics:

sumarize V133

Stata *tabstat* command can also provide some measures of central tendency and variance.

tabstat V133, stats(mean median range sd variance).

Stata *histogram* command requests histogram for the variable.

histogram V133, frequency norm

SUMMARY

This chapter introduced a range of descriptive statistics widely adopted by researchers when they summarize and describe sample characteristics using SPSS and Stata. In particular, three major tools of univariate descriptive statistics: (1) frequency distributions, (2) measures of central tendency, and (3) measures of dispersion (variability) were looked at in detail. Also addressed, in describing sample characteristics, was how to select one of these three statistical tools based on the type of variables under investigation, and how to use SPSS and Stata.

CLASS EXERCISE

- The instructor hands out a data set of sample size n=10 with three variables (gender, income, and total years of education).
- Students calculate in class the mean and standard deviation of income and total years of education, and construct a frequency distribution of the gender variable.
- Students interpret the findings narratively in class.
- Or students can use an existing data set and use SPSS, Stata or Excel to generate some descriptive statistics for at least 5 variables of interest and interpret the meanings of these statistics.

REFERENCES

IBM Software (2014). http://www-01.ibm.com/software/analytics/spss/

Stata (2014). Stata Data Analysis and Statistical Software. http://www.stata.com/

EIGHT

Survey Research Designs and Data Analysis

Survey research can be defined as a process of inquiry or investigation by asking people questions to gather information for some specific purposes. Survey research involves a planned and systematic process of asking questions, collecting data, analyzing data, and confirming answers for selected questions (Rossi, Wright, and Anderson, 1983). The survey research method has been used by various disciplines, including health sciences, management, marketing, political science, psychology, sociology, social work, and other fields outside social sciences and human services. Information from previous chapters on measurement, sampling, data collection, and descriptive statistics will be of great help to you understand the materials presented in this chapter. Students should review previous chapters in preparing for the studying of this chapter.

TYPES OF SURVEY RESEARCH DESIGNS

Survey research can be grouped into two broad categories: large-scale surveys and small-scale surveys. Large-scale surveys involve large samples or numbers of respondents such as the American Community Survey (http://www.census.gov/acs/www/), the National Health and Nutrition Examination Survey (http://www.cdc.gov/), and the California Health Interview Survey (http://healthpolicy.ucla.edu/chis/Pages/default.aspx). Researchers can gain access to numerous large-scale surveys through data archive centers such as the Inter-university Consortium for Political and Social Research (ICPSR) (http://www.icpsr.umich.edu/icpsrweb/landing.jsp). These large-scale surveys often involve thousands of respondents and are extremely expensive. Small-scale surveys are those conducted at local agencies, institutions, or organizations with a few hundred respondents.

We can also group survey research according to sampling methods: probability sampling and non-probability sampling. Probability sampling methods are scientific methods of selecting a representative sample from a larger population. Researchers can compute the probability for each respondent selected to participate in the survey. The basic principle is that each respondent in the population or the sampling frame must have an equal chance or equal probability of being selected (Levy and Lemeshow, 1999).

When respondents are selected on their availability and convenience, the researchers cannot compute their selection probability; therefore, the sample is not representative. If the survey is conducted with an entire population, however, there is no need to select a sample. Social work researchers frequently have to work with non-probability surveys when they conduct a community-based need assessment survey or a client satisfaction survey with a small sample. Social workers or human service organizations can use survey research for different purposes, including need assessment, program development feasibility, social policy outcome evaluation, program evaluation for social services in a community, and client satisfaction.

A survey design is a blueprint or a complete description of a research project from its inception to its final outcomes. When researchers talk about survey research designs, they tend to mean two major ways of administering survey questionnaires or survey instruments: cross-sectional survey and longitudinal survey. **Cross-sectional research** generally refers to a type of research that involves data collection from a cross section of a population at a single point in time. Many projects in social science research are cross-sectional survey studies designed to describe particular characteristics of a group or compare different groups drawn from the population of interest at a specific moment such as a snapshot. A longitudinal study, on the other

Table 8.1: Basic Steps of a Survey Research Design

Step 1	• Research interest or need
Step 2	• Research goal • Research goal can be operationalized in terms of specific aims, hypotheses or questions
Step 3	• Measurements • Develop a survey questionnaire or instrument to collect data that reflect the research goals, specific aims, hypotheses, and questions • Use of a reliable, valid questionnaire
Step 4	• Respondents • Drawing a sample of repondents from a larger community, or • Including all respondents in an agency or institution
Step 5	• Data collection • Use one or combination of data collection methods
Step 6	• Data analysis • Apply appropriate statistical approaches different types of analysis
Step 7	• Explaining the results and dissemination

hand, involves a series of data collection over a period of time aimed at examining changes taking place in the target population over time. Both designs involve a series of tasks and activities required for implementing a successful research project.

Cross-Sectional Survey: This type of survey design calls for a one-time data collection. The researcher selects a sample from a nationwide, statewide, local community, or entire agency population and then conducts data collection within a specified time frame. This design is often used to study the prevalence of health status, economic and social characteristics of a specific population, public opinions, and needs assessment. For example, immediately after the 2005 disaster caused by Hurricane Katrina, several agencies and institutions conducted survey research to collect data on the experiences of the survivors, their families, and their communities, especially in New Orleans and the coastal region along the Gulf of Mexico. Some of these surveys selected a probability sample of respondents; others used the convenience or purposive survey. For instance, one of the authors of this book received funding from Boston College to conduct a pilot survey using a cross-sectional design with a non-probability sample of Vietnamese Americans who live in the areas affected by Hurricane Katrina. The purpose of the survey was to collect information on the experiences of Vietnamese people living in New Orleans and the Gulf Coast communities in Mississippi. Two hundred survey questionnaires were distributed at churches, temples, community service agencies, and other locations. This type of research is classified as a cross-sectional survey study.

BIVARIATE DATA ANALYSIS FOR CROSS-SECTIONAL SURVEYS

You can apply both descriptive and inferential statistics to analyze data from cross-sectional surveys. In Chapter 7, we offered several examples on how to conduct descriptive analyses using survey data. If you conduct a need assessment, sometimes all that's needed is to perform a series of bivariate analyses (analyses of two variables at a time). Useful statistical procedures commonly used among researchers are cross tabulation (i.e., Chi-square statistics), mean comparisons (i.e., T-test and ANOVA), and simple correlation (i.e., Pearson correlation coefficient). In the following examples, we will use Stata 12.1, a statistical software that has gained popularity in health science and social science research over the past two decades. In the appendices, we also provided examples of SPSS and Stata, so that you can either learn how to perform the analyses yourself or know how to communicate with your data analyst.

This example uses a small pilot cross-sectional survey conducted, in 2009, in the New Orleans and Biloxi areas by the first author of this book. In this survey, respondents were asked several questions concerning their psychological experiences during and after Hurricane Katrina. Let's say we want to learn whether men had different reactions than women to the hurricane. In the survey, we asked respondents to report their sex, female or male. This variable is named "var2" in the data set. We also asked, "How frightened did you feel during the hurricane?" This variable is "var48" in the data set. And we asked respondents to register their experience on a scale consisting of the choices "Not at all," "A little," "Some," "Very," and "Extremely." Before you examine the association between two variables, you should always verify the data by running a frequency and appropriately taking care of the missing data.

Chi-square Statistics (Cross Tabulation): In Stata, you can run a "tabulate" procedure, or "tab" procedure. In the syntax command, you list the variable that you are interested in comparing with another variable. You can "assume" it is the dependent variable that you will compare between men and women.

Thus, sex is your independent variable. The "tab" procedure in Stata allows you to compare the association of two categorical variables.

Cross tabulation between "var2" (Sex) and "var48" (Frightened)
Stata syntax:
tab var48 var2,col chi

You always list your "dependent variable" before listing the independent variable. Thus, the program will compare the data in the rows (frightened) with data in the column (sex). The "col" option will estimate the percent for each column and the "chi" option will estimate the Pearson chi2 (Chi-square) test of significance. We will use conventional criteria to reject the "null hypothesis," or hypothesis of no association. This conventional criterion is that when the probability of a test of significance is at .05 or less, you can reject the null hypothesis, meaning the association between two variables is statistically significant.

Looking at the results in Table 8.2, you see in each cell there are two pieces of information. For example, in the row of "Not at all" and the column of Sex, there are six male respondents, and that this number made up 13.33% of the male respondents who reported they were not frightened during the hurricane compared with two female respondents, or 3.28% of the female respondents who were not frightened during the hurricane. Similarly, in the row of "Extremely" and the column of Sex, 4.44% of male respondents reported they were extremely frightened during the hurricane compared with 21.31% of female respondents. If you were testing the hypothesis of no association between sex and the feeling of being frightened during the hurricane, the Pearson chi2 would allow you to reject the null hypothesis of no association and conclude there was a significant association between the feeling of being frightened and sex in such a way that significantly more female respondents reported being extremely frightened than the male respondents. More specifically, in

Table 8.2: Association between Sex and Frightened

HOW FRIGHTENED DID YOU FEEL DURING THE GENDER	MALE	GENDER FEMALE	TOTAL
Not at all	6	2	8
	13.33	3.28	7.55
A little	14	11	25
	31.11	18.03	23.58
Some	10	18	28
	22.22	29.51	26.42
Very	13	17	30
	28.89	27.87	28.30
Extremely	2	13	15
	4.44	21.31	14.15
Total	45	61	106
	100.00	100.00	100.00

Pearson chi2 (4) = 11.0831 Pr = 0.026

the output of [Pearson chi2 (4) = 11.0831 Pr = 0.026] displayed at the bottom of Table 8.2, the number 11.0831 is the Chi-square (χ^2) value calculated using the 2 X 5 table (number of columns X number of rows); the number 4 in the parentheses is the degree of freedom determined by $(c-1) \times (r-1)$ in which "c" denotes the number of columns and "r" denotes the number of rows, and in this example $(2-1) \times (5-1) = 4$; Pr is the P value or Type I error (also called alpha significance level), which is the probability of rejecting a true null hypothesis. As cited briefly before, the null hypothesis is a statement of no association between two variables. Therefore, P values less than 0.05 $(p < 0.05)$ denote there is less than a 5% chance of rejecting the null hypothesis that is actually true. In this example, $p = 0.026$ indicates the calculated P value is less than 0.05 $(p < 0.05)$, and we can conclude that sex and level of being frightened are statistically significantly related at the $p < 0.05$ level of significance.

Independent-Samples T-test: Other statistical tests, such as the independent-samples t-test, can be used to compare the means of variables between two groups. Let's find out if the age of female and male respondents differed from each other. Since there are two groups in the independent variable, we can use the **independent-samples t-test** to compare the mean difference between male and female. In the following example, using the Vietnamese Katrina Survey, we compare the mean of age (var1) between men and women (var2).

Stata syntax:
ttest var1, by(var2)

Let's review the output results presented in Table 8.3.

The first column (Group) in Table 8.3 identifies group membership. The second column, Obs, provides the frequency for each group and two groups (combined). The third column presents the mean age, the fourth column is standard error (Std. Err.), the fifth column is standard deviation (Std. Dev.), and the sixth column is the 95% confidence interval range. The wider the range, the less precise the estimate of the mean. The statistics in the "diff" row are the differences of the mean of age and its 95% confidence interval (CI). Note that the difference of age between men and women is about 2.36 years (ignore the negative sign), or on average, men were 2.36 years younger than women. This difference, however, is not statistically significant, as the probability of Type I error is greater than 0.05 $(\Pr(|T| > |t|) = 0.4268)$. When you look at the 95%

Table 8.3: Independent Sample T-test with Equal Variances: Sex and Level of Frightened

GROUP	OBS	MEAN	STD. ERR.	STD. DEV.	[95% CONF. INTERVAL]	
Male	48	42.625	2.252	15.603	38.094	47.155
Female	65	44.984	1.922	15.500	41.143	48.825
combined	113	43.982	1.459	15.518	41.089	46.874
diff		−2.359	2.958	−8.221		3.502

diff = mean(Male) − mean(Female) $t = -0.7976$

Ho: diff = 0   degrees of freedom = 111
$\Pr(|T| > |t|) = 0.4268$

confidence interval range, you should also note there is a value of zero within the range (−8.22, 3.50). When there is a zero value inside the 95% CI range, the test of significance is not statistically significant.

One-Way Analysis of Variance (ANOVA): There are situations in which you have to compare the means of variables of interest among three or more groups. In such situations, you should use the procedure called one-way analysis of variance (ANOVA). In the following example, we compare the mean ages among three groups of Vietnamese people who came to the United States with various immigration statuses. Some came as refugees, others came to reunite with family members who were already in the United States, and others came with a host of other reasons. We use two variables in this example; "immigrant_sta" refers to reasons of arrival in the United States and "var1" is age.

Stata syntax:
oneway var1 immigrant_stat, tabulate bonferroni

In the above syntax, "*var1*" (age) can be viewed as the dependent variable that must be measured on a continuous scale. A continuous scale has a range of values, and each value should represent a degree of variation. For instance, in the age variable, 1 is one-year old. "*Immigrant_stat*" (reasons of immigration) can be viewed as the independent variable. This variable must be measured as a categorical variable in which its values are grouped into different categories. In this example, "immigrant_stat" is measured by three categories: *Refugee*, *Family Reunion*, and *Other*. The "tabulate" option will generate tables with descriptive statistics such as mean and standard deviation. The ***Bonferroni*** is a statistical test that allows the comparison of the mean difference between each pair of categories or groups. When the F statistics estimated by the analysis of variance procedure are statistically significant ($p < .05$), we can conclude their age differences are statistically significant in the three groups.

The results in Table 8.4 show the mean of age, standard deviation, and frequency or size for each group and for the sum of the three groups. Vietnamese respondents who arrived in the United States as refugees were the oldest group with an average of 50.10 years old. The youngest group came to the United States with other immigration status issues that were not specified in this sample.

In Table 8.5, we find the decomposition of variance of age for each group (within group variance) and for the three groups (between group variance). The abbreviation SS refers to sum of squared, DF refers to degree of freedom, and MS refers to mean of squared. As shown in Table 8.5, the level of significance of the F statistics is at $p = 0.0001$, which is less than 0.05. This result indicates a statistically significant difference in the mean age among the three groups.

Table 8.4: Descriptive Statistics: Mean Age by Immigration Status

IMIGRATION STATUS	SUMMARY OF 1. AGE		
	MEAN	STD. DEV.	FREQ.
Refugee	50.103448	14.018396	58
Family Reunion	40.147059	13.963442	34
Other	34.818182	16.158844	22
Total	44.184211	15.638372	114

Table 8.5: Results from One-Way Analysis of Variance Statistics

| | ANALYSIS OF VARIANCE | | | | |
SOURCE	SS	DF	MS	F	PROB > F
Between groups	4516.21484	2	2258.10742	10.84	0.0001
Within groups	23118.9167	111	208.278529		
Total	27635.1316	113	244.558687		

Bartlett's test for equal variances: chi2(2) = 0.7336 Prob>chi2 = 0.693

The analysis of variance procedure assumes that variances are equal across groups or samples. The Bartlett test can be used to verify that assumption. The above chi2 test has a significance level, or Prob level, at 0.693, indicating the variance of age is similar across the three groups.

The F statistic in Table 8.5 confirms the three groups differ significantly in their means of age. The results in Table 8.6 help social workers point out how much the difference is between the groups. For example, the age difference between the *Refugee* and *Family Reunion* groups is statistically significant. The "absolute value" of age difference is 9.95639 years (the difference between 50.10 and 40.147). The reason we have a negative value (−9.95639) is that Stata takes 40.14 minus 50.103. This does not change the absolute value of difference. The number below −9.956 is the significance level produced by the Boferroni test. In this case, p = 0.005, and this value is less than 0.05. Therefore, we can conclude that age difference between Vietnamese people who came to the United States as refugees compared with those who came to reunite with families is statistically significant. The two groups that did not have a statically significant difference in age were *Family Reunion* and *Other*. The following conclusion can be drawn from this ANOVA test performed with immigrant Vietnamese groups that experienced Hurricane Katrina:

Pearson Correlation Coefficient (r): Pearson correlation (simple correlation) measures linear relationships between two sets of continuous scores. The symbol "*r*" refers to a summary index that has a value ranging from −1 to 1. The index of −1 refers to a perfect negative linear correlation; that is, as the scores of one variable (x) increase, the scores of the corresponding variable (y) decrease, and all paired x and y scores are in a straight line. If the value of the *r* index is at +1, this refers to a perfect positive linear correlation; as the scores of one variable (x) increase, the scores of the corresponding variable (y) increase as well, and all paired x and y scores are in a straight line. When the value of the $r_{x.y}$ approaches 0, it means the linear relationship between x and y is weak (See Figure 8.1). The closer the value of *r* to −1 or 1 is, the stronger will be the linear relationship. A calculation of Pearson correlation with a real data set is included at the end of this chapter.

Table 8.6: Bonferroni Test for Pair Comparisons

ROW MEAN COL MEAN	REFUGEE	FAMILY REUNION
Family reunion	−9.95639 0.005	
Other	−15.2853 0.000	−5.32888 0.540

SAMPLE WRITE-UP FOR AN ANOVA TEST

A one-way ANOVA was computed to compare the age mean scores of three groups of Vietnamese victims of Hurricane Katrina—*Refugee*, *Family Reunion*, and *Other*. There was a significant mean difference in age among the three groups ($F(2, 111) = 10.84$, $p < 0.01$). Bartlett's test for equal variances confirmed that the variance of age is similar across the three groups. Bonferroni's test for pair comparisons was used to examine the pair age difference. It was found that the age difference between the *Refugee* group ($m = 50.10$, $sd = 14.02$) and the *Family Reunion* group ($m = 40.15$, $sd = 13.96$) was statistically significant. The most significant age difference was revealed between the *Refugee* ($m = 50.10$, $sd = 14.02$) and *Other* categories of Vietnamese immigrants ($m = 34.82$, $sd = 16.16$) at the $p < 0.000$ level.

LONGITUDINAL SURVEY DESIGNS

We will demonstrate the use of more statistical analyses for survey research with the data from studies that used longitudinal survey designs. Longitudinal design calls for more than a one-time data collection. There are three common types of longitudinal studies: trend survey, cohort survey, and panel survey.

Trend Survey: A trend survey is a repeated cross-sectional design to measure changes over time. This type of design is useful for social work researchers to study community changes for program modification and program evaluation. At state and national levels, trend surveys can provide useful information for policy making. In a trend survey, investigators ask the same questions to different samples (usually different people) of the target population at different points in time. As cited previously, the California Health Interview Survey (CHIS) is the nation's largest state health survey ever conducted in the United States. CHIS is a random-dial telephone survey conducted on an ongoing basis and covering a full scope of health topics including mental health and mental-health service utilization patterns. The CHIS study describes health and health-care needs of diverse populations in California (http://healthpolicy.ucla.edu/chis/about/Pages/about.aspx). The UCLA Center for Health Policy Research conducts the CHIS study in collaboration with the California Department of Public Health and the Department of Health Care Services. CHIS is an example of a trend survey as it began in 2001 and data collections have been repeated several times. From 2001 to 2009, CHIS collected data using similar survey questionnaires on large samples of the California population every two years: 2001, 2003, 2005, 2007, and 2009. Beginning in 2011, CHIS data collection was implemented over each two-year period. Each CHIS data set has three components: child, adolescent, and adult survey files. Using the results from the five CHIS surveys, we can examine the trend of changes in health problems and practices of Californians including children (under age 12), adolescents (ages 12–17), and adults (ages 18–85).

Data Analysis for Trend Surveys: One can merge five repeated surveys from the CHIS into one single data file and perform data analysis. Alternatively, we can perform data analysis for each year, and then present the results concurrently. We provide a simple example below to examine the prevalence of health conditions or percentage of health conditions over five surveys, from 2001 to 2009. In trend analysis, one can examine societal or community changes, but not individual changes. For example, Table 8.7 presents changes in health conditions for Californians aged eighteen and older. If we look at the percentage of respondents with

Figure 8.1: Graphs of Perfect Positive ($r = +1$), Negative ($r = -1$), & Zero Correlation

This figure illustrates three possible forms of correlation which are seldom found in data analysis. However, these illustrations are useful to visualize the directions of a possible correlation between two variables.

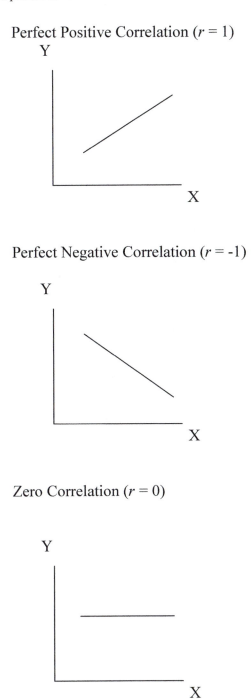

Perfect Positive Correlation ($r = 1$)

Perfect Negative Correlation ($r = -1$)

Zero Correlation ($r = 0$)

a self-rated poor health condition, it seems that more Californians reported poor health condition in 2007 and 2009 than in 2001, 2003, and 2005.

(Separate Data Analysis Using Stata for Each Survey)

Stata syntax:

tab health

This "tab" procedure can be repeated for each survey.

If the five surveys are merged, one can use the following syntax to track the changes of health conditions for Californian adults over time: [.tab health year, col].

In Table 8.7, for each health condition (excellent, very good, good, fair, and poor), we presented the percentage or prevalence. By presenting the percentage of five health conditions side by side over five survey periods, one can see general changes of health conditions over time.

Cohort Survey Design: The term "cohort" or subpopulation in research refers to a group of individuals who share certain characteristics in common, such as similar age, health/mental health condition, Afghan war veteran, and so forth. A cohort study is a type of longitudinal research in which study participants who meet certain criteria are examined over a period of time. This type of survey is similar to a trend survey, but it focuses on a particular group in the population. For example, a group of human service workers in their thirties complete a baseline questionnaire in 2015 on their job-related stress and satisfaction. In 2020, data will be collected using the same questionnaire about the topic area from those in their forties who did not participate in the baseline study in 2015. We can state that those who participated in the two surveys belong to the same age cohort with a similar occupational background. Let's say if a social service agency aims to monitor drinking behaviors of high school students in a community for better prevention planning, this agency can collect data on drinking behaviors on a sample of high school students in a school district on an ongoing basis every year, or once every two years.

The California Health Interview Survey (CHIS) and the American Community Survey (ACS) can be used to examine changes occurring among a certain age group. We can extract data from a particular group and then perform the desired analysis. For example, in the CHIS, we can examine changes in health conditions for people aged forty to fifty over the five survey cycles.

Stata syntax:

tab health if age_p >= 40 & age_p < = 50

Table 8.7: General Health Condition

YEAR SAMPLE	2001 (56,223)	2003 (42,044)	2005 (43,020)	2007 (51,048)	2009 (47,614)
EXCELLENT	19.49	21.93	21.63	19.58	19.14
VERY GOOD	32.70	31.43	31.75	32.41	32.53
GOOD	29.27	27.36	27.81	28.86	28.68
FAIR	14.02	14.18	13.83	13.95	13.45
POOR	4.53	5.10	4.97	5.20	5.20

In the syntax on the previous page, we used the "if" condition statement to select a sample of respondents aged greater (>) or equal (=) to 40 and respondents aged lower (<) or equal (=) 50.

If the data sets were merged, the syntax could be changed to:

Stata syntax:
tab health year if srage_p > = 40 & srage_p < = 50

In the above syntax, "year" refers to the survey cycles.

The results presented in Table 8.7 show changes in the prevalence of health conditions for the cohort of respondents aged forty to fifty over the five survey cycles. It appears that in 2009, about 3.50% of the respondents reported a poor health condition compared with 4.09% of the respondents in the same age cohort in 2001. Note that the 2009 respondents are not the same respondents as those from 2001. Therefore, we can only state that the results show changes in health conditions for this particular age cohort. In summary, cohort survey design can be used to monitor cohort changes of certain health, psychological, or social behaviors over time. This design can be useful for social work researchers to target particular groups of people or clients in a community for program development, monitoring, or evaluation.

Panel Survey Design: A panel survey design calls for data collection on the same group of research participants over time. Therefore, panel studies are regarded as the strongest design to study changes. This design, however, is more expensive and time consuming than cross-sectional, trend, and cohort surveys. Nonetheless, with well-designed research instruments and carefully selected samples, researchers can study not only changes taking place in the population, but also causal associations that are present among variables.

Below, we use the Children of Immigrants Longitudinal Study (CILS), 1991–2006. The principal investigators are Portes, Alejandro, and Rumbaut. Following is a description of the data set:

"Children of Immigrants Longitudinal Study (CILS) was designed to study the adaptation process of the immigrant second generation which is defined broadly as United States-born children with at least one foreign-born parent or children born abroad but brought at an early age to the United States. The original survey was conducted with large samples of second-generation immigrant children attending the 8th and 9th grades in public and private schools in the metropolitan areas of Miami/Ft. Lauderdale in Florida and San Diego, California. Conducted in 1992, the first survey had the purpose of ascertaining baseline information on immigrant families, children's demographic characteristics, language use, self-identities, and academic attainment. The total sample size was 5,262. Respondents came from 77 different nationalities, although the sample

Table 8.8: General Health Condition of 40–50 Age Cohort

YEAR SAMPLE	2001 (13,596)	2003 (9,729)	2005 (9,906)	2007 (10,327	2009 (8,589)
EXCELLENT	21.52	24.51	24.93	23.05	21.07
VERY GOOD	34.35	33.04	33.89	33.82	32.63
GOOD	27.65	25.32	25.17	28.00	28.80
FAIR	12.39	12.90	11.98	11.27	13.90
POOR	4.09	4.23	4.03	3.85	3.59

reflects the most sizable immigrant nationalities in each area. Three years later (1995), corresponding to the time in which respondents were about to graduate from high school, the first follow-up survey was conducted. Its purpose was to examine the evolution of key adaptation outcomes including language knowledge and preference, ethnic identity, self-esteem, and academic attainment over the adolescent years. The survey also sought to establish the proportion of second-generation youths who dropped out of school before graduation (see "Inter-university Consortium for Political and Social Research, ICPSR").

DATA ANALYSIS FOR LONGITUDINAL SURVEYS

How do we analyze longitudinal survey data? It depends on the questions a researcher intends to investigate. For example, in the CILS data set, investigators collected information on self-esteem using Rosenberg's well-known scale of ten items of self-esteem. If we want to look at the changes of self-esteem over time, we can use different statistical approaches. We demonstrate the use of **paired-sample t-test** and **regression analyses** to examine the changes of self-esteem among the participants.

Paired T-test to Examine Changes: This test allows researchers to test the hypothesis of "no changes" over time. We can assume the level of self-esteem using the ten-item Rosenberg scale would remain the same over time (Rosenberg 1965). The aggregate self-esteem score for each participant can range from 10 to 40. First, it is necessary to reversely recode the negative items (Item # 2, 5, 6, 8, 9) to make the scale into a uniform direction. For example, if a respondent chose the answer category of "1" (strongly disagree) in response to Question #2 (At times I think I am no good at all), it should be recoded into "4" because this person has the highest level of self-esteem on this particular question. As we reviewed in Chapter 6, the aggregate score of the Rosenberg self-esteem scale is obtained by adding the five original items and the other five recoded items altogether. The higher the score, the higher the level of self-esteem.

Before you can compare the changes of self-esteem between the 1992 survey and the 1995 survey, you must create a total score for self-esteem. You can do this in SPSS software by using the "compute" procedure. Following are two examples. The first is to generate the total score for the 1992 survey. In this survey, variables from v101 to v110 are the levels of the Rosenberg self-esteem scale. In the 1995 survey, these items are recorded as v301 to v310. They correspondent to the ten items presented in Table 8.9. To create the summative scale for self-esteem for the 1992 (SE92) survey, you can use the "Compute" command in SPSS described in Chapter 6, or use the following syntax (click on *File*, followed by *New* and *Syntax*, then type the syntax):

SPSS syntax: ["SE92" is the new variable name]
COMPUTE SE92=V101R+V102R+V103+V104R+V105+V106R+V107R+V108+V109+V110.
EXECUTE.

To create the summative score for self-esteem for the 1995 (SE95) survey, use the following syntax:

SPSS syntax:
COMPUTE SE95=V301R+V302R+V303+V304R+V305+V306R+V307R+V308+V309+V310.
EXECUTE.

Table 8.9: Rosenberg's Self-Esteem Scale

I would like to ask a few questions about how you feel about yourself. Please answer whether you strongly agree, agree, disagree, or strongly disagree with the statement.

1 = Strongly Disagree
2 = Disagree
3 = Agree
4 = Strongly Agree

	SA			SD
1. On the whole, I am satisfied with myself… … … … …	1 … ..	2 … ..	3 … ..	4 … ..
2.* At times I think I am no good at all … … … … … … .	1 … ..	2 … ..	3 … ..	4 … ..
3. I feel that I have a number of good qualities … … … …	1 … ..	2 … ..	3 … ..	4 … ..
4. I am able to do things as well as most other people …	1 … ..	2 … ..	3 … ..	4 … ..
5.* I feel I do not have much to be proud of … … … … ….	1 … ..	2 … ..	3 … ..	4 … ..
6.* I certainly feel useless at times … … … … … … … …	1 … ..	2 … ..	3 … ..	4 … ..
7. I feel that I am a person of worth … … … … … … …	1 … ..	2 … ..	3 … ..	4 … ..
8.* I wish I could have more respect for myself … … … …	1 … ..	2 … ..	3 … ..	4 … ..
9.* All in all, I am inclined to think that I am a failure … ..	1 … ..	2 … ..	3 … ..	4 … ..
10. I take a positive attitude toward myself … … … … …	1 … ..	2 … ..	3 … ..	4 … ..

After using the "compute" procedure in SPSS to create the overall scores for self-esteem in two surveys, you can perform a paired t-test to learn whether the scores of self-esteem changed significantly from 1992 to 1995 or remained the same. Following is the SPSS syntax for a paired t-test.

SPSS syntax:
T-TEST PAIRS=SE92 WITH SE95 (PAIRED)
 /CRITERIA=CI(.9500)
 /MISSING=LISTWISE.

First, SPSS will produce the flowing output descriptive statistics presented in Table 8.10, which help us understand the mean and standard deviation of overall self-esteem for each year (1992 and 1995, respectively). It appears the mean self-esteem in 1995 (SE95) is slightly higher than that of 1992 (SE92).

Table 8.10: Descriptive Statistics for 1992 and 1995 Self-Esteem Scores

Paired Samples Statstics

		MEAN	N	STD. DEVIATION	STD. ERROR MEAN
Pair 1	SE95	34.1464	4017	5.12002	.08078
	SE92	33.0941	4017	5.20134	.08207

Using SPSS, a Pearson correlation between two self-esteem scores (SE92 and SE95) can be calculated. You need to take the following SPSS steps:

---

(1) Click on *Analyze*.
(2) Click on *Correlate*.
(3) Click on *Bivariate*.
(4) Choose one variable SE92 from the variable list and move it to the *Variable* box.
(5) Choose the other variable SE95 and move it to the *Variable* box.
(6) Click on *OK*.

As reported in Table 8.11, the linear correlation of SE92 (self-esteem for 1992) and SE95 (self-esteem for 1995) is 0.44 ($r = 0.44$), and the P value (significance level) is less than 0.05 ($p < 0.000$), indicating the linear correlation is statistically significant. It also means that respondents who reported a higher sense of self-esteem in 1992 tended to consistently report a higher sense of self-esteem in 1995.

Table 8.12 shows the mean change of self-esteem from 1992 to 1995. The mean change is 1.05. This value is the difference between SE95 and SE92 ($34.1464 - 33.0941$). The paired t-test value is 12.25 ($t = 12.25$) and its level of significance is less than 0.05 ($p < 0.05$), indicating the change is statistically significant. The respondents' scores of self-esteem increased by 1.05 from 1992 to 1995.

MULTIVARIATE DATA ANALYSIS

We can use other statistical methods, such as ordinary least square (OLS) regression, logistic regression, and other multivariate statistical approaches, to analyze survey data. We can state that for most social work researchers conducting small-scale surveys, OLS regression and logistic regression analyses should be adequate for data analysis. We present examples to illustrate the applications of these two commonly used statistical approaches.

Ordinary Least Square Regression: This method of data analysis is appropriate to estimate the linear relationship between the dependent (outcome) variable and a set of independent and control variables (Mitchell 2012). The dependent variable must be measured on a continuous scale; the independent and control variables can be measured at either continuous or categorical levels. All categorical independent variables must be transformed into indicator or dummy variables (variables have two values: 0 or 1). If you use Stata, all you need to do is specify whether the variable is a continuous (c) or indicator (i) variable. In comparison with the bivariate statistical approaches such as t-test, chi-squared test, one-way analysis of

Table 8.11: Pearson Correlation of Two Self-Esteem Scores

		N	CORRELATION	SIG.
	PAIRED SAMPLES CORRELATIONS			
Pair 1	SE92 & SE95	4017	.444	.000

Table 8.12: Results of the Paired T-test for Two Sets of Self-Esteem Scores

Paired Samples Test

| | | PAIRED DIFFERENCES | | | | | | | |
| | | | | | 95% CONFIDENCE INTERVAL OF THE DIFFERENCE | | | | |
		MEAN	STD. DEVIATION	STD. ERROR MEAN	LOWER	UPPER	T	DF	SIG. (2-TAILED)
Pair 1	SE95– SE92	1.052	5.44	.08	.88	1.22	12.25	4016	.000

variance, or Pearson correlation, OLS regression is more powerful because we can examine the relationship between the dependent variable and an independent variable while controlling for possible influences of other plausible variables.

Let's say that we want to examine the causal association between English-speaking ability and self-esteem using the Children of Immigrant data set. Given that this data set is a panel data set and we have the data from the 1992 and 1995 surveys, we begin our analysis with SE95 (self-esteem measured in 1995) as our dependent variable and English-speaking ability measured in 1992 (SEA92) as our independent variable. SE95 scores range from 10 to 40; the higher the score, the greater the sense of self-esteem. SEA92 is measured on a scale from 1 to 4; the higher the score, the stronger the ability to speak English.

Stata syntax:
regress SE95 c.SEA92, beta

In the Stata syntax, "regress" is for regression, **SE95** (self-esteem measured in 1995) is the **dependent variable**, "c" refers to a continuous variable, and **SEA92** (English-speaking ability) is the **independent variable**. This is a simple regression model since it only has one dependent and one independent variable. The option "beta" refers to the estimate of the standardized regression coefficient. The "beta" coefficient has

Table 8.13: Results of the Simple Regression Analysis

SOURCE	SS	df	MS	
Model	5543.50431	1	5543.50431	Number of obs = 4195
Residual	104566.395	4193	24.9383245	F(1, 4193) = 222.29
				Prob > F = 0.0000
Total	110109.899	4194	26.2541485	R-squared = 0.0503
				Adj R-squared = 0.0501
				Root MSE = 4.9938

SE95	COEF.	STD. ERR.	t	P > |t|	BETA
SEA92	2.20761	.1480689	14.91	0.000	.2243773
cons	25.84775	.5595283	46.20	0.000	

a value ranging from −1 to 1, which is similar to the Pearson correlation coefficient. The "beta" coefficient is useful to compare the influence of independent variables in a model. It can tell you which independent variable is the strongest predictor of the dependent variable.

In Table 8.13, The **Prob of F** statistics, the **R-squared**, and the **Coef.** (unstandardized regression coefficient) indicate change in one unit of independent variable results in the change of one unit in the dependent variable. The **Beta** coefficient is useful for interpreting the linear relationship between self-esteem and English-speaking ability. The **F** statistic and its level of significance tell you whether the regression equation is statistically significant. If the **F** statistic has its **Prob >F** less than 0.05, you can conclude the regression model suggests that one or all independent and control variables are statistically different from 0. The R-squared coefficient tells you the amount of variance in the dependent variable explained by the independent variable. The "t" statistic indicates whether the relationship between a particular independent variable and the dependent variable is statistically significant from zero. In Table 8.13, we see that English-speaking ability measured in 1992 has a significant relationship with self-esteem (Coeff. = 2.20, p = 0.000, Beta = 0.22). This means that respondents who had a stronger English-speaking ability also had a greater feeling of self-esteem. This relationship can be explained as a causal relationship because of the time lag between self-esteem and English-speaking ability. But simple regression analysis can be misleading since we did not control for possible influences of other variables, such as self-esteem measured in 1992, sex, and age. Thus, we use multiple regression analysis to control for possible influences of these three variables. In the following example, additional independent variables were entered into the regression model.

Stata syntax:
regress SE95 c.SEA92 i.female c.age ,beta
Female is coded as 1 for female and 0 for male.

The results of multiple regression analysis in Table 8.14 indicate that age does not significantly influence the self-esteem score. The unstandardized regression coefficient (Coef.) and the standardized regression coefficient (Beta) on English-speaking ability on self-esteem are about the same as in simple regression

Table 8.14: Results of the Simple Regression Analysis

SOURCE	SS	df	MS	
Model	5850.49428	3	1950.16476	Number of obs = 4195
Residual	104259.405	4191	24.8769756	F(3, 4191) = 78.39
Total	110109.899	4194	26.2541485	Prob > F = 0.0000
				R-squared = 0.0531
				Adj R-squared = 0.0525
				Root MSE = 4.9877

SE95	COEF.	STD. ERR.	t	P > |t|	BETA
SEA92	2.232803	.1494656	14.94	0.000	.226938
female	−.5316758	.1542457	−3.45	0.001	−.051852
age	.0522316	.0914851	0.57	0.568	.008675
cons	25.28812	1.490731	16.96	0.000	

analysis. Females had a significant relationship with self-esteem (Coef. = −0.53, p = .001, Beta = −0.05), indicating that female respondents reported a lower level of self-esteem than male respondents. If you perform a one-way analysis of variance or a Pearson correlation between self-esteem and English-speaking ability, you will find similar results to those reported in Table 8.14. As cited previously, however, the results in Table 8.14 are more valid and meaningful than the results from simple regression or other bivariate analyses because we can examine the relationship between self-esteem and English-speaking ability simultaneously.

Logistic Regression Analysis: This statistical approach can be useful for social work research in examining dichotomous outcomes or dependent variables (Long, 1997). Sometimes it is more meaningful to have a clear cutoff point for a dependent variable. For example, it could be clinically convenient if a social worker can have a cutoff score of self-esteem for the purpose of diagnostics and decision making. If we can establish a score that indicates functional self-esteem versus poor self-esteem that might need intervention, it would make the job of a social worker easier. But the cutoff score must be sensitive and valid for proper utilization. For the purpose of illustration, we created a cutoff score for Rosenberg's self-esteem scale. We assume those with a score at 34 or higher on the Rosenberg's self-esteem scale would be considered as having a functional level of self-esteem, and those with a score below 34 may need some intervention. We then use the same three independent (or predictor) variables (age, gender, and SEA92 [English-speaking ability measured in 1992]) to explain or predict the dependent variable, which had two categories of self-esteem measured in 1995.

We used Stata for this analysis. The first thing we need to do is establish a cutoff score for self-esteem. We do this by "recoding" SE95 (self-esteem measured in 1995) into two categories. Our new variable will be SE95_2 (self-esteem measured in 1995 recoded into two categories).

Stata syntax:
recode SE95 (10/33.99 = 0) (34/40 = 1),gen (SE95_2)
logistic SE95_2 SEA92 female age

In Table 8.15, the LR chi2 and its level of significance (Prob>chi2) has a similar meaning as the F statistic in regression analysis. If the LR chi2 is significant, one or all independent and control variables are statistically significant. The "Odds Ratio" $[(Exp(B)]$ refers to the association between an independent variable

Table 8.15: Logistic Regression of Two Categories of Self-Esteem

Logistic regression
Log likelihood = −2706.9931

Number of obs = 4195
LR chi2(3) = 191.36
Prob > chi2 = 0.0000
Pseudo R2 = 0.0341

SE95_2	ODDS	RATIO	STD. ERR.	z	P > |z|	[95% CONF. INTERVAL]
SEA92	2.296286	.1498847	12.74	0.000	2.020532	2.609674
female	.7800638	.050793	−3.81	0.000	.6866021	.8862477
age	1.003143	.0386549	0.08	0.935	.9301713	1.08184
cons	.0769583	.0485739	−4.06	0.000	.0223358	.2651609

with the dependent variable in the model. The Z statistic is similar to the t statistic in regression analysis. This is the test of significance for each independent variable.

It's interesting to note the results in Table 8.15 are similar to those in Table 8.14. Respondents who had stronger English-speaking ability were about twice more likely to have greater self-esteem (Odds Ratio = 2.296, p = .00). Female respondents were less likely to have a functional self-esteem level than male respondents. Age had no significant association with self-esteem.

SUMMARY

Survey research has become a useful tool for social work researchers to conduct need assessments, monitor social changes in a community, and evaluate social service programs and social policy outcomes. Two common types of survey research design were examined in this chapter: cross-sectional and longitudinal designs. We provided data analysis examples to guide appropriate statistical approaches for social work survey research.

CLASS EXERCISE

1. Group Exercise

Depending on the class size, students should form into groups of three or more students to participate in group exercises. Each group should select a student leader to summarize the group's work to the entire class.

1.1. Your agency plans to submit a grant application to seek funding from foundation or government institutions to provide an educational training program to prevent domestic violence in its surrounding communities. You are asked by the agency director to conduct a need assessment to determine the need for such a public health educational program. The information is important for the agency to increase its chance for funding. What would you do to conceptualize, implement, and complete the need assessment? Students should also review the issues of measurement in Chapter 5 and sampling and data collection methods in Chapter 6 to complete this exercise. Group members should engage in a discussion of:

1.2. Formulating the objectives for the need assessment.

1.3. Constructing a need assessment questionnaire or survey instrument.

1.4. Sampling.

1.5. Collecting data.

1.6. Analyzing data and reporting results.

2. Individual Exercises 2. 1.   Compare and contrast cross-sectional survey and longitudinal survey designs. Illustrate the applications of these survey designs in social work and human services.

REFERENCES

California Health Interview Survey. http://healthpolicy.ucla.edu/chis/about/Pages/about.aspx & http://www.icpsr.umich.edu/icpsrweb/landing.jsp

Levy, S. P., & Lemeschow, S. (1999). *Sampling of populations: Methods and applications* (3rd ed.). New York, NY: John Wiley & Sons, Inc.

Long, J. S. (1997). *Regression models for categorical dependent variables*. College Station, TX: Stata Press.

Mitchell, M. N. (2012). *Interpreting and visualizing regression models using Stata*. College Station, TX: Stata Press.

Portes, A., & Rumbaut, R. G. "The Children of Immigrants Longitudinal Study (CILS), 1991-2006." Inter-University Consortium for Political and Social Research. From http://www.icpsr.umich.edu/icpsrweb/landing.jsp.

Rosenberg, M. (1965). *Society and the adolescent self-image*. Princeton, NJ: Princeton University Press.

Rossi, P. H., Wright, J.D., & Anderson, A. B. (1983). *Handbook of survey research*. San Diego, CA: Academic Press.

StataCorp (2007). *Stata longitudinal/panel-data reference manual, Release 10*. College Station, TX: Stata Press.

NINE

Experimental Designs, Single Subject Designs, & Data Analysis

This chapter introduces some common and practical experimental, quasi-experimental, and single-subject designs to conduct social work research and evaluate social work practice. The utmost purpose of experimental research is to examine whether the independent variable under investigation is responsible for variation in the dependent variable. Students will learn types of designs, issues concerning internal validity (causality) and external validity (generalizability), random assignments, and proper data analysis. When appropriate, we will use existing data to illustrate selected designs with appropriate statistical analyses. Similar to survey research designs addressed in Chapter 8, we will demonstrate a use of t-test (independent samples and paired t-test), analysis of variance (ANOVA), and regression analysis to analyze data for an experimental design. We will also examine the concepts of effect size and power analysis in this chapter.

In chapter 8, we cited survey research designs in which social work researchers and program evaluators used survey questionnaires to collect data from people in the community or the clients of social service agencies. Thus, data collection through survey is primarily limited to what respondents say, rather than what they actually do in the absence of others around them. Also, in survey research, investigators collect data from people or organizations without changing their existing conditions or providing some intervention.

In this chapter we examine different types of research that call for the implementation of intervention or services designed to solve particular social or psychological problems experienced by members of the community or clients who are seeking help. To implement this type of research, researchers must deliberately administer an intervention to a group of subjects (also called experimental units) and measure changes taking place in the target behavior after the intervention or service is completed. In this type of study, social work researchers must employ one of the experimental designs to determine the change in the outcomes. An **experimental design** refers to a highly controlled data collection method intended to establish causality between the independent variable and the dependent variable by examining the effect of any intervention (also called "treatment") on the variation in the dependent variable among experimental units. In this sense, experimental designs are considered the most rigorous among all existing research types. In social work practice, we often use experimental designs to evaluate the efficacy of a proposed treatment, intervention, or service before involving clients who might benefit from such treatment. We can also use experimental designs to assess the strengths or weaknesses of existing social service programs.

Prior to implementing experimental studies, people in the community, social service providers, policy makers, politicians, and researchers in academic fields, such as medicine, psychology, social work, and sociology, should realize the following three basic conditions:

1. **Acknowledgment of Problems**: People begin to acknowledge there are problems that can be either **biological** (such as treatment for AIDS victims or Alzheimer's disease), **psychological** (mental-health problems, suicidal attempts, attention deficit disorder, severe emotional disorder among children), **socioeconomic** (unemployment, working poor, domestic violence, child abuse, human trafficking), and **cultural** (acculturation issue, adjustment difficulties among immigrants, generational conflict) in essence.

2. **Orientation toward Solutions**: People begin to think that the scope and depth of the problems risk the well-being of the target populations and realize the need for planned solutions. And,

3. **Search for Desirable Outcomes**: Consumer groups and stakeholders call for solutions. In response to these demands and activities, funding becomes available at local, state, and federal levels (e.g., National Institute of Mental Health, National Institute on Health, or funding opportunities for domestic violence problems through the Department of Justice). Finally, researchers and service organizations implement experiments collaboratively to examine the effectiveness of any particular intervention in solving the identified problems.

As cited, human problems often manifest through various aspects of health and mental-health conditions. Societal problems often manifest through poverty, crime, violence, discrimination, and so forth. These problems, of course, require a variety of social intervention efforts, and we need to design research strategies to assess the outcomes of such intervention.

Following is the list of some fundamental steps in conducting an experimental research for a clinical trial or a program evaluation:

- Identify problems and needs.
- Clearly state the intervention objectives.
- Select appropriate and meaningful outcome measures (i.e., depression and anxiety scales).
- Recruit and select participants according predetermined criteria. These criteria should be based on screening information, age, mental and physical health status, and other factors.
- Determine the sample size and the sample selection procedures. The number of participants is determined by the agency's resources, and statistical power, which is addressed in the section of sample size and statistical power.
- Collect pretest data using a predetermined standardized test or measure (scale).
- Implement the intervention.
- Collect posttest data using the same standardized test as the pretest.
- Analyze the data with appropriate statistical procedures and tests.
- Draw conclusions about the effectiveness or success of the intervention.

Identify Problems and Needs: Individuals, families, and communities have different problems and needs. But often these problems are intertwined; thus, social work interventions should always reflect these aspects on designing programs and services. Identifying problems and needs sets the stage for the articulation of measurable program and service aims or objectives.

Articulate the Intervention Objectives: Well-defined aims/objectives lead to well-designed services or interventions. Aims/objectives must be measurable. For example, the aim of a social isolation intervention program is to reduce feelings of social isolation among elderly clients. The objective could be that by the end of the intervention, the levels of social isolation among the elderly participants would be significantly reduced.

Recruitment and Selection: Identifying the problem of social isolation in the community is important, but finding elderly people who would be willing and able to participate in a clinical trial is not simple. The challenge of conducting a clinical trial project is the ability to identify the proper participants. A social isolation intervention can only be successful when it is implemented for the right clients or those who have a clinical need for social isolation intervention. From our fictitious situation discussed previously, the social work researcher who is in charge of the planned intervention project should meet with her or his team to develop or find a reliable and valid screening tool to identity the elderly who are clinically isolated. This screening tool could be a well-developed standardized scale or a series of questions based on clinical knowledge of the social workers who have worked with the elderly population. A screening tool should be straightforward and simple as asking the prospective elderly participants how socially isolated he or she has felt in the last thirty days, or whether they have a strong need for social contacts but have been unable to do so because of health, transportation, or financial barriers. The agency should develop a set of well-defined criteria that could help the research team in recruiting a pool of eligible participants. Once there is a complete pool of eligible participants, the agency can either randomly select a smaller pool of participants for the pretest, and then posttest only through clinical trial or on the basis of first come, first served.

Sample Size in Experiments: One of the challenges of any social work research project is to determine the appropriate size of participants or clients for the project. First, the agency must determine in advance how much it can spend on the project and how much it would cost for each prospective participant. Second, the research or evaluation team should know which statistical test is appropriate to assess the effectiveness of the intervention, or to determine whether the project achieves its aims or objectives. We will examine this issue and demonstrate how to estimate sample size and power for the statistical tests recommended for the clinical trial designs. The agency will need to decide on the number of eligible elderly who could participate in the "pilot test" trial. The size of the group or the sample size is often determined by two factors: resources and statistical power. The availability of funding and human resources is always the first critical factor in determining how many clients or participants we can afford to enroll in a pilot test trial. The second important factor is the statistical power to reject the hypothesis that the intervention does not have any significant influence on the outcome when this assumption or hypothesis is false. A statistical power of 90% or 80% has been a common standard, and it depends on the objective of a clinical trial.

Collection of Pretest as Baseline Data: Pretest scores as baseline data are important for the assessment of changes or the effectiveness of an intervention. The agency must use the same standardized outcome measure to collect data for each participant of the intervention.

Implementation of the Intervention: Services or intervention must be well-designed to address a specific problem. The agency and staff members must use evidence-based services or interventions to ensure desirable outcomes. As our society and community have become increasingly diverse, the issue of cross-cultural comparability of services or intervention must be addressed. This can be done by conducting a thorough and thoughtful literature review and focus group meetings with prospective clients before the implementation of an intervention. Issues concerning the length and frequency of different aspects of an intervention must be standardized across clients and groups to allow an agency to draw valid comparisons of the outcomes before and after an intervention.

Collection of Posttest Data: The same standardized outcome measure used for the collection of pretest (baseline data) is used to collect posttest data. Posttest data can be collected periodically to monitor the progress of an intervention or just once at the end of an intervention.

Data Analysis: There are always at least two types of data analysis. First is the description of the participants including basic demographic characteristics such as age, sex, race/ethnicity, and the distribution of the outcome measures. This type of analysis is performed through use of descriptive statistics such as frequency distributions, and means and standard deviations. Second is the analysis of the effectiveness of the intervention. Each clinical trial design calls for different types of statistical tests. We will demonstrate these tests for the designs addressed in this chapter.

Interpretation of Outcomes and Drawing Conclusions: The interpretation of intervention outcomes should be a joint task of the agency's administrator and staff members who have direct involvement with the implementation of the intervention. There are two types of interpretation: statistical and clinical. Statistical interpretations are based on data, but clinical interpretations are based on social workers' clinical experience and wisdom. Statistical interpretations should not be the end, but only the means for the agency and its social workers to determine the effectiveness of interventions.

The detailed description of the experimental research process stated above can be condensed into the following four logically connected steps (expressed in notational form R O X O):

1. **Random Assignment (R)**: Random assignment, or "R," in an experiment refers to a technique for randomly assigning subjects to experimental or control groups. The **experimental group** (also called treatment group) is a group of subjects to which the specified treatment is provided, while the **control group** refers to a group of subjects that does not receive the treatment during the research period.

2. **Administration of Pretest (O)**: The pretest (denoted as "O" or Observation) measuring levels of a selected target behavior (i.e., level of depression, duration of attention, math skills, etc.) should be given to all subjects regardless of their membership in the experimental or control group. In an experiment, the pretest is designed to measure the dependent variable.

3. **Exposure of Subjects to Treatment (X)**: Shortly after the pretest is completed, a treatment (also called "experimental stimulus") should be provided to those who are assigned to the experimental group. Those subjects assigned to the control group are not exposed to the experimental stimulus; thus, supposedly, "exposure to the treatment condition" is the only difference between the experimental and control group. The experimental stimulus or treatment is an independent variable (denoted as X) that is manipulated by the researcher to examine its effect on the variation in the dependent variable.

4. **Administration of Posttest (O)**: Upon completion of the treatment intervention, the subjects in both groups are given the posttest using the same measurement instrument as used for the pretest.

BASIC TERMINOLOGY IN EXPERIMENT DESIGNS

When a researcher conducts an experiment, he or she should make sure the two groups—experimental and control—are nearly identical with respect to all imaginable variables (i.e., gender composition, SES, ability, etc.), except the independent variable of experimental stimulus manipulated to the experimental group subjects. The experimenter's aim is to see that variation in the dependent variable is a direct effect of the independent variable when confounding variables or extraneous variables are eliminated. The term **experimental variability** refers to the amount of variation produced by the treatment or dependent variable given to the experimental subjects. In reality, however, there are many other sources of variation in the dependent variable. For example, a researcher intends to assess the effect of behavior modification treatment on the attention span among children diagnosed with attention deficit disorder (ADD). Let's say that those children who received the specific behavior modification treatment have improved in their attention significantly. In this experiment, how do we know the behavior modification treatment is the only source that produced changes (or variations) in the children's attention span? It is very likely that some other sources, such as no sugar diet and increased hours of sleep and exercise, could also affect their attention span in addition to the independent variable of behavior medication treatment, which is the focus of this experiment.

Extraneous variables are external variables that are not being studied but affect the outcomes of the dependent variable, and, therefore, these variables must be controlled by the researcher. Extraneous variables are known, but in many cases unknown to the researcher. **Extraneous variability** refers to changes in the dependent variable produced by extraneous variables. These extraneous variables act as the confounding variables that obscure the direct relationship between the independent variable and the dependent variable. Despite the researcher's effort to minimize extraneous variability, it is impossible to remove all extraneous variables during the experiment. The presence of extraneous variability makes it difficult to infer whether variation in the dependent variable (i.e., improvement in attention span) is an effect of the independent variable (i.e., behavior modification treatment); this is the main reason why the researcher holds the values of some of the known extraneous variables constant throughout the experiment. **Control variables** are known extraneous variables whose values are kept constant throughout the experiment by the researcher. In the previous example, the researcher can keep the hours of exercise constant from the beginning of the study until the end among all research subjects.

INTERNAL VALIDITY AND EXTERNAL VALIDITY

The main purpose in any experimentation is to determine cause and effect relationships between a set of variables. The researchers' aim is to examine that the variation in the dependent variable is actually caused by the variation in the independent variable. At times, however, the change in the independent variable has little or no effect on the change in the dependent variable due to a variety of extraneous variables. **Internal validity** in experimental designs refers to the extent to which the variation in the independent variable contributes to the variation in the dependent variable. Thus, the notion of internal validity in experimentation is very important to establish causality between the independent and dependent variables. A high degree of internal validity showing that the variation in the dependent variable is attributable to the variation in the independent variable suggests strong evidence of cause and effect relationships. Likewise, a lack of internal validity suggests little or no evidence of causality.

Let's apply the concept of internal validity to a simple experimental case study. A client, who was diagnosed with clinical depression when her significant relationship with her fiancé ended abruptly, has been receiving "empowerment driven treatment" for a while. Prior to her treatment, she was given a test measuring her level of depression using the CES-D (Center of Epidemiological Studies-Depression) scale. The pretest score confirmed her clinical diagnosis of depression. The duration of treatment was six months.

At the end of her treatment she was given a posttest using the same CES-D. To our surprise, there was no change or improvement in her depression score, and this client continues to suffer from various symptoms of depression. In this case, it can very likely be concluded that the empowerment treatment (independent variable) did not work, or it did not cause any improvement in the client's depression (dependent variable). In the process of her treatment, however, it was found that she was diagnosed with breast cancer (extraneous variable, confounding variable), a factor that cannot be controlled for in advance by the researcher or counselor. It is unclear whether the treatment was effective in treating her depression because the presence of unexpected breast cancer also very likely influenced her depression as an extraneous factor. The study results are inconclusive because it is hard to determine whether the empowerment treatment was ineffective in treating her depression, or the diagnosis of breast cancer prevented her from improving. If a researcher cannot confidently state a cause and effect relationship exists between the independent and dependent variables, the degree of internal validity of the experiment is low.

Then, what jeopardizes the inter-validity in experimentation? According to Campbell and Stanley (1966), and later Cook and Campbell (1979), the researcher should identify extraneous variables that would affect the association between the independent and dependent variables under investigation, as these extraneous factors invalidate the inference of causality. Campbell and Stanley (1966) precisely identified eight extraneous factors that can jeopardize the internal validity of experimental designs. Especially when we conduct an experiment with only one experimental group (without control groups to compare), the researcher should keep in mind that he or she may not accurately conclude that the independent variable under investigation actually produced variation in the dependent variable.

Eight Threats to Internal Validity by Campbell and Stanley (1966)

1. **History**: The threat of history refers to all events that occur during the study likely to affect the outcome of the experiment. The historical event provides an alternative explanation in which, rather than the independent variable under investigation, this event causes changes in the dependent variable. Therefore, history threatens internal validity. Examples of history include earthquake, divorce, death in the family, winning a lottery, and more.

2. **Maturation**: The threat of maturation is any biological, psychological, or social change occurring in individuals while a study is progressing that influences the dependent variable. Maturation generally refers to being wiser, more tired, hungrier, more intelligent, more cooperative, more tolerant, and so on. For example, between the pretest and the posttest, the study participants may become more tolerant toward the loss of their loved ones, which is naturally acquired coping skills. Thus, the researcher is not sure whether the improvement in their depressive symptoms (dependent variable) was caused by the treatment (independent variable) or the natural tendency of maturation (extraneous variable).

3. **Testing**: The threat of testing results from a possible reactivity of measurement. When the subjects are exposed to the identical pretest and posttest material, they tend to remember the test, gain more testing skills, and subsequently would perform better on the posttest. In this case, the researcher is not sure whether the difference between pretest and posttest scores is a result of the independent variable or the subjects' exposure to the test. Especially when we conduct an experiment with only one group, namely the experimental group, "testing" becomes an obvious threat to the design.

4. **Instrumentation**: The threat of implementation refers to any changes in the way the dependent variable is measured between the pretest and the posttest, especially changes in the measuring devices between the two tests. For example, if the evaluators of the pretest and the posttest did not use the same rating criteria (i.e., more stringent ratings for the pretest, and more flexible ratings for the posttest), then the researcher is uncertain whether the score difference between the pretest and the posttest is attributable to the independent variable or to the instrumentation effect.

5. **Statistical Regression**: The threat of statistical regression refers to a natural tendency for extremely low or high pretest scores to regress toward the mean of the subsequent test. When research participants scored very low on the pretest, they are likely to achieve better scores on the posttest without any additional efforts due to the statistical regression effect. In this case, it is hard to conclude whether their improvement is attributable to the independent variable or statistical regression.

6. **Selection Biases**: When differential selections of respondents for the experimental and comparison groups take place, the two groups will be remarkable different. This difference in the composition of the experimental and control groups would act as a threat to the internal validity.

7. **Experimental Mortality**: The threat of experimental mortality, also called attrition, refers to differential dropout rates across all groups of participants. Suppose the same number of subjects remain through the entire experiment, but the experimental group lost a significant number of participants between the pretest and the posttest. It is reasonable to assume that only those who improved considerably by being exposed to the treatment tend to make it through the whole study. Experimental mortality prevents the researcher from collecting data from all participants. It is possible to infer that changes in the dependent variable are attributed to the differential dropout rates, not the independent variable.

8. **Interactions with Selection**: The term "interactions with selection" (i.e., selection-history interaction, selection-maturation interaction, and selection-testing interaction) refers to the possibility that the seven threats described so far can interact with the threat of selection biases, which eventually acts as an added threat to the internal validity of experiments. For example, the selection-testing interaction takes place when the subjects assigned to the experimental and control groups are significantly different (i.e., all male students for the experimental group and all female students for the control group), and the mean posttest score in math skills for the male group is much higher than that of the female group. Generally speaking, men tend to progress faster in math than women, and in such cases the selection-testing interaction may occur.

When data are collected from a limited number of research participants or clients, to what extent can the researcher generalize the findings to the population? This question pertains to the matter of external validity in experimental designs. **External validity** in experiments refers to the extent to which our findings obtained from participants are generalized to the overall population from which they were recruited, or the settings to which they belong. The degree of external validity is related to the extent of representativeness of the sample. In other words, if those who participated in a particular experiment are considered to represent the population, the experiment will yield a high degree of external validity; and if they do not represent the population, the results from this study will be limited to this experiment only. Selection biases can be a serious source of threats to external validity. Another source of threats to external validity is the problem of reactivity, which is a change in behavior among subjects stemming from their knowledge that they are being observed. If the research participants do not behave naturally during the experiment, the study results may not be generalized to the larger population or settings.

TYPES OF EXPERIMENTAL DESIGNS

We will examine three types of experimental designs that are widely used in clinical social work trials to assess the effectiveness of newly developed, evidence-based intervention or pilot programs implemented by community-based social service agencies.

PRE-EXPERIMENTAL DESIGNS

Pretest and Posttest-Only Designs: This design is a subtype of "pre-experimental designs." Although the design lacks a control or comparison group, it appears to be practical and feasible for social work agencies with limited human and capital resources. The design calls for a single group of clients and the measurement of their pretest and posttest scores of the dependent variable. This design can be depicted in the following notational form:

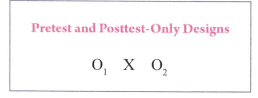

Pretest and Posttest-Only Designs

$$O_1 \quad X \quad O_2$$

X refers to the implementation of treatment. O_1 is the pretest taken at the baseline before the treatment, and O_2 refers to the posttest taken upon completion of treatment. The abbreviated symbols indicates that a group of clients is selected based on a careful selection process. This group should have a similar baseline status and shares the same need for intervention services.

ESL Study with 20 Vietnamese Refugees

Let's assume an influx of non-English–speaking refugees resettled in a local community after being admitted to the United States. Although these refugees were taught English in a refugee camp, they need further survival English skills to find employment and make successful adaptations into their new home community. A local social service agency received funding to offer English-as-a-second-language (ESL) classes to refugee adults as quickly as possible. ESL teachers were hired to develop a survival ESL program to serve five hundred newly arrived refugees. The preliminary assessment of ESL ability of former refugees suggests that for a refugee to find employment, he or she must have at least five survival English skills out of ten important ESL skills for non-English–speaking immigrants or refugees to find employment. The program director wants to make sure the program would work before offering it to the refugees. She randomly selected twenty refugee adults to enroll in a pilot class for four weeks. Through the process of random selection, these twenty participants would fairly represent the entire community of five hundred refugees. In may situations, it would be difficult to randomly select the clients or participants, thus the screening assessment must be conducted thoroughly to assure that the selected individuals have similar need. None of these twenty refugees had more than four ESL skills. The program's aim is to teach them to become fluent in at least half of the ten desirable skills. Although the selected participants were screened carefully for their English ability, all of the participants were asked to take an entry ESL exam at the beginning of their first class. The scores of this exam range from 0 to 10. The same exam will be used to assess their improvement and also the effectiveness of the program. It is assumed the exam has good internal consistency and validity. More specifically, the exam questions are consistent and have the ability to measure the students' ESL ability. The selected students attended classes four hours a day and five days a week for one month. The pilot program purpose is twofold. First, it provides preliminary outcome information to the agency to determine whether the curriculum works or needs improvement before launching the full program. Second, the outcome could help agency determine the optimal class size for program outcome assessment.

The following data are fictitious. The "Pretest" column (baseline) has ESL test scores of twenty refugee adults. The agency measured their ESL ability on the first day of class. After one month of learning, the agency measured their ESL ability again. The "Posttest" column (outcome) has their posttest ESL test scores.

Data Analysis

How would the agency assess the outcome of the pilot ESL program? The most appropriate statistical test is the paired t-test. This test allows the agency to compare the change in the pretest and posttest ESL scores of twenty adult refugees. If the ESL test scores improved significantly, the agency would have a good reason to conclude the training is successful.

Table 9.1: Fictitious ESL Data for Analysis

PRETEST SCORE ESL SKILLS	POSTEST SCORE ESL SKILLS
0	1
0	0
2	9
0	10
0	2
1	5
0	8
4	10
1	8
2	0
0	6
0	4
1	10
0	6
0	2
2	8
0	3
1	3
2	10
0	6

As presented in Table 9.1, there are two columns of ESL scores. These two columns were generated from the twenty refugees, and a pair of scores on each row belong to the same person; each person has a pretest score and a posttest score. The appropriate statistical test for these scores is the **paired t-test**. This test allows us to test the statistical significance of the average change of the ESL scores for these twenty refugees after they completed their five-week training program. As the name of the test implies, the two scores on each row are not independent, because they belong to the same individual. As such, we compare two related means of ESL scores in the paired t-test.

Stata syntax for the paired t-test is:
ttest pretest = posttest

Note that Stata syntax is case sensitive. If your variables were labeled as uppercase letters, they must be written exactly as in the syntax commands.

As presented in Table 9.2, the given variable names are "pretest" and "posttest," and "Obs" (Observation) refers to the number of participants (cases, respondents, or subjects). The descriptive statistics include the mean, standard error ("Std. Err"), standard deviation ("Std. Dev."), and 95% confidence intervals ("Conf. Interval"). If you forgot the meanings of these statistical concepts, look for their definitions in the Glossary or in Chapter 7. The difference between the mean of "posttest" and "pretest" is reported in the "diff" row. On average, the participants gained |4.75| points on the scale of 10. You see the negative size in the mean difference because Stata subtracted the posttest score from the pretest score. In the "ttest" command you could list "ttest posttest=pretest" if you want to see the positive sign of the mean difference. The results show that the change in the ESL ability was statistically significant, given the t score of |6.6522| with 19 degrees of freedom (20 – 1 = 19), and the P value of 0.000. Although the improvement or change in the ESL test scores is statistically significant, does it mean the program is beneficial to the refugees and, therefore, the agency can offer this ESL training to the entire refugee community? This question refers to the clinical significance

Table 9.2: Paired T-test Results from the Vietnamese ESL Study

Paired t-test

VARIABLE	OBS	MEAN	STD. ERR.	STD. DEV.	[95% CONF. INTERVAL]	
pretest	20	.8	.2470883	1.105013	.2828382	1.317162
posttest	20	5.55	.78296	3.501503	3.911246	7.188754
diff	20	−4.75	.7140507	3.193332	−6.244525	−3.255475

mean(diff) = mean (pretest − posttest)   t = −6.6522

Ho: mean(diff) = 0   degrees of freedom = 19

Ha: mean(diff) < 0   Ha: mean(diff) != 0   Ha: mean(diff) > 0

Pr(T < t) = 0.0000   Pr(|T| > |t|) = 0.0000   Pr(T > t) = 1.0000 of the outcome. Only the agency director, the social workers, and the ESL teachers could determine the clinical significance of the outcome.

Estimated Sample Size for Future Evaluation

For this particular example, we need to decide: How many participants should the agency need in each ESL classroom to determine the statistical significance of the outcome? What is the minimum number of participants that could give the agency adequate statistical power to reject the assumption that the training had no influence when this assumption is wrong? Following is the syntax for power analysis for the "pretest and posttest-only design" that uses the paired t-test to evaluate the outcome. The input for this power analysis is drawn from the results of the pilot training program cited previously.

Stata power analysis syntax:
power pairedmeans .8 5.55, sddiff(3.10) fpc(500)

(Note: In the power pairedmeans command, .8 is the mean of pretest, 5.55 is the mean of posttest, 3.10 is the standard deviation of the mean difference, and 500 is the population size of the refugee community.)

Power Analysis

Let's assume the agency is satisfied with the outcome of the pilot training program and is ready to open the ESL classes to the entire refugee community. What is the optimal class size that could produce a statistically significant outcome similar to the pilot program? To answer this question, the agency could perform

Table 9.3: Estimated Sample Size through Power Analysis

Estimated sample size for a two-sample paired-means test

Paired t-test
Ho: d = d0 versus Ha: d != d0

Study parameters:

alpha = 0.0500	ma1 = 0.8000
power = 0.8000	ma2 = 5.5500
delta = 1.5323	
d0 = 0.0000	
da = 4.7500	
sd_d = 3.1000	

Estimated sample size:
    N = 6

a power analysis to determine the "sample size" for each classroom. If only pretest and posttest data will be collected for each classroom, we can do a power analysis for the paired t-test using a Stata power analysis procedure. The information we need to run a power analysis is the "pretest" mean, the "posttest" mean, the standard deviation of the mean difference, and the population size of the refugee community. Since we already know the population size of five hundred refugees, the remaining statistics are found in the results of the paired t-test for the pilot program.

In Table 9.3, alpha is the significance level or the probability of making a Type I error. Conventionally, power is set at 0.80 or the probability of a Type 2 error. The power of a statistical test is the probability that the given results of a test can allow us to reject the null hypothesis (e.g., no difference) when the research hypothesis (e.g., difference) is true. The pretest and posttest means are ma1 and ma2. Delta is the effect size of the training program (4.75/3.10). The results of the power analysis suggest the required sample size to reject the null hypothesis that the training program has no significant influence on the participants is six. This could also mean that a classroom size can vary between six and twenty to produce a statistically significant change.

Clinical Implications

The result of the frequency analysis of the posttest scores as presented in Table 9.4 suggests that 45% of the participants in the pilot training grogram acquired at least five ESL skills necessary for job hunting. If the agency was satisfied with this outcome, this could be used as the standard outcome for all ESL classes.

Limitations of Pre-experimental Designs

Cook and Campbell (1979) discussed several limitations of the pretest and posttest-only, and quasi-experimental designs, which will be addressed in this chapter. Although the pretest and posttest-only designs are practical and convenient for many social work evaluation projects, they have several limitations. Thus, the results should always be interpreted with caveats and careful considerations for potential biases. This design has

Table 9.4: Frequency of Posttest Scores

POSTTEST	FREQ.	PERCENT	CUM.
0	2	10.00	10.00
1	1	5.00	15.00
2	2	10.00	25.00
3	2	10.00	35.00
4	1	5.00	40.00
5	1	5.00	45.00
6	3	15.00	60.00
8	3	15.00	75.00
9	1	5.00	80.00
10	4	20.00	100.00
Total	20	100.00	

no control group representing those who have similar service needs but receive no treatment. The comparison made for the ESL pilot training was based on the changes of ESL ability of the same group of participants. These participants were given the ESL assessment twice, and they could be familiar with the assessment, which is referred to as a threat of testing to internal validity. Thus, the change or improvement could be affected by their knowledge of the assessment. This is the problem of such testing. Because the training lasted five months, the participants could become more competent with their ESL due to being exposed to English-speaking neighbors or acquaintances, or to other sources of influence. This problem is called "maturation." If you select a sample without carefully screening, selection biases could seriously undermine the internal validity, which is the extent to which the variation in the independent variable causes the variation in the dependent variable, called causality. For example, if we selected a sample of participants who already had sufficient ESL skills, the outcome could be undermined even if the participants gained more ESL skills at the end of the program, since the main purpose of the program is to teach refugees who did not have sufficient ESL skills for employment—and not just teach ESL to refugees who already had functional ESL skills.

RANDOMIZED TRUE EXPERIMENTAL DESIGNS

There are several types of randomized true experimental designs, but we only address one standard design, the "pretest-posttest control group design with randomization." The following diagram illustrates this design:

In this design, the "R" refers to random assignments of the participants either to the experimental or control group. The "O" indicates an observation (measures) of the dependent variable (pretest and posttest). The "X" depicts the implementation of treatment (independent variable). The experiment is conducted with two groups to make accurate comparisons. In survey research, when a sample is randomly selected from a large community, the randomly selected individuals represent the larger community. In experimental or evaluation research, when *two or more* groups are randomly selected from the same population, they *are expected to* represent the larger group. More specifically, random assignment makes the two selected groups not only *statistically equivalent* to the larger community, but also statistically equivalent to each other. *Random assignment* is the key element of randomized experimental designs. Note that randomization is the process of assigning the participants or clients into the treatment (or service group) or control group randomly, that is, the selected participants or clients have an equal chance or probability to be assigned to one or the other group. The randomization process tends to "equalize" differences among the selected participants at pretest, making the comparison of the outcome stronger and more meaningful; that is, when clients or participants were recruited into the experimental and control groups, they must have similar social and/or psychological conditions. If a treatment is to reduce psychological distress, all participants should have similar levels of psychological distress before they are randomly assigned to the treatment or control groups.

Table 9.5: The Pretest-Posttest Control Group Design with Randomization

Experimental Group:	Randomization (R)	$O_{pretest}$	$X_{treatment}$	$O_{posttest}$
Control Group:	Randomization (R)	$O_{pretest}$		$O_{posttest}$

A Fictitious Clinical Trial

Let's assume that a social work agency specializes in providing counseling services and treatment to clients with severe psychological distress. A group of clinical social workers just developed a new treatment model that can better serve their clients. Although the social workers are confident on the efficacy of their newly developed treatment, they were not sure whether its efficacy is statistically significant; that is, whether the treatment really caused the desirable outcome or it occurred by chance. They decided to conduct a pilot test before advocating for use of this treatment. The agency recruited twenty volunteers who met the psychological distress profile that would benefit from the treatment. They were then randomly assigned to two groups: treatment group and control group. The treatment will run two weeks. Participants of both groups were given a short psychological distress assessment with scores ranging from 0 to 24. Those with a score at 13 or higher would be considered as "severe distress" (all of the participants should have a score from 13 or higher at pretest). Both groups were assessed again after two weeks. Ideally, the two groups should have very similar pretest scores on psychological distress, or at least all selected participants must have a score of 13 or higher (see Table 9.6).

Table 9.6: Fictitious Data Examining the Effectiveness of a New Treatment Model

ID	GROUP	PRETEST	POSTTEST
1	treatment	13	12
2	control	15	16
3	treatment	16	14
3	control	17	18
5	treatment	18	16
6	control	19	20
7	treatment	22	15
8	control	15	15
9	treatment	24	13
10	control	20	21
11	treatment	20	12
12	control	20	23
13	treatment	19	11
14	control	19	12
15	treatment	20	11
16	control	20	22
17	treatment	19	12
18	control	19	19
19	treatment	19	19
20	control	19	19

Data Analysis

To determine whether the treatment had a statistically significant influence on the participants' psychological distress, we can perform a series of statistical analyses. After checking and verifying the data entry to make sure no data entry mistake was made, we can proceed with the following analyses using Stata or other statistical packages.

First, it is necessary to estimate the **mean psychological distress scores** of the treatment and control groups for both pretest and posttest to overview the nature of this experiment.

Stata syntax:
mean Pretest Posttest, over (Experimental_Group)

In the above syntax, in your "do file" or syntax file, you list the variables you want to estimate their mean, and the variable representing the groups or categories that you want to compare the means. In the above syntax, there are three variables: "Pretest" representing the pretest scores, "Posttest" representing the posttest scores, and "Experimental_Group" representing the treatment and control groups. In this example, we want to estimate the psychological distress means for the treatment group and the control group.

The results shown in Table 9.7 indicate that at the baseline or pretest, both groups had somewhat similar means of psychological distress, but the two groups had different posttest means of psychological distress after the treatment. This information is not sufficient to conclude that the two groups were statistically equal at the pretest and statistically different at the posttest. We need to perform another test to examine the statistical differences.

T-test to Compare Means

"Statistical significance" and "effect size" are the two primary outputs of the t-test. Statistical significance indicates whether the difference between the two sample means is likely to represent an actual difference between two groups of the population, and the effect size indicates whether that difference is large enough to be practically meaningful.

Table 9.7: Mean Score of Pretest and Posttest for Treatment Group & Control Group

Mean estimation Number of obs = 20

treatment: treatment group

control: control group

OVER	MEAN	STD. ERR.	[95% CONF. INTERVAL]	
Pretest				
treatment	19	.9545214	17.00216	20.99784
control	18.3	.6155395	17.01166	19.58834
Posttest				
treatment	13.5	.8062258	11.81255	15.18745
control	18.5	1.067187	16.26635	20.73365

A *two-sided* (or two-tailed) P value is appropriate when the difference between the two means can occur in both directions. It may be either negative or positive; the mean of one sample may either be smaller or larger than that of the other sample.

A *one-sided* test should only be performed when—before the start of the study—it has already been established that a difference can only occur in one direction. For example, when the mean of group *A* must be greater than the mean of group *B,* or vice verse.

To determine whether the difference between the means of two groups or the association between two variables is statistically significant, you look at the significance level or the P value of a given statistical test. The conventional cutoff value of P is .05 or less. Some researchers report the exact P values as found on the results, other often report three traditional values (* p < .05, ** p < .01, and *** p < .001). You should not interpret the P values too strictly; the P value at .001 does not mean the association between two variables is stronger than the P value at .05. With large sample sizes, you are more likely to find the difference or the association is statistically significant. Therefore, given the small sample size of many social work agencies, you should pay more attention to the 95% confidence levels (Altman, Gore, Gardner, and Pocock 1983). The narrower the 95% confidence intervals is, the more precise the difference or association. Also, clinical significance should play an important role in your interpretation; that is, regardless of the statistical result, do you find the outcome meaningful based on your own or your peers' clinical observations, wisdom, or experiences? Let's perform t-tests to examine whether there is no difference in the pretest scores between the treatment and the control group, and also whether there is a significant difference in the posttest scores between the two groups. Pretest and posttest t-test results are presented in Table 9.8 and Table 9.9, respectively. Results indicate the mean difference in pretests between the two groups is statistically insignificant, while there is a significant mean difference between the treatment and the control group on the posttest.

Stata syntax for t-test (comparing pretest mean scores between two groups):
ttest Pretest, by (Experimental_Group)

Table 9.8: Pretest Score of Treatment & Control Groups

Two-sample t-tests with equal variances

GROUP	OBS	MEAN	STD. ERR.	STD. DEV.	[95% CONF. INTERVAL]	
treatmen	10	19	.9545214	3.018462	16.84072	21.15928
control	10	18.3	.6155395	1.946507	16.90755	19.69245
combined	20	18.65	.558546	2.497894	17.48095	19.81905
diff		.7	1.135782		−1.686189	3.086189

diff = mean(treatmen) − mean(control)   t = 0.6163
Ho: diff = 0   degrees of freedom = 18

Ha: diff < 0   Ha: diff = 0   Ha: diff > 0
Pr(T < t) = 0.7273 Pr(|T| > |t|) = 0.5454 Pr(T > t) = 0.2727

Table 9.9: Posttest Score of Treatment Group & Control Group

Two-sample t-tests with equal variances

GROUP	OBS	MEAN	STD. ERR.	STD. DEV.	[95% CONF. INTERVAL]	
treatmen	10	13.5	.8062258	2.54951	11.67619	15.32381
control	10	18.5	1.067187	3.374743	16.08585	20.91415
combined	20	16	.8675434	3.879772	14.18421	17.81579
diff		−5	1.337494		−7.80997	−2.19003

diff = mean(treatmen) − mean(control)   t = −3.7383
Ho: diff = 0   degrees of freedom = 18

Ha: diff < 0   Ha: diff = 0   Ha: diff > 0
Pr(T < t) = 0.0008   Pr(|T| > |t|) = 0.0015   Pr(T > t) = 0.9992

Stata syntax for t-test (comparing posttest mean scores between two groups):
ttest Posttest, by (Experimental_Group)

QUASI-EXPERIMENTAL DESIGNS

Sometimes, random assignments are not possible due to a variety of reasons that can be either ethical or practical. Experiments that do not randomly assign participants into experimental conditions are called quasi-experiments. Thus, **quasi-experimental designs**, also called field experiments, refer to experiments that use manipulated independent variables but lack random assignments. Quasi-experiments are often conducted in natural settings, such as schools, agencies, clinics, various practice settings, and so forth. Participants are assigned to the treatment group or control group by availability or convenience. There are many types of quasi-experimental designs but we discuss one of the most common ones in this chapter, the "pretest-posttest with a comparison group design." Its notational form is illustrated in Table 9.10.

Let's use the previous psychological distress treatment example to illustrate quasi-experimental designs. The agency cannot randomly select clients for the study nor provide more than one treatment session. Only a limited number of clients can participate, and other clients will have to be placed on a waiting list. Clients on the waiting list could be viewed as the control or comparison group, and can participate in the treatment session when spaces are available. One of the key problems of quasi-experimental design is selection bias,

Table 9.10: The Pretest-Posttest with a Comparison Group Design

Experimental Group: O$_{pretest}$ X$_{treatment}$ O$_{posttest}$
Control Group: O$_{pretest}$ O$_{posttest}$

Note: The design lacks random assignment, but includes two groups.

which is an extrinsic threat to internal validity. In many aspects, participants in the experimental and control groups are not equivalent, and their differences could affect the outcomes. The researchers should identify potential selection biases and incorporate these potential sources of bias in the analysis and interpretation of the results. Therefore, key background information such as age, sex, race/ethnicity, education, and other demographic variables should be taken into consideration.

Let's use the previous data to illustrate how one can use regression analysis to control for background information when examining the effect of the psychological treatment program. In the analysis of the outcome, we will take a sex variable into consideration. Sex is viewed as a control variable or a covariate. We will use multiple regression analysis to analyze the data. Simply speaking, multiple regression analysis is a statistical method that allows us to examine the linear association between a set of independent variables and one continuous dependent or outcome variable. The independent variables can be continuous or discrete. A discrete variable has a finite number of categories such as group membership, sex, race/ethnicity, and likewise (indicator, categorical, nominal, dummy (0/1), or dichotomous). In the data set, the pretest scores and posttest scores are continuous variables, and experimental groups and sex are discrete variables.

We can express the association of the dependent variable (outcome variable) and the independent variable in the following regression equation:

$$Y = a + X_1 b_1 + X_2 b_2 + X_3 b_3 + e$$

Notes:

Y = posttest scores

a = constant (intercept): starting value of Y

X_1 = group (treatment vs. no treatment)

X_2 = pretest scores

X_3 = sex (male, female)

b_1 = regression coefficient (linear association) of posttest scores on experimental groups

b_2 = regression coefficient of posttest score on pretest scores

b_3 = regression coefficient of posttest scores on sex

In the above equation, "group" is the independent variable, and the control variables are "pretest scores" and "sex." In explaining the association between "groups" and "posttest scores," we can say that we examined the posttest scores between the treatment group and the control group controlling for the possible confounding effect of the pretest scores and participants' sex identification.

Let's look at the results of a regression analysis of the fictitious data used in the true experimental design, and the difference is the addition of the sex variable in the analysis. We use regression analysis instead of the independent sample t-test that was used to compare the posttest scores in the previous analysis. If we run it, the regression model would be:

$$Y = a + X_1 b_{1\ \text{(experimental groups)}} + X_2 b_{2\ \text{(pretest scores)}} + X_3 b_{3\ \text{(sex)}} + e$$

This regression model or equation includes one dependent variable (Y) and three independent variables (X_1, X_2, and X_3). It's more proper to say the model has one independent variable (group) and two covariates or control variables (pretest scores and sex).

Stata syntax of regression analysis:
regres Posttest i.experimental_groups Pretest i.sex
Note: We place "i." before each discrete variable in the syntax.

Multiple regression analysis results are presented in Table 9.11.

In Table 9.10, the regression coefficient of posttest on the group variable is -5.21 with the t score of |3.95| and $p = 0.001$. The t-test is the test of statistical significance for each independent variable and control (covariate) variable in the regression analysis. The t score is the result of the ratio of the regression coefficient over its standard error (i.e., $5.21/1.32 = 3.95$). The values of the 95% confidence (Conf.) interval refer to the precision of the regression coefficient. The narrower the interval, the more precise the regression coefficient. The regression coefficient must fall inside the confidence interval to be meaningful. The significant association between the treatment group and the posttest indicates that, on average, those who received psychological treatment were able to lower their level of psychological distress by 5.21 compared with those who were in the comparison group. The regression coefficient of the pretest scores and sex were not statistically significant, indicating that participants' pretest psychological distress scores and sex did not influence the posttest psychological distress scores. Thus, we can rule out the possible confounding effect of the pretest psychological distress scores and clients' sex. Note that the results in this analysis are similar to

Table 9.11: Multiple Regression Analysis Result

SOURCE	SS	DF	MS	NUMBER OF OBS = 20	
				F(3, 16) = 5.81	
Model	149.068569	3	49.689523	Prob > F = 0.0070	
Residual	136.931431	16	8.55821444	R-squared = 0.5212	
				Adj R-squared = 0.4314	
Total	286	19	15.0526316	Root MSE = 2.9254	

POSTTEST	COEF.	STD. ERR.	T	P>|T|	[95% CONF. INTERVAL]	
Group						
Treatment	−5.218504	1.322083	−3.95	0.001	−8.021195	−2.415813
Pretest	.3121487	.2720312	1.15	0.268	−0.2645317	.8888292
sex						
Male	−1.506355	1.310841	−1.15	0.267	−4.285213	1.272502
cons	13.54086	5.145275	2.63	0.018	2.63336	24.44835

* Prob of F or the P value of F statistics indicate the regression model or equation is statistically significant, suggesting at least one or all independent and control variables is (are) statistically significant.

those using the t-test because both the pretest and sex variables did not have a statistically significant effect on the outcome. Multiple regression analysis, however, is more powerful than independent samples t-test because we can take possible confounding variables into consideration in performing a regression analysis.

SINGLE SUBJECT DESIGNS

A **single subject design**, also called single case research design, is essentially a quasi-experimental design that involves repeated multiple observations of a client's target behavior, with the same measurement techniques used throughout the experiment period of no-intervention baseline and intervention phases. Single subject designs are more appropriate to monitor treatment or intervention outcomes in clinical settings compared with other research designs (Kazdin, 1982). Social work researchers can also use single subject designs to collect preliminary data for a larger study or to explore the evidence-based result of a specific intervention. We will analyze three types of single subject designs that can be useful and feasible for social work practice. Unlike other experimental research designs in which data are collected from a group of multiple subjects, which allow the researcher to examine the mean score of the group on a target behavior, in single subject research each participant acts as his or her own control entity without any separate comparison or control groups. Clinicians or researchers can compare changes of the outcomes using data from the same client. This is similar to the "one group pretest and posttest design" we examined earlier in this chapter.

Steps in Single Subject Designs

1. Preliminary Assessment: This phase includes a collection of personal background data, a client's self-assessment of his or her situation, and a clinician's preliminary assessment. If the client was referred for a specified condition, the clinician should verify the information.
2. Selection of Treatment and Outcome Measures and Treatment Plan: A clinician selects an evidence-based treatment model or intervention strategy as well as an appropriate outcome measure designed to measure the selected target behavior (i.e., depression, anxiety, low self-esteem, coping strategies, etc.). A comprehensive treatment plan is developed with approval of the client or legal guardian.
3. Establish the Baseline Data: A clinician should meet with the prospective client at least three times and administer the selected outcome measure to collect baseline data (data collected prior to treatment). Baseline data will be used as a basis to compare the changes in the target behavior after the treatment is introduced.
4. Treatment Implementation: A clear procedure of implementation must be established and followed carefully.
5. Post Baseline or Outcome Observations: Outcome data must be collected after each treatment session. The same measure of outcome must be repeated. The number of treatment sessions is determined by the clinician's and agency's policy.
6. Data Recording: Baseline and treatment outcome data must be recorded accurately on a predesigned graph (See the graphs below).
7. Narrative Report: Each data point should be supplemented by a narrative report from the clinician. This in-depth information is important to explain the changes in the client's condition.

8. Termination: There are three conditions that warrant a termination of the case—first, if the client's situation becomes more severe after three intervention sessions; second, if the client's condition remains unchanged after three intervention sessions; and third, when the client's condition changes in the desired direction and stabilizes over at least three sessions.

Types of Single Subject Designs

Figures 1 and 2 in this chapter illustrate two single subject designs that can be used in social work practice.

Basic AB Design

This is the basic single subject design that requires a baseline phase (A) and a treatment phase (B). At least three baseline observations must be made unless it's an emergency situation that requires an immediate crisis intervention. Three observations provide the minimum condition to verify the changes or stability of the client's condition. The time intervals between observations are determined by the clinician and the client's condition.

The AB design in Figure 1 demonstrates how a treatment of depression for one client was implemented and recorded. First, the client had a depression score above the cutoff score at the baseline phase. The clinician assessed the client's depression over three periods or intervals depending on the severity of the client's condition. As illustrated in Figure 1, the client's depression continued to increase, suggesting that treatment should be implemented. In Phase B, the client's depression must be recorded shortly after the first session. It is reasonable to measure the client's depression within the twenty-four- to forty-eight-hour period after each treatment session. As recorded in the Basic AB design graph in Figure 1, the client's depression continued to decrease to a level under the cutoff score and became stabilized. It is preferable to have the client's condition become stabilized over three consecutive sessions before the termination of treatment.

The use of a scale or measure with a clear cutoff score is convenient for social workers to decide whether a continued treatment is needed, but this decision must be evaluated with clinical evidence and a careful scrutiny of the case supplemented by a case conference. Social work interventions are not based on the medical model. Thus, the decision to select and implement a treatment should be carefully considered and evaluated with peer and/or team contributions.

Treatment and Withdrawal Design: ABWB

This design is also designated as the ABAB design, which calls for four alternating phases: baseline, treatment, withdrawal, and treatment. Data are recorded for all phases. The special feature of this design is the withdrawal or "time-out" phase that clearly shows the effect of treatment on the client's condition. For example, if the client's condition becomes worse shortly after the withdrawal of the treatment, we can see that treatment produces changes in the client's condition. This design might not be appropriate for some clinical situations due to both ethical considerations and the nature of the problem. The clinician, however, can substitute the treatment with an alternative temporary intervention strategy to observe changes in the client. The second graph in Figure 1 illustrates this design.

Figure 9.1: AB and ABWB Designs

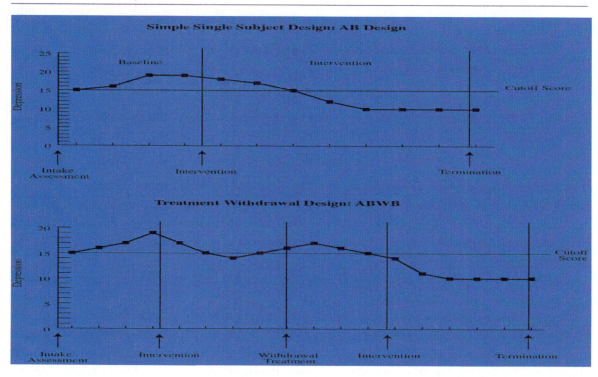

Complementary Outcomes AB Design

As illustrated in Figure 2, social workers can use two outcome measures to assess the client's changes in psychological distress or behavior. The use of two opposite measures can improve the validity of the efficacy of the treatment. For example, life satisfaction and depression are two opposite measures, and their relationship has been verified in numerous studies. Conceptually, it makes sense to observe these two outcome measures change in the opposite direction. If the goal of the treatment is to reduce the client's depression, it is also expected that once the client's depression decreases, he or she would be more satisfied with life.

Strengths and weaknesses of Single Subject Designs

Single subject designs provide a practical framework for the social worker to monitor and evaluate the treatment outcomes. Since the single subject design focuses on one client at a time, the social worker can be creative and flexible in the process of data collection, such as the use of different outcome measures targeting the same problem and outcome purpose. For example, Figure 2 illustrates a combined use of depression and life satisfaction scales as outcome measures. This design can be used as a pilot test of a treatment or intervention before it is implemented in a larger study. The researcher can compile the outcome data from several individuals to verify the efficacy of a treatment or service program. The comparison of outcomes of the same program or services, using the data from clients of different racial/ethnic and socioeconomic

Figure 9.2. Complementary Outcomes AB Design

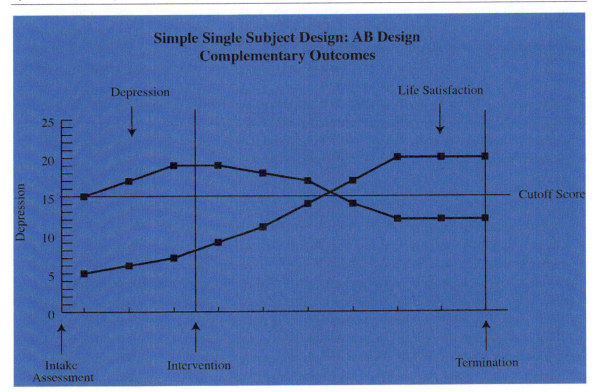

backgrounds, can help the social work researcher assess the cross-cultural comparability of certain treatments or programs.

It should be noted that while single subject designs are convenient and practical, there are drawbacks to this type of research: it has a low degree of internal validity, data generated for single subject designs are not generalizable, and it is difficult to ascertain causality between the treatment and the outcome variable.

POSSIBLE BIASES IN EXPERIMENTAL DESIGNS

Social Desirability: Social desirability refers to the possible biases caused by the untruthful reactions or responses to a treatment or intervention by participants whose intention is to please the evaluator/researcher or avoid revealing their true feelings. The untruthful responses from clients or participants distorts the effectiveness of a treatment, program, or service. The only option a researcher has is to request that the participant be truthful and sincere in his or her responses as much as possible.

Selection Bias: Selection bias arises when participants or clients are not randomly selected from a community or a pool of eligible clients.

Implementation Problem: This occurs when treatment or intervention is not implemented systematically and consistently.

Measurement: This bias arises when the researcher uses outcome measures that have poor reliability and validity including cross-cultural appropriateness or sensitivity. This bias can also be caused by the repetition of data collection. When data are collected more than once, participants can become familiar or tired of being exposed to the same measure over time.

Environmental Influences: Unexpected circumstances from the surrounding environment can influence the effectiveness of a treatment or intervention.

Biases can be caused by the researcher and the participants. There is no perfect research design. Nonetheless, social work researchers and evaluators need to foresee possible biases and make every effort to avoid them. When the researcher cannot rule out or control for possible biases, it is important to take this into consideration in the report and interpretation of the results.

SUMMARY

This chapter addressed some practical and feasible experimental research designs that can be used in social work research and evaluation. Experimental design is the systematic and highly controlled process of examining the effect of the independent variable (also called experimental stimulus or treatment) on the variation in the dependent variable (outcome or target behavior). It is important to plan an experimental design carefully. The social work researcher needs to have the right type of data, a sufficient sample size, and statistical power to answer the research or evaluation questions of interest. For each selected design, the students learn how to work with the data and use the appropriate statistical test to evaluate the project outcomes or test the research hypothesis. We demonstrated the use of Stata for both statistical analysis and power analysis. The key difference between experimental research and other type of research designs examined in this chapter is implementation of the well-designed independent variable, i.e., the experimental or treatment conditions. The social work researcher implements an intervention, manipulates experimental conditions, and then observes the outcome or dependent variable. The chapter also addressed the use of single subject designs in social work research and evaluation.

CLASS EXERCISE

The instructor divides the class into groups of two or more students and assigns each group the following group tasks:

- Groups will choose a topic relevant to evidence-based multicultural social work practice.
- Discuss the application of experimental research designs to the chosen topic.
- Develop research questions and hypotheses.
- Find appropriate statistical tools to answer the research questions and test the hypotheses.

REFERENCES

Altman, D. G., Gore, S. M., Gardner, M. J., & Pocock, S. J. (1983). Statistical guidelines for contributors to medical journals. *British Medical Journal (Clinical Research Ed.), 286*(6376), 1489.

Campbell, D. T., & Stanley, J. C. (1966). *Experimental and quasi-experimental designs for research.* Chicago, IL: Rand McNally.

Cook, T. D., & Campbell, D. T. (1979). *Quasi-experimentation: Design & analysis issues for field settings.* Chicago, IL: Rand McNally.

Frankfort-Nachmias, C., & Nachmias, D. (2008). *Research methods in the social sciences.* New York, NY: Worth Publishers, Macmillan Higher Education.

Kazdin, A. (1982). *Single-case research designs.* New York, NY: Oxford University Press.

TEN

Secondary Research and Data Analysis

In this chapter, we will introduce students to many sources of secondary data analysis. Students will learn how to identify existing data at social work agencies as well as local health and human services institutions. And we will teach students how to use US Bureau of the Census data to identify different racial/ethnic groups for social and economic information. Students will learn how to use local census data for need assessments and grant writing activities. And they will learn techniques to compile and prepare the existing data into manageable data files for statistical analyses.

PUBLIC DATA FOR SECONDARY DATA RESEARCH

Secondary data research is defined as any research that uses data from existing sources (Smith, Ayanian, Covinsky, Landon, Wee, and Steinman 2011). With development of the Internet, the deposit of public-funded data on major data archives during the past two decades has greatly aided social work researchers and other health scientists in examining racial and ethnic differences on health status, health-service utilization, health disparities, economic achievements, poverty, disability, and a host of important social issues through the use of large-scale data, and with more credible and valid outcomes. There are many public data archives available for seeking the information that suits your research project. For example, researchers who receive funding from most government institutions are required to store their data for public use. Specifically, the National Institute on Health (NIH) made its position clear regarding publicly funded data sharing:

> In NIH's view, all data should be considered for data sharing. **Data should be made as widely and freely available as possible while safeguarding the privacy of participants, and protecting confidential and proprietary data.** To facilitate data sharing, investigators submitting a research application requesting $500,000 or more of direct costs in any single year to NIH on or after October 1, 2003 are expected to include a plan for sharing final research data for research purposes, or state why data sharing is not possible (http://www.grants.nih.gov/grants/policy/data_sharing/data_sharing_guidance.htm#archive).

The availability and easy accessibility of large-scale data sets allow social worker researchers to conduct quality comparative research, especially research concerning racial and ethnic differences in health disparities, poverty, and other important social and psychological problems.

STEPS IN SECONDARY DATA RESEARCH

Following is a guide that can be used to conduct a secondary data-research project. These steps are not linear. The researcher should always go back to previous stages to reassess his or her actions.

1. Identify research questions or interests. This can be done through brainstorming with coworkers, or responding to requests for research proposals from external funding agencies.
2. Conduct literature review. This is a process of learning what has been done and what remains to be investigated in your research area.
3. Develop specific aims and hypotheses. If your agency is the sole source of funding for your research project, you need to discuss with administrators and coworkers to decide what needs to be investigated and develop specific aims, hypotheses, or objectives.
4. Clearly state the research variables in the context of a conceptual framework. Based on the specific aims, hypotheses, or objectives, you can choose the variables that best reflect the project aims.
5. Update and expand your literature review. Once you and your agency know exactly what to do, further literature review is needed to help you refine your rationale, articulate the theoretical framework, or establish a knowledge base to explain what you will do.
6. Search for the data. You need to develop a guide to help you and your team identify the appropriate data for your projects. For example, identify a list of key words that can be used for the data search.
7. Study the data codebook or data dictionary. Once you select a data set, you need to become familiar with the variables contained in the data. It could take a few weeks to become familiar with the data set.
8. Review the existing literature published from the data set you chose. You should know who used the data and what they reported in journals or research reports.
9. Analyze the data to test your hypotheses or find information for your questions. Most large-scale data use complex sampling designs; thus, you need to account for sampling designs in your analysis. The codebook will provide information on the weighted information and you should be able to use this information in your analysis.
10. Summarize, interpret, and disseminate your results. The purpose of your study will dictate how you present and disseminate the results.

ADVANTAGES AND DISADVANTAGES OF SECONDARY DATA RESEARCH

There are some key advantages of the use of secondary data. First, its use is inexpensive or free. Second, it saves time. You just need to download the data from the data archive websites to your laptop, desktop, or external hard drive. This can be done in a few minutes. Third, most large-scale data sets are well designed and high quality. On the other hand, you have no control over the data collection process, and the existing variables in the data set might not be exactly what you would want. Thus, the use of secondary data requires flexibility from the researchers in terms of measurement selection. Following is a list of types of data that social work researchers can use for their research:

1. Client records are a rich source for social work evaluation of evidence-based practice. For example, the first author of this book is collaborating with a local mental-health hospital to study the correlation of patients' length of stay and the frequency of their family visits. We hypothesize that those patients who had family visits would be released faster than those without or very few family visits. To find data for this research question, we reviewed a sample of closed patient records. This type of research requires a careful review of records and use of predetermined criteria to retrieve data from patients' records.

2. The **American Community Survey** (ACS) is a great source of data for social workers to study various socioeconomic issues that have policy implications at local, state, and national levels. This could be a great source for social service agencies to identify socioeconomic needs such as poverty and unemployment in local communities.

The following overview of the ACS data source will help us understand what type of data are available through the ACS:

> *The American Community Survey (ACS) is an ongoing survey that provides data every year—giving communities the current information they need to plan investments and services. Information from the survey generates data that help determine how more than $400 billion in federal and state funds are distributed each year* (https://www.census.gov/acs/www/about_the_survey/american_community_survey/).

Social researchers and social work researchers can certainly use this large national-scale data to test hypotheses or describe a particular social problem or issue. For example, Minkler and Fuller-Thomson (2005) used the ASC data to "determine the prevalence, sociodemographic characteristics, and service utilization patterns of African American grandparents raising grandchildren compared with noncaregiving peers." Their research, titled "African American Grandparents Raising Grandchildren: A National Study Using the Census 2000 American Community Survey," was published in the *Journal of Gerontology*, Series B, Psychological Sciences and Social Sciences, in 2005.

3. Another example of using US census data to study economic assimilation of immigrants and refugees is the study by Tran and Phan (2003). They used the **census data from 1980, 1990, and 2000** to examine homeownership among single Vietnamese Americans adults aged twenty-five to sixty-four. They found two factors that personal income and number of siblings had a consistent association with homeownership over time. They suggested that their results highlight the role of economic achievement and family support in impacting the successful assimilation of newly arrived immigrants or refugees.

LARGE SCALE SECONDARY DATA RESOURCES

You can find data from data archives at many universities and government institutions. Some of the largest scale data sets can be downloaded from the following sources:

*   **Health Service Research Data Sets: Society of General Internal Medicine (SGIM) Research Dataset Compendium**
    www.sgim.org/go/datasets

- **National Information Center on Health Services Research and Health Care Technology (NICHSR)**
  http://www.nlm.nih.gov/nichsr/index.html

- **University Consortium for Political and Social Research (ICPSR):**
  World's largest archive of digital social science. This data archive contains thousands of data sets in all aspects health, human services, and social sciences.
  https://www.icpsr.umich.edu

- **Directory of Health and Human Services Data Resources (US Dept. of Health and Human Services)**
  This website has links to nearly all data sets from the National Institutes of Health, Centers for Disease Control and Prevention, Centers for Medicare and Medicaid Services (CMS), Agency for Healthcare Research and Quality (AHRQ), Food and Drug Administration (FDA), and other agencies of the US Department of Health and Human Services. http://aspe.hhs.gov/datacncl/DataDir/index.shtml

- **National Center for Health Statistics (NCHS)**
  http://www.cdc.gov/nchs/index.htm This site links to a variety of data sets from the Veterans Affairs (VA) data. http://www.virec.research.va.gov/index.htm

- **US Bureau of Census Data**
  Important resource for social work research to learn about demographic characteristics of the US population and the local communities. Data on poverty, employment, educational attainment, race, ethnicity, linguistic diversity, and more can be found from the US census data. http://www.census.gov/

CONTENT ANALYSIS OF SOCIAL SERVICE AGENCY WRITTEN RECORDS

Content Analysis is a systematic method "for analyzing textual information in a standardized way that allows evaluators to make inferences about that information" (Weber 1990, 9–12; Krippendorff 1980, 21–27). This is a method of organizing existing information from various sources (i.e., written records, media records, newspaper stories, and others) into fewer meaningful categories or themes and presenting them in a logical report. There is a rich tradition to keep narrative reports in social service agencies. These historical narrative reports can be analyzed for educational and evaluation purposes. For example, one can use content analysis to reconstruct past client records (1) to describe the interaction between social workers and clients across different historical periods, (2) identify intervention processes used over time, and (3) establish evidence-based practice or best practice and other purposes.

Krippendorff (1980) recommended the following six questions that must be addressed in every content analysis:

1. Which data are analyzed?
2. How are they defined?
3. What is the population from which they are drawn?

4. What is the context relative to which the data are analyzed?
5. What are the boundaries of the analysis?
6. What is the target of the inferences?

In addition to the restructuring of written records to produce a logical and cohesive report, social workers can use charts and figures to present the results.

Strengths and Weaknesses of Content Analysis

There are a few strengths of content analysis research: (1) it is an unobtrusive method of research and analysis, allowing researchers to avoid the biases of interaction between researcher and participants; (2) access to exiting historical data is often more convenient and less expensive than other methods of data collection; and (3) a good content analysis provides an objective account of what happened in the past.

The content analysis method, however, suffers from some obvious weaknesses: (1) researchers are constrained to the availability and the quality of existing records–poor data will never produce good reports; (2) regardless of how systematic and objective the researcher strives to be, the results of content analysis are always subjective to certain degrees; and (3) content analysis can be time consuming.

CONTENT ANALYSIS AND SOCIAL WORK APPLICATION

Most, if not all, social service agencies have rich archives of narrative reports, pictures, newsletters, brochures, and other types of information useful for content analysis research projects. For example, researchers can review the intake forms from many decades to examine the types of information collected from clients over time. Client records are good data sources to understand the change in community population, needs, problems, and treatments or services provided by social workers and agencies over time. Following is a list of possible social work content analysis research projects:

1. The use of evidence-based treatments or services.
2. Changes in outreach methods.
3. Changes in client population.
4. Changes in social service funding.
5. Changes in the expertise or training of staff.
6. Changes in staff composition, recruitments, and hiring practice.

SUMMARY

This chapter presented both quantitative and qualitative approaches of secondary data analysis. Social work researchers can perform low-cost, large-scale secondary data analyses to address many social issues or problems relevant to social work. The American Community Survey from the US Bureau of the Census (http://www.census.gov/) provides data for social work researchers to study issues important to social work such as poverty, housing problems, health insurance, immigration, disability, and other social issues across many racial and ethnic groups.

CLASS EXERCISE

Go online and identify at least two public data archives. For each data archive, write a brief report on the availability of data that can be used in social work research.

REFERENCES

Krippendorff, K. (1980). *Content analysis: An introduction to its methodology*. Newbury Park, CA: Sage.

Minkler, M., & Fuller-Thomson, E. (2005). African American grandparents raising grandchildren: A national study using the Census 2000 American Community Survey. *The Journals of Gerontology Series B: Psychological Sciences and Social Sciences, 60*(2), S82–S92.

Smith, A. K., Ayanian, J. Z., Covinsky, K. E., Landon, B. E., Wee, C. C., & Steinman, M. A. (2011). Conducting high-value secondary dataset analysis: an introductory guide and resources. *Journal of General Internal Medicine, 26*(8), 920-929.

Tran, T. V., & Phan, P. T. (2011). Homeownership among single Vietnamese American adults. *Journal of Comparative Social Welfare, 27*(3), 243–252.

Weber, R. P. (1990). *Basic content analysis* (2nd ed.). Newbury Park, CA: Sage.

ELEVEN

Qualitative Research

In this chapter, we introduce basic concepts of qualitative research and illustrate how social workers can use qualitative research in social work research and practice. This method of inquiry seeks to understand a problem or topic from the perspectives of people in their own natural environment. Qualitative research is especially effective in collecting culturally relevant information about the values, opinions, behaviors, social interactions, and lifestyles of racial, ethnic, or subculture groups.

As cited in Chapter 1, qualitative research is an inductive reasoning process that uses scientific methods to generate knowledge. The basic scientific method of qualitative research involves:

- asking meaningful and relevant questions;
- using appropriate procedures to collect data;
- analyzing and making sense of the collected data; and
- producing knowledge that is cohesive, logical, and meaningful.

We will examine three approaches in qualitative research that can be useful for social work research and evaluation: ethnography, focus groups, and case study.

ETHNOGRAPHY

Ethnography is a type of qualitative research method employed by anthropologists to study human society and culture. A definition given by the 2013 Encyclopædia Britannica Inc., stated that ethnography is a "*descriptive study of a particular human society or the process of making such a study. Contemporary ethnography is based almost entirely on fieldwork and requires the complete immersion of the anthropologist in the culture and everyday life of the people*" that she or he studies (htp://www.britannica.com/EBchecked/topic/194292/ethnography). It should be noted that contemporary ethnographies tend to focus on a community, current situations, and circumstances of a community rather than individuals and historical events. Ethnographic studies are no longer restricted to small primitive societies but have expanded to urban communities and groups. Today, ethnographers employ a variety of technological tools to collect and record fieldwork data.

The United States General Accounting Office (2003) provided this definition of ethnography:

> *Ethnography is a social science method developed within cultural anthropology for studying communities in natural settings. Although ethnography is commonly associated with lengthy research aimed at understanding cultures remote from our own, it can also be used to inform the design, implementation, and evaluation of public programs* (http://www.gao.gov/new. items/d03455.pdf, p. 4).

The US government has used ethnography to provide information for various federal policies and program. The Administration for Children and Families in the Department of Health and Human Services has used ethnography to examine how Early Head Start children and families experienced a Montessori preschool program in order to interpret results from quantitative data. It's important to note that ethnographic researchers seek to understand culturally based behaviors and beliefs from the perspective of community members, and use local perspectives as the foundation for building testable theories. The ethnographic researchers actively collect their data by engaging in the lives of the people in their own living environment. Therefore, it's probable their data can be subjective and suffer from numerous potential biases that can compromise the reliability and validity.

Steps in Ethnographic Social Work Research

1. Develop feasible research questions.

2. Select the study site and prepare for gaining entry. Identify and select a research site. This can be a social service agency, a client family, local church, club, or any natural environment where the research subjects (participants) live, work, or engage in social activities. In the preparation stage, the researcher or her or his team assembles existing information about the local community to be studied, seeking permission to conduct the study.

3. Collect field data. Ethnographic social work researchers collect data by means of human observation and interaction in a local setting. The researcher himself or herself is the primary data collection tool. The researcher can employ any means of data recording (i.e., note taking, audio recording, video recording, etc.) to collect data.

4. Analyze field data. Data analysis requires the researcher to transcribe the collected data into text, review the data, code the data, and organize the data in terms of themes under a meaningful framework with

ETHNOGRAPHIC DATA COLLECTION TECHNIQUES

- Exploratory or participant observation requires the social worker researcher to be present at, participating in, and recording the daily activities in the natural research environment.
- In-depth, open-ended interviewing aims to collect in-depth information of the research topic. The researcher is open to all relevant responses and welcomes new topics as they arise.
- Semi-structured interviewing aims to collect data using predetermined questions but seeks open-ended answers and allows the researcher to expand questions through probes.

which the researcher can support the analysis and reach conclusions. In general, ethnographic data analysis produces a narrative description of the cultural behaviors, symbols, and interactions of a group or agency from data collected and recorded by researchers over a long period.

5. Report and disseminate results. This step requires the researcher to produce a narrative portrait of what is collected and recorded from the data. The narrative may include stories or in-depth descriptions intended to describe and convey typical event situations. A researcher can use tables, graphs, and other visual means to substantiate the narrative report.

Lenette, Brough and Cox (2013) reported an ethnographic study of single refugee women in Brisbane, Australia. Their specific aim was to contextualize the concept of resilience of single refugee women with children. The principle investigator, Caroline Lenette, spent the entire year with four refugee women to collect the data. She explored this concept of resilience through the ethnographic research approach. The researcher "was immersed in the women's everyday lives, to establish genuine relationships of trust." They used "a combination of participant observation, in-depth interviews, and visual ethnography" approaches to collect their data. As you can see, ethnographic research is time consuming and labor intensive.

FOCUS GROUPS

Another type of qualitative research approach that can be useful for social work research is focus groups (Morgan, 1996). This method employs interviews on a specific topic with a small group of clients or prospective participants. Patton (2002) suggested a focus group method might provide cross-validation of data because participants can offer checks and balances on one another that can serve to screen out extreme information. The researcher can use note taking, audio recording or video recording to collect data. It is important for the researcher to prepare a well-thought list of questions and rules of discussions before the meeting. A focus group is composed of a moderator and respective participants.

Focus Group Moderator: The researcher herself or himself or a trained person can be the moderator to lead the group discussions.

Focus Group Participants: A small group of selected individuals provide data relevant to the research purposes.

Size of Focus Group: Typically six to twelve participants should be recruited for focus group meetings. It is important to have equal numbers of female and male participants. A minimum of three group meetings should be conducted. More meetings are required if the information collected from the meeting does not satisfy the purposes of the study.

Length of Focus: Group meetings typically last one to two hours in length.

Meeting Format and Data Recording: Focus groups can be held in person (face-to-face) or conducted remotely by teleconferencing, videoconferencing, or through the use of other modern communication technologies.

Data Analysis: A content analysis of narrative information generated from focus group discussions can be performed as part of data analysis.

Selection Criteria for a Moderator

The focus group moderator plays an important role in the collection of data for the study. The quality of the data collected from the focus groups also depends upon the quality of the focus group moderator. Thus, in planning and conducting focus group meetings, the researcher should be mindful of the following considerations when selecting a moderator. Tran (2009) recommended a list of selection criteria that can be used to recruit and select the focus group moderator and focus group participants.

An effective focus moderator should have the following qualifications:

Cultural Competency: The moderator should have an in-depth knowledge of the culture of the target population.

Language Competency: If the target population has a different linguistic background, the moderator is expected to be fluent in their languages to fully enhance the focus group meetings.

Analytical Skills: The moderator should have good analytical skills to raise meaningful questions and guide participants in the right direction.

Verbal skills: The moderator who is able to communicate and define the research aims and meanings of the research variables and instruments will stimulate participants to stay focused on their tasks during the focus group meetings.

Listening Skills: The success of a focus group largely depends on the ability of the moderator to listen to the participants. Showing respect to participants' ideas will help them reveal the information that they would not reveal if they thought the moderator were not interested in them.

Empathy: Being able to share participants' feelings and appreciate their attitudes in a group setting will attract more attention from participants and boost their willingness to share their views and thoughts concerning the purpose of the focus group meeting.

Selection Criteria for Focus Group Participants

The quality of focus group data is largely determined by the participants who provide the information relevant to the research purposes. As recommended by Tran (2009), the researcher should consider the following criteria to recruit and select the prospective participants for focus group meetings:

Socioeconomic Background Representative of the Target Population: Although the sample of a focus group is small, the research team should make every effort to recruit participants who are representative of the target population or community.

Good Communication Skills: Focus group participants need to have the ability to communicate in group settings. They must be willing and able to share their ideas and thoughts with others by engaging in the group discussion.

Personal Experiences: Focus group participants need to have personal experiences that are relevant to the goal of the focus group. For example, if the team wants to develop an instrument to study the effects of natural disaster on psychological well-being, the participants should come from the section of the community that experienced a nature disaster in the past.

Tolerance and Respect for Different Opinions: Participants should have a sense of tolerance and respect for different opinions. Although it is difficult to screen participants for this criterion, the research team can provide instructions and clear rules of engagement in group interaction and discussion.

The focus group method can provide valuable data for social work researchers at lower cost if conducted appropriately. Social workers can use this method at social service agencies for need assessment, program development, program evaluation, and other purposes.

CASE STUDY

The third type of qualitative research methods addressed in this book is case study. We examine this research approach because of its potential applications in social work research and evaluation. We use the definition of case study as defined by the United States General Accounting Office (1990):

> *A case study is a method for learning about a complex instance, based on a comprehensive understanding of that instance obtained by extensive description and analysis of that instance taken as a whole and in its context.*

This definition of case study indicates that **case study is particularistic, descriptive, and heuristic**. It is particularistic because it aims to study a particular instance or situation. It is descriptive because it describes the elements of an instance or situation. Finally, it is heuristic because it attempts to explain how and why things happened in a particular situation. For example, a social worker can use case study to describe an instance of child abuse and explain what and how the abuse occurred. Case study seems to be appropriate and applicable to social work evaluations.

Steps in Case Study

In general, a case study involves the following steps:

1. *Define the research/evaluation questions and the specific aims.* Research questions are often presented to social workers from their interactions with clients and the community. Research questions should be discussed among peers to prioritize their importance and relevance to the need of the agency or the community. A research question can be broad and general. Therefore, it is important to expand the research question into specific aims or objectives.

2. *Select a case or cases to study.* Once the research/evaluation questions are identified and defined, the researcher or the research team needs to decide on the selection of a case or cases to investigate. Each case should be investigated independently. The selected case must be relevant to the research/evaluation questions and specific aims or objectives.

3. *Determine on the data collection approach.* There are a few approaches of data collection that can be used in case study. These approaches can be used simultaneously to enhance the reliability and validity of the data. The following are some types of data collection techniques employed in case studies (Yin, 2010): Face-to-Face, Participation Observations, and Documents (See Page 154 for details).

4. *Analyse the Data.* Data collected or compiled from various sources can be transcribed, edited, and then organized into themes reflecting the research questions and specific aims. The research can compare or triangulate data from different sources into common themes under a meaningful framework.

5. *Interpret the Information and Report the Results.* Information developed from the data should be interpreted in such a way that readers can find the meaningful and logical link between what the researcher found and the research questions. The researcher needs to explain whether the results provide answers to the research questions in general and the specific aims.

CASE STUDY DATA COLLECTION TECHNIQUES (YIN 2010)

- Face-to-Face Interviews: Both structured and open-ended interviews can be used. Structured interviews are good to collect factual information. Open-ended interviews are good to collect data on personal experience, emotion, feelings, and attitudes.
- Participation Observations: There are issues or situations that require the researcher to actively engage with the clients or community to observe and record the data for the study. This approach is time consuming, expensive, and could be impractical in some situations.
- Documents: Existing multimedia records including memos, letters, e-mails, stills or motion pictures, newspaper stories, and news can be a great source of data for case study.

SUMMARY

In this chapter, we briefly presented and examined three approaches of qualitative research that can be used in social work research and evaluation. The three types of qualitative research relevant for social work researchers are ethnography, focus group, and case study. Specific steps involved in data collection methods were presented in this chapter. Each approach has its inherited strengths and weakness.

CLASS EXERCISE

A class can be divided into a few groups consisting of eight members. One of the eight students will serve as moderator for a focus group, six students will be the participants, and one student will take notes. The instructor will choose topics for focus group meetings, such as experience as a social work student intern at a field agency, attitudes toward current health policies for the working poor, etc. The moderator needs to follow the rules as moderator (i.e., respect for the participants, listening attentively, etc.) in conducting the meeting. Also, the participants need to communicate clearly with other participants, and the note taker needs to write precisely what is discussed at the meeting.

REFERENCES

Lenette, C., Brough, M., & Cox, L. (2013). Everyday resilience: Narratives of single refugee women with children. *Qualitative Social Work, 12,* 637–653.

Morgan, D. L. (1997). *Focus groups as qualitative research.* Thousand Oaks, CA: Sage.

Patton, M. Q. (2002). Two decades of developments in qualitative inquiry a personal, experiential perspective. *Qualitative Social Work, 1*(3), 261–283.

Tran, T. V. (2009). *Developing cross-cultural measurement.* New York, NY: Oxford University Press.

U.S. General Accounting Office (1990). *Case study evaluation.* http://www.gao.gov/search?search_type=Solr&o=0&facets=&q=case+study+evaluation&adv=0.

Yin, R. K. (2010). *Qualitative research from start to finish.* New York, NY: Guilford Press.

TWELVE

Mixed Methods Research

In previous chapters, we examined both quantitative and qualitative research methods. Qualitative research is considered an inductive process of inquiry or a theory-development–driven research that focuses on the meaning of human lives and experiences in natural environments. Qualitative social work research uses different methods of data collection including in-depth interviews, ethnographic observation, and review of documents or case histories. The in-depth nature of qualitative data helps social work researchers understand processes of human and social interactions. Social workers can use qualitative approaches such as case studies, grounded theory, and ethnography. Grounded theory, coined by Glaser and Strauss (1967), refers to an inductive research method that guides us in developing a theory that is grounded in data. When a research topic of interest is not well documented, and little is known, it will be especially difficult to develop research hypotheses from the existing literature. In this situation, guided by the qualitative grounded theory approach, researchers can make individual observations with little preconceived ideas about the topic area and identify patterns, themes, and categories of their main concerns.

On the other hand, quantitative research is considered a deductive process of inquiry. Social work researchers use quantitative research methods to test theories or hypotheses, gather descriptive information, examine relationships among variables, or evaluate intervention outcomes. Unlike qualitative research, quantitative research uses systematic measurement instruments to collect data and statistical tests to analyze the data. Quantitative data provide us with measurable evidence for objective comparisons and replications. We can establish possible cause and effect relationships of social work interventions or evaluate the strength and direction of the relationships among the research variables. Typical quantitative approaches used in social work research are descriptive surveys and program evaluations.

Mixed methods research can be viewed as the integration and utilization of available research methods, designs, and statistical analytical approaches to study psychological and social phenomena. This chapter will briefly address and illustrate the integration of quantitative and qualitative research methods in social work research. The students will learn to appreciate the combination of different complimentary research approaches that can enhance the quality of research findings.

WHEN TO USE MIXED METHODS RESEARCH

We recommend three situations in which social work researchers might consider using mixed methods in their research/evaluation project: triangulation, complementarity, and development. **Triangulation** occurs when a researcher wants to converge results from various research methods. This can also be used to cross-validate the outcomes of an intervention or social service program. **Complementarity** refers to a situation in which the researcher wants to use the results from one method to explain, illustrate, clarify, or enhance the results from another method. For example, you can conduct a focus group to explain the correlation or association of research variables found in a survey research project. **Development** refers to the use of more than one research method at different phases of a project such as measurement development (Greene, Caracelli, and Graham, 1989). For example, social work researchers should employ both qualitative and quantitative methods to develop their research instruments or to construct a specific scale to measure a research concept or construct (Tran, 2009). One can use a focus group method to identify the instrument items (i.e., scale) and quantitative method (survey) to test the validity and reliability of the instrument.

As social workers attempt to understand and explain the relationship between our clients and the environments, we quickly learn and realize there is no such thing as a "complete" or "absolute" method of inquiry or understanding. Since gathering data, processing information, and making sense of the information are fundamental steps in social work practice regardless of the situations presented to us, the use of different methods of inquiry or investigation can further expand our knowledge and improve the reliability and validity of our decisions.

In a paper published in the *International Journal of Social Psychiatry*, Tran, Manalo and Nguyen (2007) employed survey research using a standardized questionnaire to collect data on acculturation and depression among a sample of Vietnamese refugees. They used multiple regression analysis to test a hypothesis that the association between the length of residence and depression is a nonlinear association; that is, depression tended to increase during the first decade of resettlement and gradually declined. This hypothesis was supported by the data statistically. But the authors were not sure if this phenomenon reflects the refugees' experiences and whether the findings could provide insightful information for practitioners. They further conducted an opened-ended telephone interview with a dozen social service staff members, managers, and directors who have worked with the refugee and immigrant community. They presented the research findings to the social service providers and asked them if what they found in their study reflected what they had observed from their clients in the past. The qualitative data they collected from the social service practitioners overwhelmingly supported their statistical results. This is a simple example of how social workers can use different research methods in the pursuit of research and practice.

BASIC STEPS IN MIXED METHODS RESEARCH

1. Identify research questions and develop specific aims.
2. Determine whether the use of mixed methods is necessary to answer the research questions and the specific aims.
3. Justify the use of mixed methods.
4. Select the methods and decide when each method should be used in the research process.

5. Collect data. Each selected design requires different approaches for data collection.

6. Process and compile data from the selected research methods.

7. Analyze data for each method separately, and then triangulate the results or compare the results from all methods used in the study (Onwuegbuzie and Teddlie, 2003).

8. Report, interpret, and disseminate the results.

In conclusion, mixed methods research is useful in social work research and evaluation; however, this research approach can be complicated, expensive, and time consuming. As with other research methods, social work research needs to assess the feasibility and the justification of mixed methods approach before it can be implemented.

SUMMARY

This chapter illustrated the growing trend of integrating quantitative and qualitative research methods in social work research. This integrated approach can bridge the gap between quantitative and qualitative research methods and enhance the quality of research findings. Grounded theory, coined by Glaser and Strauss (1967), provides an analytical framework for mixed methods research. We presented real examples of research that used both qualitative and quantitative methods.

CLASS EXERCISE

Find a research article that used mixed research methods, and describe the methods reported by the author(s). Discuss how the researchers integrated the methods used in the study. In addition, students can brainstorm collaboratively on possible research topics that would benefit from the mixed methods approaches in social work and human services.

REFERENCES

Glaser, B. G., & Strauss, A. L. (1967). *The discovery of grounded theory: Strategies for qualitative research*. New York, NY: Aldine de Gruyter.

Greene, J. C., Caracelli, V. J., & Graham, W. F. (1989). Toward a conceptual framework for mixed-method evaluation designs. *Educational Evaluation and Policy Analysis, 11*(3), 255–274.

Onwuegbuzie, A. J., & Teddlie, C. (2003). A framework for analyzing data in mixed methods research. In A. Tashakkori & C. Teddlie (Eds.), *Handbook of mixed methods in social and behavioral research* (351–383). Belmont, CA: Sage.

Tran, T. V., Manalo, V., & Nguyen, V. T. (2007). Nonlinear relationship between length of residence and depression in a community-based sample of Vietnamese Americans. *International Journal of Social Psychiatry, 53*(1), 85–94.

THIRTEEN

Program Evaluation

This chapter introduces the field of program evaluation, which involves various dimensions of assessment on the design, implementation, and outcomes of a wide range of social service programs. The phenomenal increase in government spending on welfare and health-care expenditures in the United States has produced millions of public and private social service agencies and health-care programs, including family service agencies, community-based mental health services, health organizations (i.e., adult day health centers and nonprofit health-care agencies), programs designed for the homeless and runaway youths, drug-rehabilitation agencies, programs for the developmentally disabled, and more. In the beginning of the twentieth century, the United States spent less than 0.5 percent of the country's gross domestic product (GDP) on welfare and health care. In 2010, government spent more than 8 percent of its GDP on welfare including Medicare and Medicaid health-care expenditures (http://www.usgovernmentspending. com/us_welfare_spending_40.html).

The rapid expansion of human services and health-care programs calls for heightened needs for program evaluation. Service consumers and providers, stakeholders, policy makers, and government-funding entities recognize the importance of program evaluations and raise the following questions: (1) what is the impact of the program, both intended or unintended, on the target population, and whether the program is based on a well-defined mission statement and measurable goals and objectives (impact evaluation); (2) whether the publicly funded program is responsive to the unique needs of the target population (needs assessment); (3) whether the program implements evidence-based effective intervention strategies (monitoring service delivery); (4) whether the program is cost-effective (cost-effectiveness evaluation); (5) whether the program operates on the basis of well-established procedures that guide the documentation process of its service activities (process evaluation); (6) whether the program achieves goals and objectives as planned (outcome evaluation); and (7) whether clients and workers are satisfied with the overall program performance (client satisfaction and worker-retention research) (Harrell et al., 2014; Rossi, Lipsey, and Freeman, 2004; Weaver et al., 2007).

The term "program evaluation" can be defined differently by different program designers and researchers. But no matter who carries out the evaluation project, evaluation research will most likely address some of the seven dimensions cited above. **Program evaluation** generally refers to the systematic collection and analysis of data collected from clients, service providers, administrators, and stakeholders as well as agency document sources to assess a variety of aspects of the program, including the program structure, staffing patterns, bilingual and bicultural staff capacity, mission statement and measurable goals and objectives, service documentation procedures, availability and quality of supervision, compiling annual service statistics, client satisfaction, worker-retention patterns, and so forth. Today, government funding sources require grant applicants to describe rigorous plans for program evaluation in their funding proposals, as presented in the following example:

> "Specify expected outcomes or impacts for project activities and interventions (i.e., the results). As grant applicants consider and plan their proposed activities and interventions, they need to identify the *outcomes and/or impacts* (i.e., the results) that might be expected to take place following implementation of their projects and such activities and interventions. The outcomes/impacts identified will guide the design and selection of methods for evaluating the effectiveness of project activities and interventions" (Office of Minority Health 2007, p. 4).

TYPES OF PROGRAM EVALUATION

To evaluate social service programs, researchers can employ a variety of research designs including quantitative surveys, experimental designs, qualitative in-depth interviews, observational techniques, and mixed methods. There are numerous types of program evaluation, but the following three types are widely cited in the field of program evaluation research: goal-attainment impact evaluation (or outcome evaluation, outcome monitoring), needs assessment, and process evaluation (or program process monitoring, performance evaluation).

GOAL-ATTAINMENT IMPACT EVALUATION

Goal-attainment impact evaluation focuses on the extent to which the program enabled changes in target problems by examining the overall consequences of the program and its goal attainment. To evaluate the scope and nature of impact and goal attainment, many evaluation projects employ longitudinal research designs. For example, the Office of Planning, Research & Evaluation (OPRE), which belongs to an Office of the Administration for Children & Families, posted a national longitudinal study report on the Head Start impact, 2000–2013, on its website (http://www.acf.hhs.gov/programs/opre/research/project/head-start-impact-study-and-follow-up). One of the foremost program goals of Head Start is to provide early development services to children from underprivileged families. This large-scale longitudinal evaluation research was conducted by Westat and its associates (Chesapeake Research Associates, Abt Associates, American Institutes for Research, University of Virginia Center for the Advanced Study of Teaching and Learning, and AMSAQ), and the impact assessment utilized a quasi-experimental field design. The purpose of this research was twofold: (1) to determine whether Head Start actually impacts school readiness among children participating in the program in the areas of cognitive development, general knowledge, social/emotional functioning, communication skills, and parents' support; and (2) to examine what circumstances led Head Start to achieve its success. According to the Executive Summary released by the Office of Planning, Research & Evaluation (2012), Head Start significantly improved children's preschool outcomes, but "there was little evidence of systematic differences in children's elementary school experiences through 3rd grade between children provided access to Head Start and their counterparts in the control group" (OPRE, 2012, iv). The detailed process of the national Head Start impact study is presented in Table 13.1.

Table 13.1: Sample Impact Study

U.S. Department of Health and Human Services / Office of Planning / Public Domain.

Source: (1) http://www.acf.hhs.gov/programs/opre/research/project/head-start-impact-study-and-follow-up

(2) http://www.acf.hhs.gov/sites/default/files/opre/head_start_report.pdf

Office of Planning, Research & Evaluation (OPRE)
An Office of the Administration for Children and Families

Head Start Impact Study and Follow-up, 2000–2013

Project Overview

Head Start provides comprehensive early child development services to low-income children, their families, and communities. In 1998, Congress determined, as part of Head Start's reauthorization, that the Department of Health and Human Services (DHHS) should conduct a national study to determine the impact of Head Start on the children it serves. In October 2000, DHHS awarded a contract to Westat in collaboration with the Urban Institute, American Institutes for Research, and Decision Information Resources to conduct this study through spring of the children's first-grade year.

Evaluation Goals

The National Head Start Impact Study has two primary goals: (1) determine the impact of Head Start on children's school readiness and parental practices that support children's development; and (2) determine under what circumstances Head Start achieves its greatest impact and for which children.

The National Head Start Impact Study is a longitudinal study that involves approximately 5,000 three- and four-year-old preschool children across eighty-four nationally representative grantee/delegate agencies in communities where there are more eligible children and families than can be served by the program. The children participating were randomly assigned to either a treatment group (which had access to Head Start services) or a comparison group (which did not have access to Head Start services, but could receive other community resources).

Data Collection

Data collection began in fall 2002 and ended in spring 2006, following children through the spring of their first-grade year. It includes in-person interviews with parents, in-person child assessments, direct observations of the quality of different early childhood care settings, and teacher ratings of children.

Third Grade Follow-up

In 2006, DHHS awarded another contract to Westat and its colleagues (Chesapeake Research Associates, Abt Associates, American Institutes for Research, University of Virginia Center for the Advanced Study of Teaching and Learning, and AMSAQ) to follow the Head Start Impact Study children and their families through the spring of their third-grade year.

This follow-up will examine the following questions: What is the impact of Head Start on children's well-being and on parental practices that contribute to children's well-being, through their third-grade year? For whom and under what circumstances does Head Start have its greatest impact?

Key Findings

Head Start significantly improved children's preschool outcomes, but "there was little evidence of systematic differences in children's elementary school experiences through 3rd grade, between children provided access to Head Start and their counterparts in the control group."

As seen in this Head Start study, the aim of program impact evaluation is to determine whether the program under investigation has achieved its intended effects by examining its program objectives. Impact assessments are often used as baseline data to determine whether it is essential to continue the program, expand its coverage to other geographic areas and diverse populations, or terminate the program. As every social service program has both strengths and weaknesses, findings from impact assessments can guide the ongoing program toward a program modification. And high-cost established programs should be especially subject to periodic impact assessment (Rossi, Lipsey, and Freeman, 2004).

NEEDS ASSESSMENT

While impact evaluations focus on existing programs that have been implemented for a certain period of time, needs assessment is usually conducted at the early stage of program planning prior to implementation. And needs assessment can be also performed when a need to improve the existing program is expressed by community leaders, stakeholders, policy makers, and other concerned individuals and groups. Focus groups are often used to identify the types of problems experienced by the target population, and to develop culturally appropriate remedies to address those issues.

Let's suppose there are many problems expressed by monolingual immigrant Hispanic women who previously utilized domestic violence (DV) shelters in the Hispanic community (i.e., East Los Angeles). To respond to their growing needs for better DV shelter services and ameliorate the quality of the existing programs, it is critical to conduct a series of focus group discussions with former DV shelter residents and focus group facilitators. The topic areas for group discussions would include: (1) initial difficulty in finding and accessing the shelters they utilized; (2) the nature of treatment strategies adopted by the program; (3) children's experience at the shelter; (4) the most and least helpful programs offered by the shelter; (5) their self-rated psychological well-being; and (6) the availability of follow-up services. One of the authors of this book conducted a focus group study with eight former DV shelter residents regarding their experiences in utilizing DV shelters in the Korean community in the Greater Los Angeles area. Table 13.2 presents a list of actual questions explored at the focus group meeting, held in 2012. It was found from this focus group needs assessment that, though most programs offered by the existing shelters in the Korean community significantly helped them in gaining self-confidence and independence, it was somewhat difficult to get support for permanent housing. This was due to housing shortages and also because treatment programs for dependent children, who resided in the shelters with their parents, did not reflect their needs. This information obtained from the focus group participants can help various DV programs to modify their service priorities and strategies by reflecting what their consumers actually experience and need.

PROCESS EVALUATION

As seen previously, impact evaluations are largely concerned about whether the program has influenced the target population as intended. On the other hand, program process evaluation focuses on how and whether services are delivered to consumers as intended (Scheirer 1994). The term **process evaluation** refers to monitoring the process of program implementation. When evaluation research emerged as an important field of applied research, Washington (1980) pointed out that "Process evaluation is a measure of input

Table 13.2: Sample Focus Group Needs Assessment Topics for Former DV Shelter Residents

1. What organization did you utilize?

2. When did you receive services at the organization, and how long did you stay there?

3. Was it difficult/easy to find agencies, shelters, or other DV services?

4. How did you learn about the organization? (i.e., community directory, newspaper, public announcement, relative/friend, church, etc.).

5. Did you stay at the shelter alone or with your child(ren)? Did you receive services by yourself or with your child(ren)?

6. What types of services did you receive while you stayed there?

7. What types of services did your children receive during their residence at the shelter?

8. How was the treatment by the staff?

9. How were your children's experiences at the organization?

10. What was (were) the most helpful program(s)/classes/services provided by the organization?

11. What was (were) the least helpful programs offered by that organization?

12. How would you (the client) change the organization's program, if any?

13. In what way did the shelter help you, if it did?

14. Please describe how you are doing now in terms of employment, independent living skills, school, hobby, emotional stability, etc.

15. Has there been a change in your knowledge about domestic violence?

16. How is your self-esteem when compared with the past?

17. What types of follow-up service did the organization provide after you left the program?

18. How can we improve accessibility to existing shelter programs/services?

19. Please make final comments on the existing DV programs in your community in general.

and … it is an essential step in program evaluation. We cannot measure outcomes without first having some understanding of the process of implementation" (p. 129).

Generally, there are two main areas of assessment within the program process evaluation: the infrastructure of the program, and service utilization patterns. Process evaluations are quite different from outcome evaluations in such a way that process evaluation focuses on monitoring the infrastructure (also called "operation" or "in-house functioning") of the program. The analytical framework of infrastructural assessments includes the following key aspects of service delivery:

- Availability of the mission statement that informs what types of services the program intends to provide
- Feasibility of measurable goals and objectives
- Development of criteria and measures of goal attainment (i.e., pretests and posttests)
- Quality and comprehensiveness of agency forms (i.e., consent form, authorization of release form and intake form)
- Documentation procedures of service activities
- Types of in-service training for practitioners and administrators
- Availability of agency procedural manuals
- Availability and quality of staff supervision
- Qualifications of staff members
- Staff turnover rates, and guidelines for case opening and closure
- Updated outreach plans

One of the authors of this book conducted a process evaluation project aimed at assessing the strengths and weaknesses of the existing shelters designed for monolingual victims of domestic violence in the Los Angeles Asian community. As shown in Table 13.3, the survey instrument reflects the above cited key areas of the agency's internal structure of program implementation.

SUMMARY

This chapter emphasized the importance of program evaluation to measure whether the program achieves the effects as intended. There are many different types of program evaluation, but three main forms of evaluation research are widely utilized among program evaluators: goal-attainment impact evaluation (or outcome evaluation, outcome monitoring), needs assessment, and process evaluation (or program process monitoring, performance evaluation). Each of these types of evaluation was examined based on real examples of evaluation research.

CLASS EXERCISE

The instructor divides the class into two groups and chooses a community-based family service agency in the neighborhood. Ask the first group to design a process evaluation project, and the second group to design an outcome impact evaluation project.

Table 13.3: Sample Process Evaluation Instrument

Strength & Needs Assessment (2012)
Domestic Violence Shelters in the Asian Community

The main purpose of this survey is to assess strengths as well as needs of community-based domestic violence (DV) shelters designed to serve Asian American immigrant victims and their families. The specific objectives of this research are to obtain in-depth information that is useful in planning, implementing, and improving the performance of the participating DV shelters in an effort to promote the accessibility of DV shelter services in the underserved Asian American community in Greater Los Angeles. Your participation in this study is very important because we hope that the data collected in this survey will help identify effective service strategies, areas needing improvement, and resources for Asian American immigrant families.

PART I: AGENCY INFORMATION

(1) Name of the Agency and Address/Phone Number/Fax Number/E-Mail Address:

Name of Contact person:

Name of Agency:

Address:

Phone #   Fax #   E-mail

(2) When was your agency established? Year:

(3) Please provide the **mission statement** of your program:

_____

(4) What are(is) the funding source(s) in operating your program?

1. _____

2. _____

3. _____

(5) Is your shelter faith-based?

     1. Yes _____ (Please Specify: _____)   2. No _____

(6) What is the maximum and average client capacity and average capacity at a given time?

    Maximum: _____ Persons   Average: _____ Persons

(7) What is the maximum and average length of the client's stay in your shelter?

    Maximum _____ Months   Average _____ Months

PART II: PROGRAM DESCRIPTION: Goals/Objectives/Referral Sources/Eligibility

(8) Please provide the **goal(s)** of your program for 2011.

1. _____

2. _____

(9) What are the specific **objectives** of your program to accomplish your goal(s) for 2011. (i.e., To accomplish the program goals, the program targets to improve clients' *knowledge of spouse abuse, coping skills, emotional stability, self-esteem, job interview skills*, etc.) (If you need additional space, please use the reverse side.)

1. _____

2. _____

3. _____

(10) How were your clients referred to your program (**referral sources**)?
(Please check all that apply.)

    1. Walk-in (self-referral) _____
    2. Police _____
    3. Court _____
    4. Social Service Agency _____
    5. Faith Organizations (i.e., church, temple, etc.) _____
    6. Friends/Relatives _____
    7. Other (please specify:) _____

Table 13.3: Continued.

(11) What are the eligibility requirements for clients?

PART III: ADMINISTRATOR & STAFF INFORMATION AND HUMAN RESOURCE DEVELOPMENT

(13) In total, how many paid staff members including administrator(s), counselor(s), and support staff are working at your agency?

_____Persons

(14) Among the total number of staff members and volunteers, please provide the number of the staff members in each of the following categories:

Number of Administrators: _____Persons

Number of Counselors: _____Persons

Support Staff: _____Persons

Volunteers: _____Persons

(15) What are your staff's educational backgrounds and credentials?

Position	Terminal Degree	Major	Gender	Position	Years at Current Position	Bilingual
Administrator						Yes/ No
Administrator						Yes/ No
Counselor (1)						Yes/ No
Counselor (2)						Yes/ No
Counselor (3)						Yes/ No
Counselor (4)						Yes/ No
Counselor (5)						Yes/ No
Counselor (6)						Yes/ No

(16) Please describe the volunteers who are currently working at your program (number, career/educational background, gender, duties, etc.).

1. _____

2. _____

(17) Do you have written agency procedural manuals or handbook designed to train your counselors or case managers on referral sources, routine intervention procedures, and practice approaches?

      1. Yes _____   2. No _____

(18) Is training available for all staff and volunteers who are involved in the direct care of the clients? _____ Yes _____ No

    (18a) If yes, what type of training is provided (please mark all that apply)?

        _____ In-service
        _____ Manual/Handbook
        _____ Outside Provider (specify: _____)
        _____ Other (specify: _____)

(19) Is supervision available for staff and volunteers? _____ Yes _____ No

    (19a) If yes, what type of supervision is provided?
        Group _____ Individual _____ Clinical _____ Other _____ (Specify:)
        _____

    (19b) How often? _____

    (19c) How long? _____

(20) What types of volunteers do you often utilize in the agency (please mark all that apply)?

        _____ Office Duties (filing, answering phone calls, making copies, etc.)
        _____ Professional Counseling
        _____ Leisure Activities (knitting, yoga, etc.)
        _____ Instructors (ESL teachers, job skill development, etc.)
        _____ Religious Activities (worship service, prayer groups, etc.)
        _____ Special Events (luncheon, yard sale, tea party, etc.)
        _____ Other (specify) _____

(21) How often does your program hold case conferences? (i.e., once a week, once a month, etc.)

_____

PART IV: PROGRAM IMPLEMENTATION

A. CASE MANAGEMENT SERVICES (linkages to internal/external resources):

(22) Do you make an initial written assessment at the time of case opening?

      1. Yes _____   2. No _____

(23) Do you keep case files as part of record keeping maintenance?

      1. Yes _____   2. No _____

Table 13.3: Continued.

(24) Do you provide the following case management services offered by your agency/shelter?

		Yes (1)	No (2)
1.	Emergency Supportive Counseling:	____	____
2.	Employment Services:	____	____
3.	Running Support Groups:	____	____
4.	Legal Services (obtaining TRO, etc.):	____	____
5.	Advocacy Services:	____	____
6.	DV Education Services:	____	____
7.	Life Skill/Coping Skill Training:	____	____
8.	Anger Management Training:	____	____
9.	Transportation (Escorting) Services by Staff:	____	____
10.	Interpretation/Translation Services:	____	____
11.	ESL	____	____
12.	Family Planning Counseling:	____	____
13.	Other Case Management Services (please specify):	_____	

(25) Did your shelter/agency refer clients to the following outside services?

Type of Services		Number of Clients Referred to These Programs	Referral Rate (Total Clients) ÷ (# of Referral)
1. Emergency Shelter	Yes( ) / No ( )		
2. Transitional Shelter (Board & Care Home)	Yes( ) / No ( )		
3. Well Baby Care	Yes( ) / No ( )		
4. Emergency Infant Supplies	Yes( ) / No ( )		
5. Hospital/Clinics	Yes( ) / No ( )		
6. Housing Assistance (i.e., Section 8 Housing)	Yes( ) / No ( )		
7. WIC	Yes( ) / No ( )		
8. Mental Health Clinic	Yes( ) / No ( )		
9. Child Day Care	Yes( ) / No ( )		
10. Emergency Food	Yes( ) / No ( )		
11. Public Assistance (CalWorks, Medi-Cal)	Yes( ) / No ( )		
12. Outside Job Training	Yes( ) / No ( )		
13. Food Stamps	Yes( ) / No ( )		
14. Food Banks	Yes( ) / No ( )		
15. Transportation Assistance (i.e., ACCESS, Para ACCESS, etc.)	Yes( ) / No ( )		
16. Legal Assistance (i.e., legal aid, law offices)	Yes( ) / No ( )		
17. Educational Institutions (vocational colleges, ESL, etc.)	Yes( ) / No ( )		
18. Other (please specify)			

B. TREATMENT METHODS TO EMPOWER CLIENTS:

(26) What intervention approaches/steps do your counselors use when they provide individual/group counseling to clients to achieve your goals and objectives?

_____

_____

(27) How do you measure whether the above-mentioned goals/objectives/expected client outcomes are achieved (i.e., pretest and posttest, survey, qualitative interview, counselor's impression of the client progress, etc.)?

1. _____

2. _____

3. _____

(31) Number of clients served by the agency in each category of **internal** case management services in 2011:

Type of Case Management Services	Number of Clients
1. Emergency Supportive Counseling	
2. Employment Services	
3. Running Support Groups	
4. Legal Services (obtaining TRO, etc.)	
5. Advocacy Services	
6. DV Education Services	
7. Life Skill/Coping Skill Training	
8. Anger Management Training	
9. Transportation (Escorting) Services by Staff	
10. Interpretation/Translation Services	
11. ESL	
12. Family Planning Counseling	
13. Other Case Management Services	

REFERENCES

Harrell, A., Burt, M., Hatry, H., Rossman, S., Roth, J., & Sabol, W. "Evaluation Strategies for Human Services Program: A Guide for Policy Makers and Provides." Retrieved February 23, 2014, from https://www.bja.gov/evaluation/guide/documents/evaluation_strategies.html

Office of Planning, Research & Evaluation. "Head Start Research: Third Grade Follow-up to the Head Start Impact Study, Executive Summary. OPRE Report 2012-45b." Retrieved February 20, 2014, from http://www.acf.hhs.gov/sites/default/files/opre/head_start_report.pdf

Office of Planning, Research & Evaluation. "Head Start Impact Study and Follow-up, 2000–2013." Retrieved February 21, 2014, from http://www.acf.hhs.gov/programs/opre/research/project/head-start-impact-study-and-follow-up

Rossi, P. H., Lipsey, M. W., & Freeman, H. E. (2004). Evaluation: *A systematic approach* (7th ed.). Thousand Oaks, CA: Sage Publications.

Scheirer, M. A. (1994). Designing and using process evaluation. In J. S. Wholey, H. P. Hatry, & K. E. Newcomer (Eds.), *Handbook of practical program evaluation* (40–68). San Francisco, CA: Jossey-Bass.

The Office for Minority Health. "Evaluation Planning Guidelines for Grant Applicants. US Department of Health and Human Services, Rockville, MD 20852." Retrieved February 23, 2014, from http://minorityhealth.hhs.gov/Assets/pdf/Checked/1/Evaluation%20Planning%20Guidelines%20for%20Grant%20Applicants.pdf

US Welfare Spending for 2014. Retrieved on February 23, 2014, from http://www.usgovernmentspending.com/us_welfare_spending_40.html

Washington, R. O. (1980). *Program evaluation in the human services*. Lanham, MD: University Press of America.

Weaver, D., Chang, J., Clark, S., & Rhee, S. (2007). Keeping public child welfare workers on the job. *Administration in Social Work, 31*(2), 5-25. http://www.acf.hhs.gov/programs/opre/research/project/head-start-impact-study-and-follow-up

FOURTEEN

Writing Research Proposals & Research Reports

This chapter discusses the process of grant writing for research and program evaluation. The students will learn to read the research announcement, request for proposal (RFP), and program announcement. The grant writing process from writing the specific aims to implementing and reporting will be addressed. We will use examples of real grant proposals to illustrate the grant writing process.

WHAT IS A RESEARCH OR SERVICE PROPOSAL?

A research proposal can be defined as a comprehensive description of a systematic and logical plan of investigation. This plan should outline and describe all necessary steps to investigate a research problem. With respect to service and intervention, a service proposal describes all necessary steps to develop and deliver a specific service to a group of clients or to a community.

A good research proposal must have specific, well-defined aims as well as innovative, interesting, and novel approachs of investigation or service delivery. A good proposal also must have potentials to benefit society and clients. And the researcher or service provider must be able to demonstrate her or his knowledge of the proposed area and have a well-designed approach for investigation or service delivery. Finally, the researcher or provider must demonstrate the ability to implement the proposed project successfully.

STEPS IN WRITING RESEARCH OR SERVICE PROPOSAL

1. Identify funding sources or funding opportunities. This information can be found on the websites of government institutes or nonprofit foundations.
2. Study the research funding or service funding announcement. It is important to know what funding is available and the specific requests from the funding agencies.

3. Examine the ability and feasibility. The researcher or the agency needs to know if she or he, or the agency, has the ability to compete for the funding, and whether it is feasible to carry out what the funding agency requires.

4. Identify the problem and clearly define specific aims for the proposal.

5. Review the existing literature on the topic and the evidence-based services or interventions.

6. Develop a sound approach to find answers to the research aims or to deliver and evaluate the proposed services.

7. Follow the instructions of the funding agencies, foundations, or institutions.

8. Have peer review before submitting the proposal.

REVIEW CRITERIA FOR FUNDING

The best way to learn how to write a research proposal or service proposal is to write it. Proposal writing requires practice and experience. Trial and error is the most practical approach of learning how to write a successful proposal. Following is the proposal review criteria used by the National Institute of Health (NIH).* You can visit its website to have a general idea about the process of grant writing in general. These criteria are useful for researchers to develop their grant application. According to the NIH website, grant proposal reviewers consider the following five areas as NIH review criteria: (1) significance of the problem, (2) qualification of the investigator(s), (3) innovation of the project, (4) implementation approach, and (5) the environment in which a proposed research project will be implemented. The established review criteria currently adopted by NIH in verbatim is as follows (http://grants.nih.gov/grants/peer_review_process. htm#PeerReview):

Significance: *Does the project address an important problem or a critical barrier to progress in the field? If the aims of the project are achieved, how will scientific knowledge, technical capability, and/or clinical practice be improved? How will successful completion of the aims change the concepts, methods, technologies, treatments, services, or preventative interventions that drive this field?*

Investigator(s): *Are the PD/PIs (Program Director/ Principal Investigator), collaborators, and other researchers well suited to the project? If early stage investigators, new investigators, or in the early stages of independent careers, do they have appropriate experience and training? If established, have they demonstrated an ongoing record of accomplishments that have advanced their field(s)? If the project is collaborative or multi-PD/PI, do the investigators have complementary and integrated expertise; are their leadership approach, governance and organizational structure appropriate for the project?*

Innovation: *Does the application challenge and seek to shift current research or clinical practice paradigms by utilizing novel theoretical concepts, approaches or methodologies, instrumentation, or interventions? Are the concepts, approaches or methodologies, instrumentation, or interventions novel to only one field of research or novel in a broad sense? Is a refinement, improvement, or new application of theoretical concepts, approaches or methodologies, instrumentation, or interventions proposed?*

Approach: *Are the overall strategy, methodology, and analyses well-reasoned and appropriate to accomplish the specific aims of the project? Are potential problems, alternative strategies, and benchmarks for success presented? If the project is in the early stages of development, will the strategy establish feasibility and will particularly risky aspects be managed? If the project involves clinical research, are the plans for 1) protection of human subjects*

*National Institutes of Health / Public Domain

from research risks, and 2) inclusion of minorities and members of both sexes/genders, as well as the inclusion of children, justified in terms of the scientific goals and research strategy proposed?

Environment: Will the scientific environment in which the work will be done contribute to the probability of success? Are the institutional support, equipment and other physical resources available to the investigators adequate for the project proposed? Will the project benefit from unique features of the scientific environment, subject populations, or collaborative arrangements?"

The Health Resources and Services Administration of the US Department of Human Services provides ten important tips for grant proposal writing. You can visit the website to read more about these tips and other related information (http://www.hrsa.gov/grants/apply/granttips.html).

US Department of Health and Human Services

Health Resources and Services Administration

Apply for a Grant: 10 Tips

1. **Start preparing the application early.**
2. **Follow the instructions in the Funding Opportunity Announcement carefully.**
3. **Keep your audience in mind.** Reviewers will use only the information contained in the application to assess the application. Keep the review criteria in mind when writing the application.
4. **Be brief, concise, and clear.** Make your points understandable. Provide accurate and honest information, including candid accounts of problems and realistic plans to address them. If any required information or data is omitted, explain why. Your budget should reflect back to the proposed activities, and all forms should be filled in accurately and completely.
5. **Be organized and logical.**
6. **Show evidence of fiscal stability and sound fiscal management.** Your application should demonstrate your ability to be a responsible steward of public funds.
7. **Attend to technical details.** Read instructions and follow them.
8. **Be careful in the use of attachments.** Do not use the attachments for information that is required in the body of the application.
9. **Print out and carefully proofread and review your electronic application to ensure accuracy and completion.** When submitting electronically, print out the application before submitting it to ensure appropriate formatting and adherence to page limit requirements. Check to ensure that all attachments are included before sending the application forward.
10. **Submit all information at the same time.**

Source: U.S. Department of Health and Human Services / Public Domain.

RESEARCH PROPOSAL EXAMPLE

Following is an outline of an example of a research proposal. It has all elements required by most government institutions and foundations; however, the format of the proposal can vary according to the requirements of the funding institutions. The main content of the proposal can be found in Appendix B.

Project Title

"Confronting Social Isolation and Depression among Older Vietnamese Americans"

Project Significance

Highlights from the 2000 US Bureau of the Census indicated that 74.1% of Vietnamese living in the United States are foreign-born. More than 6% of the Vietnamese American population is sixty-five and older. In addition, data from the American Community Survey in 2008 indicated a large proportion of Vietnamese elders experiences some form of physical disability (44.3%), and a great majority of them cannot speak English well or not at all (73.8%). This background information suggests older Vietnamese Americans are potentially at risk of being socially isolated and depressed (US Bureau of the Census 2000; US Bureau of Census 2008).

Statement of Objectives

This proposed study will implement and evaluate a multifaceted intervention to alleviate social isolation and reduce depression for Vietnamese Americans age sixty years or older, recruited from a Vietnamese Catholic community in the Greater Boston area.

Description of Methodology

- **Experimental Design**

We will randomly assign eligible participants to either the experimental group or the parallel intervention control group. Both groups will have the same number of females and males.

The key elements of the proposed experimental intervention consist of a series of two-hour sessions that utilize attribution-retraining techniques from the field of motivational psychology, in combination with behavioral strategies derived from social cognitive theory, organized religious activities, and physical activity (Hilt 2004; Weiner 1985).

- **Screening for Social Isolation**

We will use version 3 of the UCLA ten-item Loneliness Scale (Russell 1996). The UCLA Loneliness Scale was developed to assess subjective feelings of loneliness or social isolation.

- **Sample Size**

Sixty Vietnamese (30 men and 30 women) aged sixty and older living in the Greater Boston area will be recruited to participate in this proposed study.

- **Eligibility Criteria.** The participants will need to meet the following eligibility criteria:
    (1) Self-identified Vietnamese and Catholic sixty years and older.
    (2) Have a score of 30 or greater on the UCLA Loneliness Scale.
    (3) Not currently participating in any organized physical activities.
    (4) Have approval from a physician to engage in physical activities such as tai chi.
- **Experimental Group.** Thirty participants (15 men and 15 women) will participate in a series of experimental sessions, which will include four sessions a month (weekly) for three months and two sessions a month (biweekly) for another three months.

- **Parallel Control Group.** Thirty randomly assigned participants (15 men and 15 women) in the parallel control group will participate in a series of planned tai chi exercise sessions four times a month (weekly) for three months, followed by twice a month (biweekly) for another three months.
- **Data Collection**

We will collect data using a bilingual English–Vietnamese questionnaire consisting of basic demographic characteristics such as age, sex, length of residence, along with outcome measures. The baseline data collection will be conducted through telephone interviews by our bilingual research assistant at the participants' residences.

- **Outcome Measures**
    (1) The UCLA Loneliness Scale.
    (2) Lubben Social Support Scale.
    (3) The Center for Epidemiologic Studies Depression Scale (CES-D)
    (4) Religiosity Scale
    (5) Self-Efficacy Scale
- **Statistical Power and Data Analysis.** We assessed the statistical power for the proposed sample size of this study using existing pilot survey data. We will employ paired sample t-tests to examine changes in outcome measures in each group for our within-group analysis. We will use t-tests for the two independent samples to compare the changes in scores of the outcome measures between the two groups. Repeated measures ANOVA will be used to examine the changes in scores in each group from baseline, at three months, and six months.
- **Dissemination**

For the details of this proposal, please see Appendix B.

SEEKING FUNDING TO PROVIDE SERVICES

Throughout your career as a social worker, you may need to seek funding to provide services to your clients. Unlike a research proposal, you ask for funding to bring new services to a community or a particular group of clients with unique needs. You will have to describe the purpose of the proposed project, demonstrate the need for services, describe the clients or community, location of the proposed project, the target population or the clients that you serve, the proposed service and its potential benefits, your agency's staff and professional qualifications, your approach to deliver the service, and your plan to monitor and evaluate.

Real Example of Social Service Proposal

Next, we will present another example of a real proposal, titled "**Defending Childhood Initiative Family Nurturing program" and** prepared by an ethnic community service agency. Again, due to consideration of space, here we only provide an outline of the proposal. For details, see Appendix C. Viet-AID - Vietnamese American Initiative for Development - http://www.vietaid.org/)

Outline of the Project

Over the past few years, police officers, court personnel, parents, and community leaders have expressed concerns over an increasing number of runaway and homeless youth in poor Southeast Asian communities of

Greater Boston. These young people have run away from homes due to cultural differences and parental abuse and neglect. Once on the streets, they are at risk of being sexually exploited or abused by adults for pleasure or profit. In addition, they often engage in shoplifting, survival sex or drug dealing to provide for their basic needs.

This approach incorporates youth development principles and provides shelter and support services in a culturally and linguistically appropriate manner. We will conduct a community outreach and prevention education campaign to increase awareness about our services, runaway and homeless issues, and prevention strategies. Youth who are interested in our program will receive individualized assessment and develop a service plan to reconnect with their families and develop skills and knowledge to become self-sufficient. They will receive shelter and support services, including individual and group counseling, family counseling when appropriate, and referral services to education, employment, health care, housing, recreational, and cultural programs and services.

Our project will increase community awareness among the 30,000-plus Southeast Asian immigrants and refugees living in Greater Boston. They will help at least one hundred runaway and homeless Southeast Asian youths transition to a safe and appropriate living arrangement, reconnect with their families, and develop knowledge and skills to become self-sufficient and contributing members of their community and families. They will also prevent at-risk youth from running away from their families.

Project Description

A. Objectives and Need for Assistance

(1) Project Goals and Objectives

The overcharging goal of the shelter is to help youth transition to safe and appropriate living arrangements where they receive supportive and caring services, build lasting relationships with adults, reconnect with their families, and develop knowledge and skills to become independent, self-sufficient, contributing members of society.

We intend to accomplish this overarching goal through the following objectives. (To save space only first two objectives are listed here. For other objectives, please see Appendix C.)

Objective A: Conduct community outreach and education among the 30,000-plus Southeast Asian community members in Greater Boston to increase awareness about our services and to prevent youth from running away from home.

Objective B: Provide information about our services—and on how to prevent youth from running away from home—to three hundred youths and parents who contact our program.

In Section B of this application, we detail the measurable outcomes and long-term results that we expect to achieve through program activities, which are tailored to address this critical community issue and accomplish these objectives.

(2) Needs for Assistance

In response to the cry for help by Southeast Asian parents and community leaders, Viet-AID worked with the Boston Police Department, Dorchester Youth Collaborative (DYC), Dorchester House Multi-Service Center (Dorchester House), Vietnamese American Civic Association (VACA), Close to Home (C2O), and Southeast Asian community-based, faith-based organizations to conduct a needs assessment to gain a better understanding of the problems and causes of increased youth violence and runaway teens.

The needs assessment revealed that Southeast Asian children and youth today have become more prone to violence, poor academic performance, substance abuse, gang involvement, and running away. Southeast Asian runaways, homeless, and street youth share many background characteristics and experiences often associated with runaways and homeless youth.

The assessment further found a steady decline in academic performance among Southeast Asian students. Due to socioeconomic, cultural conflicts, and other cultural factors, many poor Southeast Asian children and youth do not receive adequate support from their families.

(3) Service Location

The proposed Southeast Asian shelter is located within walking distance of the facilities and offices operated by Viet-AID and our partners. The shelter as well as our offices and facilities are located in Fields Corner, Dorchester, and adjacent to a subway station and several major bus lines, making our services easily accessible by all Southeast Asian families and youth. As described above, Dorchester is home to a majority of low-income Southeast Asian families in Greater Boston and is a destination for all Southeast Asian families in Greater Boston and Massachusetts for the following reasons:

(4) Data on Runaways, Homeless, and Street Youth

In recent years, data and reports from the Boston Police Department, Dorchester Youth Collaborative, and Boston Juvenile Court show an annual average of 200-plus Asian runaways reported along the Dorchester Avenue Corridor in Greater Boston. We have learned, however, though our community meetings and one-on-one interviews with parents, religious leaders, and community members, that the runaway problem among Southeast Asian children and youth is much more severe than reported. The Boston Police Department and the community-based organizations believe the actual number of runaways is higher than documented since many runaways are unreported. Oftentimes parents do not report their children as having run away due to fear of involvement with law enforcement agencies and shame on their family. Parents are also often frightened into silence by the adult leaders of Asian gangs with whom Southeast Asian runaway youth often become affiliated. In addition, juvenile courts have very stringent guidelines regarding what constitutes a "runaway." They will not process a runaway youth who has not been reported to a law enforcement agency, or a runaway who claims he or she was told to leave home, or a runaway who has returned home voluntarily or involuntarily.

B. Results or Benefits Expected

(1) Number of Youth to be Served

A minimum of one hundred youths will receive bilingual and bicultural emergency shelter and support services each year through the proposed Southeast Asian shelter. Our shelter, while available to all runaway and homeless youth, will target Southeast Asian youth thirteen through eighteen years of age who are having serious family problems that prompted them to leave home or threaten to do so. Further, we will serve three hundred youths through nonresidential services.

(2) Overall Quantitative Outcomes and Relationships between Activities and Outcomes

Through a comprehensive continuum of services, this joint project between Viet-AID and our partners seeks to accomplish the following qualitative and quantitative outcomes:

Activities	Outputs	Outcomes/Impact
Conduct community outreach and prevention education: Conduct street-based outreach to identify and establish relationship with runaway/homeless youth. **Conduct presentations at community-based organizations, civic groups, courts, etc.:** Conduct parenting education workshops. Distribute program brochures and fliers at Southeast Asian and other business establishments. Conduct interviews and publish articles in Southeast Asian print and electronic media. **Provide shelter and support services to runaway and homeless youth and their families:** Conduct individual assessment and create a service plan. Provide shelter and support services. Provide individual and group counseling services to youth. Provide referral services to connect youth to education, recreational, health care, and other support services: Sexual/substance abuse counseling and treatment. Education and/or career development. Health care (including health, mental health, dental, etc.) Access to social, recreational, and community service activities. Housing search Provide aftercare services to youth who have been discharged.	**Community outreach and prevention education:** 150 contacts with runaway and homeless youth. Conduct 12 monthly presentations at nonprofit organizations, civic associations, etc. Publish/conduct 12 monthly newspaper articles and interviews. Distribute 5,000 brochures and fliers. Conduct four quarterly parenting workshops. **Intake, assessment, and service plan development:** 100 youths complete intake and assessment and develop a service plan. Emergency shelter and support services: 100 youths receive emergency shelter service. 100 youths receive one-on-one and group counseling. 75 receive family counseling services. 75 youths are connected to services including vocational/educational training, drug/substance abuse counseling, housing search, health care, recreational, and community service. **Aftercare service:** 50 youths will receive aftercare services following discharge.	**Outcome 1:** 30,000-plus Southeast Asian youths and families with increased awareness about our services and issues related to homeless and runaway youth. **Indicators:** # of contacts with runaway and homeless youth; # of presentations conducted; # of newspaper articles published and interviews conducted; # of brochures and fliers distributed; # of parenting workshops conducted. **Outcome 2:** Youth reconnect with families and return home. **Indicators:** # of youth who reconnect with their families and return home. **Outcome 3:** Youth secure safe, stable, and permanent housing. **Indicator:** # of youth who secure long-term, stable and safe living arrangements. **Outcome 4:** Youth become independent, self-sufficient, and contributing members of community. **Indicator:** # of youth who become engaged in education; # of youth who become employed or participate in vocational training program; # of youth who participate in recreational activities and community service projects. **Outcome 3:** Decrease number of youth who run away from home. **Indicator:** # and % of reported runaway youth per year; # of at-risk youth who decide not to run away after receiving prevention counseling and support.

(3) Evaluation Plan

Viet-AID will use the above logic model as a foundation for our evaluation plan. The logic model describes the relationship between the project's goal, objectives, and activities, and the project's short- and long-term benefit.

The Project Team will initially use the following mechanisms to evaluate the project:

- Team evaluation
- Case management data participant feedback
- Program impact surveys—survey and interview with partner referral agencies, existing data collection, and citywide trends.

Findings from these team evaluation and participant feedbacks will be used to adjust program design and improve program effectiveness.

Approach

Viet-AID and our partners will implement a comprehensive approach that helps Southeast Asian youth transition to safe and appropriate living arrangements where they will receive shelter and support services, build lasting relationships with adults, reconnect with their families, and develop knowledge and skills to become independent, self-sufficient, contributing members of the community. Our approach incorporates youth development principles and provides comprehensive services in a linguistically and culturally appropriate manner.

Youth Development Approach

Viet-AID and our partners incorporate the Family and Youth Services Bureau's youth development approach in our program design. This program design is holistic, strengths-based, and comprehensive, giving power back to the community to resolve issues.

Viet-AID and our partners propose to use the youth development approach to engage youth in leadership, social, recreational, cultural, and employment activities that will promote their emotional, cultural, social and character development.

Program Operation (Mandatory Services)

Youth come to Viet-AID through a variety of means—on the recommendation of a friend, parental decision, referral from another agency or institutions, or through another program of Viet-AID and our partners, most notably the street outreach program.

Outreach and Prevention Education Campaign

We will conduct a comprehensive outreach and prevention education campaign to inform youth and families about our services, increase community awareness and response to the problems with runaway and homeless youth, establish and maintain community linkages, expand and develop new resources, and solicit community support. The campaign will consist of a number of key activities, listed as follows:

- Street-based outreach
- Agency-based outreach
- Media-based outreach
- Parenting workshops.

Individual Intake Process

Every youth who seeks admission is given an individual, confidential intake interview. The first objective of the intake interview is to address emergency/immediate needs of the youth, such as food, clothing, warmth or medical care. If there is an emergency need beyond the scope of the shelter—e.g., a medical/psychiatric emergency, the youth is unwilling to enter the program, doesn't meet eligibility criteria for the shelter, or no beds are available—appropriate referral or nonresidential services are immediately provided.

Once the intake is completed, the youth is introduced to staff members and residents, given a shelter tour, assigned a bedroom, given any needed personal hygiene supplies, and assigned a case manager who will assist in securing all needed services and provide individual and family counseling.

Temporary Shelter

Viet-AID will apply for a state license to provide emergency shelter to runway and homeless youth.

Individual and Group Counseling

Each youth is assigned an individual case manager at intake, with whom he or she collaboratively develops a service plan to identify needed services and crisis intervention counseling. The goal is to expand the frequency of their effective behavior, instead of a traditional approach that focuses on deficits. This is a solution-focused, youth development approach. Youth attend a weekly house meeting to offer their thoughts on shelter routines, policies, and procedures.

Family Counseling

Family counseling by the family case manager is strongly encouraged for each family as a means to explore family reunification, or if this is not an option, to enlist family support and improve relationships.

Service Linkages

As part of the intake process, in the weekly case review and during a youth's residency, staff members assess and inquire whether a youth requires additional services. Case managers make referrals with the written consent of youth and families, and involve other agencies in the provision of services whenever possible. In all instances, Viet-AID staff members coordinate with all involved agencies, the youth, and family.

- **Recreational and Fitness Activities:** Youth will be connected to health, nutrition, fitness, and physical activity programs.
- **Mental and Physical Health Care:** Youth will have access to mental health and physical care, including individual and group counseling, routine physicals, health assessments, and emergency treatment.
- **Education:** Youth will be enrolled in public school, provided assistance with application for free lunch and other services, and provided transportation. Youth interested in furthering their education at college or a technical or vocational school will receive assistance in the application and financial aid processes, and will be provided transportation.
- **Employment:** We will provide services to assist youth in finding employment.
- **Life Skills Training:** Training will be provided on skills the youth needs to become self-sufficient.

- **Mentoring Program**: Because social skills are a critical component of success, youth will have an opportunity to participate in a formal mentoring program designed to increase their ease in social settings, communication skills, and interpersonal relations. Youth will be assisted in obtaining other benefits such as housing, food stamps, and Medicaid.
- **Aftercare Services:** An aftercare plan is developed with each youth to assure continuity of services to youth and their families post–discharge.
- **Ongoing Center Planning**: Each year, Viet-AID and our partners plan to conduct a retreat to review agency and program goals and develop plans for the coming year. This includes a review of crisis counseling, temporary shelter, aftercare needs of those youth served, and existing services available to meet those needs. We review the summary of all evaluation surveys completed by parents and youth during the year to ascertain achievement of projected outcomes and recommendations for improvement.

Sub-Grant or Contract

Viet-AID serves as an applicant for this grant and sub-grants a significant portion of the proposed project to our partners (DYC, Dorchester House, and VACA).

Service Linkages with Local Agencies

Viet-AID and our partners have established written cooperative working agreements with community agencies, most of which are enclosed in this application. The agreements were developed for the purpose of coordinating comprehensive services for runway, homeless, and street youth. We also work very closely with the Boston Police Department, Boston School Police, and juvenile courts.

Finally, Viet-AID and our partners have formed relationships with other nonprofit agencies to provide appropriate career development, education, legal services, housing services, and other services and support that are essential to help runaway and homeless youth reconnect to their families and communities.

School Coordination

Viet-AID and our partners have strong relationships with several local schools with high enrollments of Southeast Asian students. These schools have agreed to work collaboratively with Viet-AID and our partners to provide support to help students who are at risk of dropping out and running away from home, and runaway youth who desire to return to school and reconnect with their families.

Dealing with Youth Who Have Run Away from Foster Care and/or Correctional Institutions

Viet-AID follows procedures in accordance with federal, state, and local laws involving youth who have run away from foster care or correctional institutions. The Boston Police Department is contacted to check missing person reports or arrest warrants for all youth admitted. If a youth has run from the foster care system, the state social worker is contacted so the youth can be placed in an alternative placement.

Confidentiality of Records

Viet-AID and our partners will ensure the security of client files as required by state and federal laws regarding confidentiality.

Home-Based Services

While the program does not provide home-based services, our outreach and prevention education activities are designed to educate parents about appropriate parenting skills to better communicate with their children and to prevent conflicts.

Organizational Profiles

Viet-AID and our partners collaborate to offer a comprehensive range of supports and opportunities to runaway and homeless Southeast Asian youth and families.

(1) Organizational Capacity and Experience in Managing Federal Grants

Founded in 1994, Viet-AID is the first and only grassroots community development corporation founded and operated by Vietnamese refugees and immigrants in the United States. Over fifteen years, Viet-AID has worked with mainstream organizations and long-time residents to improve the lives of hundreds of Vietnamese immigrants and refugees; increased the participation of Vietnamese residents in civic life; revitalized the once blighted Fields Corner residential area; and contributed to the economic vitality of the neighborhood. Our current programs and their accomplishments include:

Viet-AID: As the lead applicant, Viet-Aid has more than ten years of experience in managing federal grants and maintains a financial management system. Viet-AID is a community-based organization, with membership open to anyone eighteen years or older.

Close to Home: Since 2002, Close to Home has focused on community organizing and domestic and sexual violence prevention in Fields Corner. Close to Home has formed partnerships with youth organizations, police officers, local businesses, and service providers to enable the organization to deepen its organizing work with youth in Fields Corner. Close to Home engages local youth and adults as leaders by asking current leaders to reach out to their social networks, engaging residents of all ages who live in the Fields Corner area, and letting the local community know we are seeking new leaders.

Vietnamese American Civic Association (VACA): VACA was founded in 1984 to help Vietnamese refugees resettle and rebuild their lives in America.

Dorchester House Multi-Service Center: Dorchester House provides a full range of health care, public health, and community services to the poor and underserved community in Dorchester.

(2) Proposal to Sub-Grant and/or Contract

Viet-AID serves as an applicant for this grant and sub-grants a significant portion of the proposed project to our partners Dorchester Youth Collaborative, Dorchester House Health Center, and VACA. Viet-AID will hold a lead role in the administration and delivery of project services. Viet-AID will be responsible for all contractual, fiscal, and programmatic management. We will be responsible for all programmatic and financial reports. Viet-AID will work closely with DYC, Dorchester House Health Center, and VACA to ensure that these agencies follow and comply with all programmatic and grant management requirements.

(3) Knowledge of State and Local Licensing Requirements

Viet-AID plans to apply to the Massachusetts Department of Early Care and Education to operate a temporary shelter facility for Southeast Asian youth. The facility meets and exceeds all licensing requirements.

(4) Agency's Experience Working with Runaway and Homeless Youth

Our partner, Dorchester Youth Collaborative, has twenty years of experience working with runaway and homeless youth. DYC was founded in 1981 to reduce fear and hopelessness among low-income urban teens through positive youth development activities and access to educational, recreational, and employment opportunities. DYC has operated a successful culturally competent Asian gang diversion and intervention programs for teens living along the Dorchester Avenue corridor.

Sustainability Plan

Viet-AID and our partners are committed to continued operation of the proposed project once federal funding for the project has ended. We plan to leverage other sources of funding to supplement the grant award and to support services through collaborative partnerships, which results in cost-effectiveness, efficiency, and increased resources. Our diverse portfolio of funding sources includes government, private foundation, and corporations. We offer high-quality programs and proven results.

Positive Youth Development Philosophy

Viet-AID incorporates the Family and Youth Services Bureau's youth development approach in our organizational culture. As described in more detail in the subsection above, we view children/youth as positive, creative, and resourceful individuals with an amazing ability for emotional resiliency. Services provided by Viet-AID have always honored the developmental needs of youth. As such, we have an organizational culture that seeks to involve youth in all aspects of our organization. These include serving on the board of directors, as a member of an advisory or steering committee responsible for planning and implementing community initiatives, involving youth in planning and implementing a community service project, and volunteering in one or more of our program activities. One of the potential project ideas is to present, through performance art or digital photography, how cultural differences influence decisions by young people to run away from homes.

Staff and Position Data

Key Staff

Viet-AID has assembled an experienced and committed team consisting of staff members and consultants to implement this project. The key staff positions include one part-time project administrator, one part-time project director, two youth case managers, one family case manager, and one youth worker. The program staff is supported by a team of street outreach workers (DYC), youth workers (all partners), and a clinical counselor (Dorchester House).

Staff Ratio

There will always be a minimum of two professional paid staff members on duty at all time for a staff-to-youth ratio of 1 to 4 or 1 to 6.

Agency's Policy for Criminal History or Child Abuse Registry Checks

All staff members must agree to be subject to initial and annual Massachusetts CORI criminal offender and sexual offender record information checks.

(5) Staff Training Plan

We have a detailed and well-designed staff training plan. Staff training is required of all staff, volunteers, and youth peer counselors at a minimum of forty hours annually. The initial training is a rigorous, in-depth orientation for new staff members, conducted by the supervisory team. The training is both didactic and experiential and employs different media for communicating the information, addressing the spectrum of learning styles. The initial training and mandatory shadowing for a new staff member totals forty hours of education.

Budget and Budget Justifications

The total annual budget for the Southeast Asian shelter is $455,038. Viet-AID and our partners request $188,675 yearly in federal funding and will provide $266,363 in matching funds, or 59 percent. Matching funds consist of in-kind and cash. Viet-AID and our partners have secured funding commitments from the Charles Hayden Foundation, Boston Foundation, Hyams Foundation, and Schraffts Foundation. We have proposals pending with the Peabody and Smith family foundations to support the case manager position to provide case management services and support to parents of program participants. We also plan to approach state agencies for funding support.

As cited earlier, the detailed service proposal briefly discussed above can be found in Appendix C.

WRITING RESEARCH REPORTS

Social workers need to write reports containing factual and objective information collected through their research practice. Many social workers struggle to prepare and write reports. Similar to other phases of research, reports need to be constructed on the basis of culturally sensitive, anti-discriminatory, and non-judgmental ways of thinking. Reports should clearly identify objective facts. Without published research reports, the claim of a scientific knowledge base for social work might be difficult to substantiate (Grinnell, 2001). Research reports can be in a variety of forms and be of different lengths.

Bogg (2012) suggests some key points that need to be applied for a good report even though no single set of standards is recognized and many organizations have their own guidelines and standards. The key points that should be addressed in any research report include:

- The purpose of the report is clear.
- All information provided is based on evidence.
- All sources of information are clearly identified.
- Any opinions or third-party information are identified.
- Appropriate language is used for the report's purpose.
- The report is within appropriate length and concise.

Prepare the Report

Before drafting a report, you need to keep in mind several things, including determining whether the report is for aiding decision making or guiding future planning, and also determining who will read the report and the proper scope of the report. Social workers and MSW candidates are encouraged to get reports of their studies published in an academic journal. Most unpublished social work reports, however, are used for conference presentations, student projects, or presented to sponsoring agencies. The audiences to whom reports are directed are an even more important source of variation in the report. And keeping in mind who will be the audience will help you in using the appropriate language and terminology in the report. A useful way to prepare a report prior to actually writing it is to generate the outline with major headings. This outline is helpful in organizing divisions to be used in writing the report.

Organization of Report Content

A general framework of a research report for publication consists four parts (Grinnell, 2001).

- *Problem:* context and background, significance of the study; review of relevant literature and theory; research problem and research question, hypotheses, and variables.
- *Method:* research design, description of the setting, sampling; data collection procedure, measures, and instruments.
- *Findings:* summarizing main findings, including textual exposition and appropriate data displays using tables and graphs.
- *Discussion:* discussion of findings, interpretation of data, implications for policy and practice; limitations and recommendations; summary and conclusions.

For each of the four parts, after outlining the major headings, you may break them down to subheadings according to your specific project. As Grinnell (2001) cited, there could be a significant deviation from the four-part report structure when an evaluation study is conducted. In such studies, there may be one problem to address, but each stage might use a different method including objectives, data collection procedure, and results.

Due to the limitation of space, here we focus on how to write results or findings and discussions. The presentation of findings should be directly linked to the research question or hypotheses and an explanation of the research method. The formats include data display and text description and interpretation. It is important to report the results and display the data objectively, and to make sure your data are clear and easy to understand. Very often, you will need to present the data with the help of tables, charts, and graphs to enhance readers' understanding of the data and results. But remember that the text is primary, and the graphics support and help explain the text. Textual commentary on data displays should be used to emphasize the main points of the data or to draw attention to the data that might be overlooked.

In reporting your analysis result, you need go beyond just presenting data, and you need to interpret the data, i.e., stating what it means, especially in relation to your research question. For example, in describing a correlation between self-esteem scale and depression scale, the report might state: "The correlation coefficient between self-esteem scale and depression scale was -0.56, which suggests a moderately high degree of negative association between these two variables." Complex methods such as multiple regression and logistic regression that are not in common use should be fully explained. Chapter 9 provides good examples of textual interpreting the results of these two methods.

After reporting the findings, the discussion section is primarily concerned with the meaning and importance of the findings, implications, and conclusions. At this point we do not repeat the findings, but we need to provide explanations of what was learned from the study. Since many social work research projects use relatively small and nonrepresentative samples, when we discuss causal relationships, it is not always possible to generalize the findings to larger populations. Findings from most studies, however, still have some implications for social work practice. They may provide some evidence supporting or challenging certain hypotheses, or raise further questions about something. In the report's conclusion, limitations including major shortcomings that affect the internal and external validity should be explicitly stated such as sampling methods and size.

SUMMARY

In this chapter, we provided some practical tips for proposal writing with two examples. One example pertains to research, and the other to the service grant proposal. Proposal writing is a trial and error process. The best way to learn how to write a proposal is to write one. Through the writing process you will learn what to do and what to avoid. Always seek consultation and critiques from your peers and from others in writing or revising your proposal. Note that a good proposal might not be funded because it does not address what the funding agencies or instructions are seeking. We also provide a brief guidance for writing a research report.

CLASS EXERCISE

Students are divided into 2 groups: One works on an outline for a research proposal of interest; the other works on a service proposal of interest. Group leaders should present their group's outline for the entire class.

REFERENCES

Bogg, D. (2012). *Report Writing*. New York, NY: McGraw-Hill International.

Grinell, R. M. (2001). Social work research and evaluation: Quantitative and qualitative approaches (6th ed.). Itasca, IL: F. E. Peacock Publishers, Inc.

U.S. Department of Health and Human Services, National Institute of Health, Office of Extramural Research. "Peer Review Process." Retrieved February 19, 2014, from http://grants.nih.gov/grants/peer_review_process.htm#Initial. This page updated on August 15, 2013.

U.S. Department of Health and Human Services, Health Resources and Services Administration. "Apply for Grant." Retrieved February 19, 2014, from http://www.hrsa.gov/grants/apply/granttips.html.

FIFTEEN

Summary and New Frontiers for Social Work Research

This book is an introduction to research methods and data analysis for social work students. We begin with basic concepts of research, types of research, measurement issues, survey research, experimental research, qualitative research, mixed methods, and end with examples of research and service grant proposals. For each research design or approach, we give examples to illustrate how researchers used these methods to test hypotheses or evaluate the outcomes of social services or interventions. We emphasize the importance of measurement in multicultural social work research and services. Social work researchers and social services providers should not ignore the importance of the use of culturally comparable and culturally appropriate research instruments and services or interventions.

Multicultural society requires multicultural social services to address a variety of problems and social service needs. Social work researchers and services providers play an important role in finding the best solutions to prevent and eliminate social problems. This requires the collaboration of researchers and practitioners in the investigation of social problems, the development and implementation of social services and treatments, and evaluation of social services.

TRAINING FOR RESEARCH AND EVALUATION

It is always difficult for any graduate social work program to have more than two courses of research and evaluation in the curriculum; however, all graduate social work programs should equip students with a solid foundation of research and evaluation skills by the time they graduate from the program. Continuing social work education programs around the country, for the most part, have not paid attention to the offering of courses in research and evaluation. If evidence-based social work is the choice of practice, all social workers should be trained to have adequate knowledge and skills in research and evaluation to evaluate their own practice, and to evaluate the current research literature for evidence-based interventions and services.

Social work students often complain they don't know why they have to take research and evaluation courses, especially those involving data analysis skills. Students' negative attitude toward the subject has become a learning and effective teaching barrier. What should be done about this? As listed below, there are a few things that academic administrators and instructors can do to change social work students' attitude toward research and evaluation:

1. The importance of research and evaluation must be articulated in the curriculum and admission requirements.
2. Instructors must use relevant examples in their teaching of research methods, statistical analysis, and evaluation.
3. Research concepts must be explained from social work perspectives.
4. Instructors should provide opportunities for students to be exposed to social work research projects.

DEVELOPING AND TESTING NEW TREATMENT MODELS

It is important for social workers to possess skills to develop and test new treatment or service models. The current training in both master's and doctoral levels of social work lacks an element of treatment development. Social work programs have not paid adequate attention to providing future social workers with an ability to "invent" or "develop" a new therapeutic treatment approach and submit for a rigorous testing process.

Developing Outcome Measures

Many people seem to have a vague understanding of what social workers do. Since social workers can perform a variety of roles and functions in the community, from school to prison, it's often difficult to define their roles and tasks. One way to define the uniqueness of social work is to develop outcome measures (i.e., improvement in clients' target behaviors and symptoms) to assess the quality of social work services. Developing social work outcome measures is a way to define the contributions of social workers in the community.

Research on the Quality of Social Work Mental Health Services

It's known that social workers have played a prominent role in mental health services in the United States (Gibelman, 2005). But if you ask a mental health social work professional to describe the unique contribution of social work in the overall mental health services system, she or he might find it difficult to explain. How does a mental health social worker differ from other nonmedical mental health professionals? This is an important question for future research. If we were able to develop what we do best in the mental-health services system, we could demand better compensation and professional autonomy. The discipline of social work can emphasize such a unique field as measuring the quality of human services, including client satisfaction, psychological distress experienced by clients, and the quality of services provided by mental-health service professionals in response to clients' needs.

Social Work in the Military System.

With regard to military social work, the National Association of Social Workers (2014) states, "*There are many opportunities available to professional social workers interested in serving veterans and military families.*

Regardless of practice area, chances are that nearly all social workers will serve this population in some capacity whether through mental and behavioral health therapy, social services, housing, health care, care coordination, or a variety of other services." As reflected in this statement, social workers can play an important role in serving this special population. Social work research can also play a critical role in enhancing the quality of military social work by exploring the types of services that can best be performed by social workers in the military systems. The discipline of social work needs to develop and test different models of treatment and intervention for different social and psychological problems often experienced by the service personnel and their families. One knowledge gap in the existing literature involves the unique issues and needs concerning LBTG service personnel and their families. Thus, this topic must be examined.

School Social Work

What do school social workers do? The School Social Work Association of America (SSWAA) defines school social work as follows:

> *School social work is a specialized area of practice within the broad field of the social work profession. School social workers bring unique knowledge and skills to the school system and the student services team. In particular, School Social Workers are trained in mental health concerns, behavioral concerns, positive behavioral support, academic and classroom support, consultation with teachers, parents and administrators as well as with individual and group counseling techniques"* (SSWAA, 2013).

This area of social work requires further investigation on the working relationship among interdisciplinary team members consisting of school social workers, teachers, administrators, and parents. There should be research on the quality of school social work with respect to the overall quality of the school system. For example, would school social workers be able to prevent dropout, alcohol and drug use, bulling, and other school-related problems? Can school social workers help improve testing and other educational achievements? Can school social workers help teachers and administrators promote and maintain diversity, cultural sensitivity, and cultural competency for the school system?

Social Work Research and the Affordable Health-Care Law

Health disparity is a fact of life in the United States. Research has well documented that certain minority populations and people who are economically and educationally disadvantaged have poorer health status or suffer from chronic health conditions (Adler and Rehkopf, 2008; Braveman, 2006; Mensah, Mokdad, Ford, Greenlund, and Croft, 2005). With the passage of the Affordable Health Care Law (https://www.healthcare.gov/), more people in poverty will have health coverage. This presents new opportunities for social work research and practices in community health care systems. Social work researchers should investigate racial/ethnic differences in prevention and use of community health-care services, especially community mental-health services.

SUMMARY

The new generation of social workers should be well equipped with both quantitative and qualitative research skills. Cross-cultural social work requires cross-cultural evidence-based knowledge and interventions. Research and data analytical skills are important for evidence-based social work practice. The social work profession needs to develop unique approaches to confront and alleviate social and psychological problems at all levels. We hope that this introductory textbook helps social work students appreciate the importance of learning research for their future career in social work, a noble profession that deserves more societal recognition.

CLASS EXERCISE

Students are encouraged to choose the area(s) they intend to work upon graduation, and explore, in their own words, what their roles might involve. They will also be encouraged to explore how to research the quality of their own practice as well as the quality of their agency, public or private, in the context of what they have learned from this research course.

REFERENCES

Adler, N. E., & Rehkopf, D. H. (2008). US disparities in health: Descriptions, causes, and mechanisms. *Annual Review of Public Health, 29*, 235–252.

Braveman, P. (2006). Health disparities and health equity: Concepts and measurement. *Annual Review of Public Health, 27*, 167–194.

Gibelman, M. (2005). *What social workers do* (2nd ed.). Washington, DC: NASW Press.

Mensah, G. A., Mokdad, A. H., Ford, E. S., Greenlund, K. J., & Croft, J. B. (2005). State of disparities in cardiovascular health in the United States. *Circulation, 111*(10), 1233–1241.

National Association of Social Workers. "Social Work and Service Members: Joining Forces to Support Veterans and Military Families." Retrieved February 17, 2014, from http://www.socialworkers.org/military.asp

School Social Work Association of America. "About School Social Work." Retrieved February 17, 2014, from http://www.sswaa.org/displaycommon.cfm?an=1&subarticlenbr=1

APPENDIX A

Using Excel for Statistical Analysis:

An Introduction to Data Analysis Using Excel

In many small human service agencies, social workers have no access to popular statistical sofware such as SPSS or STATA for basic data analysis. Fortunately, most if not all human service agencies have access to Microsoft Office Excel with built-in statistical functions of data analysis. Although there are limitations with the use of Excel for statistical analysis, the Add-ins statistical tools should be sufficient for simple data analysis. This Appendix will use Excel 2010 for Windows to demonstrate the use of:

- Descriptive statistics
- Cross-tabulation and chi-square analysis
- Paired samples t-test
- Independent samples t-test
- One-way analysis of variance
- Pearson correlation
- Linear regression analysis

To perform statistical analysis using Excel, we first need to install **Analysis ToolPak**.

1. Open **Excel**.
2. Click the green **File** tab in the upper-left corner of the Excel screen.
3. On the File tab, click **Options.**
4. On the **Excel options** menu, click **Add-ins**, then select **Analysis Toolpak**. Then click the **Go** button at the bottom:

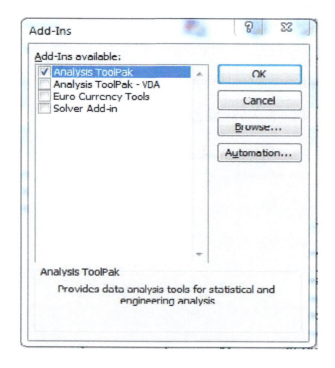

5. You'll see the **Add-ins** window. In this window, you'll see a check for **Analysis ToolPak.** Click the **OK** button.

6. By now, the **Analysis ToolPak** is installed.
7. Under the **Data** tab in Excel, on the far right side on the screen, click the **Data Analysis** option. The **Data Analysis** dialogue box will appear. The Analysis Tools list nineteen options for various data analyses.

The nineteen analysis tests include:

Anova: Single Factor

Anova: Two-Factor With Replication

Anova: Two-Factor Without Replication

Correlation

Covariance

Descriptive Statistics

Exponential Smoothing

F-Test Two Samples for Variances

Fourier Analysis

Histogram

Moving Average

Random Number Generation

Rank and Percentile

Regression

Sampling

T-Test: Paired Two Sample for Means

T-Test: Two Sample Assuming Equal Variances

T-Test: Two Sample Assuming Unequal Variances

Z-Test: Two Samples for Means

In this Appendix, we provide selected hands-on data analyses listed at the beginning of the Appendix, using a fictitous and simple Excel data set. This data set has twenty cases and five variables: Age, Sex (1=Female, 2=Male), Employment Status (1=Employed, 2=Not employed), Type of Need (1=Food, 2=Clothing, 3=Housing), and Family Size (a coninuous variable).

DESCRIPTIVE ANALYSIS

To perform a descriptive analysis of the variables of the sample data set:

1. Open the Excel data.

2. Click on **Data** (on top of the screen). You will then see the **Data Analysis** on the upper-right corner. Click on **Data Analysis**, then select **Descriptive Statistics,** as follows:

3. Click **OK** and you'll see a **Descriptive Statistics** window, as follows:

4. As shown, to select your **Input Range**, you need to move your mouse outside the **Descriptive Statistics** dialogue box and back over the work sheet. For our example, select Age and Sex so that they have a black dotted line around them. You can also type in the range after Input Range, in this case, $B$1:$C1$21.

5. For output options, it is probably best to select **New Worksheet Ply** and give it a meaningful title such as Output 1.

6. Make sure the box next to **Summary statistics** is checked.

7. You can also check the box next to **Confidence Level for Mean**, which is set by default to 95%.

8. Then click the **OK** button.

9. Once you click **OK**, a new work sheet titled **Output 1** appears with all descriptive statistics such as the one below, including mean, standard deviation, median, mode, and so on.

	A	B	C	D
1	*Age*		*Sex: 1=Female; 2=Male*	
2				
3	Mean	34.2	Mean	1.45
4	Standard Error	1.422747527	Standard Error	0.114132887
5	Median	32.5	Median	1
6	Mode	30	Mode	1
7	Standard Deviation	6.362720372	Standard Deviation	0.510417786
8	Sample Variance	40.48421053	Sample Variance	0.260526316
9	Kurtosis	-1.164877016	Kurtosis	-2.182610418
10	Skewness	0.172612321	Skewness	0.217686598
11	Range	21	Range	1
12	Minimum	24	Minimum	1
13	Maximum	45	Maximum	2
14	Sum	684	Sum	29
15	Count	20	Count	20
16	Confidence Level(95.0%)	2.977844798	Confidence Level(95.0%)	0.238882877

HOW TO CREATE A HISTOGRAM

Excel is well known for creating a nice box plot, pine chart, line chart, and so on. In describing data, we may need to create a histogram to help check the distribution of a variable specifically for a continuous or approximately interval variable. Here we'll create a histogram for age based on our fictitious data. The process to create a histogram in Excel is more complicated than obtaining it from SPSS or STATA.

1. Open the data set in Excel.
2. To prepare your data for the age histogram, we first need to create a new variable labeled Age Range, which lists all possible age values from minimum to maximum value (24 to 48, as shown in the previous table). In Sheet 2, we copied age data from Sheet 1, then put it next to the column of the new variable Age Range.
3. From the Data menu, select **Data Analysis** on the far right, then select **Histogram**.
4. Highlight the range for variable age as the **Input Range.** Then highlight the range for variable Age Range as the **Bin Range**.
5. Check the button next to Labels.
6. Check the box next to Chart **Output**.

7. Finally, type a meaningful name for the new worksheet next to **New Worksheet Ply**, such as "Histogram for Age." We'll then have something very similar to:

	A	B	C	D	E	F	G	H	I
1	Age Range	Age							
2	24	25							
3	25	30							
4	26	30							
5	27	36							
6	28	42							
7	29	37							
8	30	40							
9	31	41							
10	32	44							
11	33	32							
12	34	33							
13	35	45							
14	36	28							
15	37	40							
16	38	28							
17	39	32							
18	40	24							
19	41	29							
20	42	38							
21	43	30							
22	44								
23	45								

Histogram

Input

Input Range: $B$1:$B$21

Bin Range: $A$1:$A$23

☑ Labels

Output options

○ Output Range:

● New Worksheet Ply: Histogram for Age

○ New Workbook

☐ Pareto (sorted histogram)
☐ Cumulative Percentage
☑ Chart Output

OK
Cancel
Help

8. Then click **OK.** You'll get the new work sheet and the age histogram. It shows that three cases are 30 years old and two cases are 28, 32, and 40 years old.

	A	B	C	D	E	F	G	H	I
1	Age Range	Frequency							
2	24	1							
3	25	1							
4	26	0							
5	27	0							
6	28	2							
7	29	1							
8	30	3							
9	31	0							
10	32	2							
11	33	1							
12	34	0							
13	35	0							
14	36	1							
15	37	1							
16	38	1							
17	39	0							
18	40	2							
19	41	1							
20	42	1							
21	43	0							
22	44	1							
23	45	1							
24	More	0							

Histogram — bar chart of Frequency by Age Range

HOW TO PERFORM CROSS-TABULATION ANALYSIS AND CHI-SQUARE TEST OF INDEPENDENCE

This type of analysis requires two categorical variables (nominal or ordinal). In the following fictitious data, we have two variables: sex and employment status (unemployed or employed). We will compare types of need (dependent variable) between female and male clients (sex). Cross tabulation produces the frequency for the table's cells, column total, and row total. Once you compute these frequency values, you can compute chi-square statistics (χ^2) to test the hypothesis that two variables of interest are not associated with each other or are independent from each other. Following is the formula of the chi-square statistics test:

$$\chi^2 = \Sigma \frac{(Observed - Expected)^2}{Expected}$$

The chi-square test measures the difference of the observed data (data that you collected) from the expected data—the values that you would *expect to find* if there was no association between the independent and the dependent variables (e.g., the null hypothesis of no association). The expected value for each cell in a two-way table is equal to:

$$(row\ total*column\ total)/n$$

where n is the total number of observations included in the table.

Excel does not include chi-square analysis in the nineteen analyses listed under **Data Analysis**. Given the complexity of using Excel, we demonstrate the application of cross tabulation (cross classification) of a 2-by-2 table for two dichotomous variables. SPSS and STATA would give you more statistical options for this type of cross-tabulation table.

1. Open the existing data or enter data into a new Excel work sheet.
2. Click on **Insert**, and then **PitvotTable**. You'll see a **Create PivotTable** dialogue box open.
3. In the **Table/Range** box select the two variables you would like to examine and the data in the box. For this example, we will use sex and employment status as the **Table/Range**. Under "Choose where you want the PivotTable report to be placed," you're asked to pick a **New Worksheet** or somewhere in the same work sheet. For this example, we want to display it in the same work sheet.

4. Then press the **OK** button.

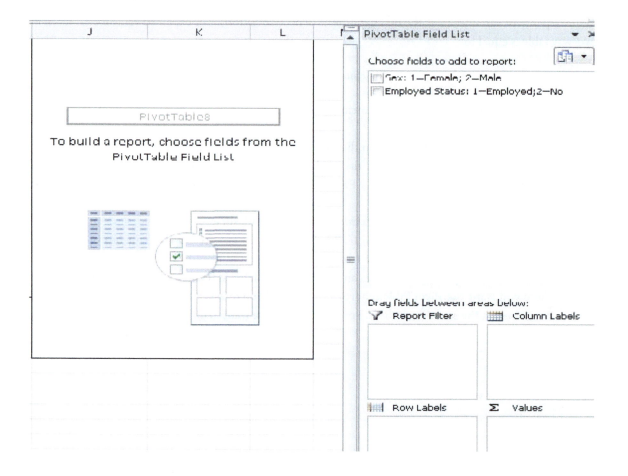

5. In the **PivotTable Field List** dialogue box on the right side of the PivotTable work sheet, check the box next to Sex.
6. Click and drag the variable name Employment Status, hold and drag it to the **Row Labels** box. Click, hold, and drag variable name Sex to the **Column Labels** box.
7. In the **Σ Values** box in the lower-right side of **the PivotTable Field List** dialogue box, click **Sum of…**. Select **Value Field Settings** dialogue box.
8. In the dialogue box, under the **Summarize Values By** tab, select **Count**.

Value Field Settings

Source Name: Employed Status: 1=Employed;0=No

Custom Name: Count of Employed Status: 1=Employed;0=No

Summarize Values By | Show Values As

Summarize value field by

Choose the type of calculation that you want to use to summarize data from the selected field

Sum
Count
Average
Max
Min
Procuct

Number Format   OK   Cancel

9.   After you click **OK,** you'll see the table below:

Count of Employed Status Column Labels ▼			
Row Labels ▼	1	2	Grand Total
0	6	4	10
1	5	5	10
Grand Total	**11**	**9**	**20**

10. You may type value labels to replace the numerical values, as shown below:

	J	K	L	M
Count of Employed Status Column Labe ▼				
Row Labels ▼		Female	Male	Grand Total
Unemployed		6	4	10
Employed		5	5	10
Grand Total		**11**	**9**	**20**

These numbers are observed data: Among 11 females, 5 employed and 6 unemployed; and among 9 males, 5 employed and 4 unemployed. Among 20 total cases, 10 employed and 10 unemployed.

11. To calculate chi-square, we need to have expected data for each cell. Write the formula of expected value (**row total*column total**)/**n**) on the work sheet to make it easier to compute the expected values. (You do not have to do this with SPSS or STATA.) As shown in the previous output table, Excel uses **"Grand Total"** instead of "**n**." Write the name of the cells that contain data for "row total," "column total," and "Grand Total" or "n." You need to type the equal sign "=" at the beginning of each formula. For example, to calculate the expected value of "Unemployed" for "Female," type =b7 (cell b7 in the work sheet)*d5(cell d5 in the work sheet)/d7 (cell d7 in the work sheet), and then hit **Enter**.

	Female	Male
Expected Value for Unemployed	=M3*K5/M5	=M3*L5/M5
Expected Value for Employed	=M4*L5/M5	=M4*L5/M5

Then you need to do the following:
1. Set Alpha equal to 0.05. See cell K12.
2. Calculate the degree of freedom, (number of columns-1 * number of rows-1). For our example: (2-1) * (2-1) = 1. See cell K13.
3. Calculate critical chi square value. In cell K15, type =c. You will see a list of options. Double-click on **CHINV** and you will see: =CHINV (probability, degree of freedom). Here you type the set Alpha value (0.05), and after the comma, type 1 (the degree of freedom for our example), as shown below:

J	K	L	M
Count of Employed Status: Column Labe ▾			
Row Labels ▾	Female	Male	Grand Total
Unemployed	6	4	10
Employed	5	5	10
Grand Total	**11**	**9**	**20**
Expected value for unemp	5.5	4.5	
Expected vaue for emp.	5.5	4.5	
Alpha	0.05		
degree of fredom	1		
Critical chi-square	=CHIINV(.05,1)		

4. Then press **Enter**. You'll have the critical chi-square value, which is 3.84. It tells us that based on the calculation of our observed data and expected data, if the calculated chi-square value is greater than 3.84, it would be statistically significant at p=.05 level.

5. To get the actual P value based on our data, type =c. in cell K15. You will see a list of options, then double-click on CHITEST. It will show CHITES (actual range, expected range). You need to select the two ranges. For our case, first select K3:L4, and after typing a comma, select K8:L9.

6. Then hit **Enter**. You'll get the actual P value, which is .653.

7. To calculate the observed chi-square, type =c. You will see a list of options, then double-click CHINV again. This time you will need to type the actual P value and the degree of freedom. You just need to type K15 (our actual P value), then type K13 (the degree of freedom).

8. Then press **Enter**. You'll have the following:

J	K	L	M
Count of Employed Status: Column Labe ▼			
Row Labels ▼	**Female**	**Male**	**Grand Total**
Unemployed	6	4	10
Employed	5	5	10
Grand Total	**11**	**9**	**20**
Expected value for unemp	5.5	4.5	
Expected vaue for emp.	5.5	4.5	
Alpha	0.05		
degree of fredom	1		
Critical chi-square	3.841458821		
P-value	0.653095115		
Observed chi-square	0.202020202		

The result reveals the actual chi-square value is .202 with p=.653, far from the critical chi-square and set P value. For this example, we conclude there is no difference in the employment status between female and male clients. Or you can say that female and male clients have similar employment status.

HOW TO PERFORM A T-TEST FOR TWO INDEPENDENT SAMPLES (GROUPS)

We will use the t-test to compare the average of age between female and male clients using our fictitious data set. Prior to doing the independent form of t-tests that either assumes equal or unequal variances, you must check **Levene's F statistic** between samples to determine whether the variances of the two samples are equal.

1. Open the data set.

2. We need to create two new variables: Female's Age and Male's Age. First, we need to sort the data by sex. To do this, under Data menu, click **Sort** and you'll see the **Sort** window, as on page 206:

3. Select Sex after sort by. Click **OK**.
4. You will then see that Age (column B) is arranged by Sex: 1=Female, and 2=Male (column C).
5. Highlight age for female clients (B2–B12), copy the data, and paste on column G.
6. Highlight age for male clients (B13–B21), copy the data, and paste on column H.
7. Make sure to type the label "Female's Age" to column G and "Male's Age" to column H.

Now your Sheet 1 looks like:

	A	B	C	D	E	F	G	H
1	Case ID	Age	Sex: 1=Female; 2=Male	Types of Need: 1=Food;2 = Clothing 3 =Housing	Family Size: # Person(s)	Employed Status: 1=Employed;2=No	Female's Age	Male's Age
2	1	25	1	3	5	2	25	45
3	2	30	1	1	4	2	30	28
4	4	30	1	3	2	2	30	40
5	5	36	1	3	4	1	36	28
6	8	42	1	3	1	2	42	32
7	10	37	1	3	1	1	37	24
8	12	40	1	1	5	2	40	29
9	13	41	1	2	3	1	41	38
10	14	44	1	3	4	1	44	30
11	17	32	1	1	1	1	32	
12	19	33	1	2	5	2	33	
13	3	45	2	2	3	1		
14	6	28	2	1	3	1		
15	7	40	2	2	3	2		
16	9	28	2	1	4	1		
17	11	32	2	3	5	2		
18	15	24	2	1	5	2		
19	16	29	2	1	2	1		
20	18	38	2	2	4	2		
21	20	30	2	3	5	1		

8. From Sheet 1 open the **Data Analysis** dialogue box on the **Data** menu tab, select **F-Test: Two Sample for Variance**. After clicking the **OK** button, you'll see a new **F-Test Two Sample for Variance** dialogue box.

9. You need to check **Labels** and set **Alpha** at 0.05 by default.

10. In the **Input** section, make sure your cursor is in the **Variable 1 Range** text field, then go back to the Excel work sheet with your mouse and select G1 to G12 for **Variable 1 Range.**

11. Next, click your cursor in the **Variable 2 Range** text field, then go back to the Excel work sheet with your mouse and select the H1 to H10 for **Variable 2 Range** so that the range appears in the **Variable 2 Range** text field.

12. If you want to have the output in a new work sheet, type a meaningful name in **New Worksheet Ply** after you check it.

13. If you want to have your output in the same work sheet, check Output Range and type something such as $I$1. After clicking **OK**, you'll have your Levene's test result in the same work sheet from column I to column K.

F-Test Two-Sample for Variances

	Female's Age	Male's Age
Mean	35.45454545	32.66666667
Variance	35.67272727	46.75
Observations	11	9
df	10	8
F	0.76305299	
P(F<=f) one-tail	0.33774724	
F Critical one-tail	0.325557036	

The output above shows the F statistic (F = 0.763, p =.323) between variables Female's Age and Male's Age, indicating the variances are not significantly different. Then we should perform the independent t-test assuming equal variances (see below).

14. Click on **Data** menu. Click **Data Analysis** on the top-left corner and select **t-Test: Two Sample Assuming Equal Variance**, then click **OK**. (If the Levene's F statistic is significant, you should select **t-Test: Two Sample Assuming Unequal Variance.**)

15. Fill in the **Variable 1 Range** and **Variable 2 Range**: Female's Age and Male's Age (columns G and H). To have the label of each column you should:

   a. Select G1 to G12 for **Variable 1 Range,** and H1 to H10 for **Variable 2 Range**.

   b. Check the **Labels** box.

   c. If you want the output to appear from column I, select **Ouput Range** and type $I$1 in the blank box or highlight column I1 and click it.

The following is the output:

	I	J	K
t-Test: Two-Sample Assuming Equal Variances			
		Female's Age	Male's Age
Mean		35.45454545	32.66666667
Variance		35.67272727	46.75
Observations		11	9
Pooled Variance		40.5959596	
Hypothesized Mean Difference		0	
df		18	
t Stat		0.973498039	
P(T<=t) one-tail		0.171603826	
t Critical one-tail		1.734063607	
P(T<=t) two-tail		0.343207652	
t Critical two-tail		2.10092204	

Interpretations:

Mean: Average age of female and average age of male respondents.

Variance: Sample variance of age for females and males.

Observations: Group size or the number of clients in each group.

Pooled Variance: Estimated variance of two groups assumed to be equal.

Hypothesis Mean Difference: The value zero (0) means the difference of the average of age equals zero or that females and males have the same age average.

df: Degrees of freedom equal n1+n2–2 (total number of females and males minus 2). There are two groups, therefore we take the total sample size (20) minus 2.

t Stat: Value of the t-test.

P(T<=t) one t-tail: The t-test value for one-tailed probability. This is used when you hypothesize that one group would be older (greater age average) than the other group or vice versa.

t Critical one-tail: The obtained t Stat value between the two groups must be greater than this value to be statistically significant at .05.

Similar interpretations are applied for the two-tailed test. This is the situation when you do not specify in your hypothesis which group would be older (having a greater average value) than the other and vice versa.

HOW TO PERFORM A PAIRED T-TEST

We create another fictitious data set to demonstrate the use of a paired t-test to compare the means of depression between baseline and post-intervention (O X O). This is a pretest and posttest-only design. Because the means of depression are from the same clients, they are not independent. The appropriate statistical procedure is the paired t-test In **Excel ToolPak** the name of this procedure is **t-Test: Paired Two Sample for Means**.

Here are the steps:

1. Open the Excel data sheet. Click on **Data**, click on **Data Analysis**, select **t-Test: Paired Two Sample Means**, and then click **OK**. You'll see a **t-Test: Paired Two Sample Means** dialogue box.

2. For the **Input**, when your cursor is in the **Variable 1 Range** box, move your mouse back over the Excel work sheet and highlight the variable name Baseline and data values for your first variable.

3. Highlight the second variable name Post Intervention and data values to the **Variable 2 Range** box.

4. Make sure **Labels** is checked. Also check the **New Worksheet PLY** box and type in a meaningful name, such as paired t-test.

5. Then click **OK**. You'll get the output in a work sheet for a paired samples t-test:

	A	B	C
1	t-Test: Paired Two Sample for Means		
2			
3		*Baseline Depression*	*Post Intervetion Depression*
4	Mean	31.92857143	25.71428571
5	Variance	3.763736264	4.835164835
6	Observations	14	14
7	Pearson Correlation	0.499741141	
8	Hypothesized Mean Difference	0	
9	df	13	
10	t Stat	11.16740913	
11	P(T<=t) one-tail	2.46313E-08	
12	t Critical one-tail	1.770933396	
13	P(T<=t) two-tail	4.92626E-08	
14	t Critical two-tail	2.160368656	

The results show that the baseline depression mean is 31.928 (column B) and the post-intervention depression mean is 25.714 (column C). The t value is 11.167 with a P value of 2.46313E-08 for the one-tail t-test and 4.92626E-08 for the two-tail t-test. This is the scientific notation for a number with eight zeroes after the decimal point. You should rewrite it as p = 0 .00000002 or p= 0.000. Given the P value of the paired t-test is at .000 (p = .000), we can conclude that the clients' depression reduced significantly for both one-tail and two-tail tests.

HOW TO PERFORM ONE-WAY ANALYSIS OF VARIANCE (ANOVA)

In this example, we run a one-way ANOVA to compare the means of age across three types of needs.

1. To do so you need to sort Age by Types of Need, as was done with t-test for two independent samples.

2. Once you complete the sorting of age according to need types, you then copy age for each type of need and paste three new columns in the data sheet as three new variables. Give a label for each new column of data.

I	J	K
Age for Need=1	Age for need=2	Age for need=3
30	41	25
40	33	30
32	45	36
28	40	42
28	38	37
24		44
29		32
		30

3. Click on **Data Analysis**, select **ANOVA: Single Factor**, then click **OK**.
4. Highlight the ranges of data (your dependent variable) to include in the analysis: **Input Range.**
5. Mark the **Label** box to include the label of the selected variable.
6. Type a meaningful name for **New Worksheet PLY** to store the results in a different sheet.

I	J	K	L
Age for Need=1	Age for need=2	Age for need=3	
30	41	25	
40	33	30	
32	45	36	
28	40	42	
28	38	37	
24		44	
29		32	
		30	

Anova: Single Factor

Input
Input Range: $I$1:$K$9
Grouped By: ● Columns
              ○ Rows
☑ Labels in First Row
Alpha: 0.05

Output options
○ Output Range:
● New Worksheet Ply: ANOVA
○ New Workbook

OK
Cancel
Help

7. Click **OK** and you'll get the following results:

	A	B	C	D	E	F	G
	Anova: Single Factor						
	SUMMARY						
	Groups	*Count*	*Sum*	*Average*	*Variance*		
	Age for Need=1	7	211	30.14286	24.80952		
	Age for need=2	5	197	39.4	19.3		
	Age for need=3	8	276	34.5	41.71429		
	ANOVA						
	Source of Variation	*SS*	*df*	*MS*	*F*	*P-value*	*F crit*
	Between Groups	251.1429	2	125.5714	4.120615	0.034744	3.591531
	Within Groups	518.0571	17	30.47395			
	Total	769.2	19				

In this analysis, the results show a statistically significant difference in the average of age across three types of need (the P value of F is at .034, which is smaller than .05), but there is no way to compare age between food and clothing, food and housing, and clothing and housing. The limitations of using Excel for ANOVA is the lack of post-hoc comparison procedures to examine the difference between two groups. Both SPSS and STATA have multiple options for two-group comparisons in ANOVA.

HOW TO PERFORM PEARSON CORRELATION USING EXCEL

When we examine the relationship or association between two continuous variables, we run correlation. In the fictitious data sets we used earlier, there are two continuous variables: age and family size (number of family members).

1. Click on **Data Analysis**, select **Correlation,** click **OK**.
2. Make sure the data of the two variables are side by side.
3. Highlight the data to insert in **Input Range**. For our example, it is B1:C21.
4. Check **Labels in First Row** box.
5. Check the **New Worksheet PLY** box and type a meaningful name such as "Correlation."

	A	B	C	D	E	F	G	H
	Case ID	Age	Family Size: # Person(s)	Sex: 1=Female; 2=Male	Employed Status: 1=Employed;0=No	Need: 1=Food;2=Clothing 3		
	2	30	4	1	0	1		
	12	40	5	1	0	1		
	17	32	1	1	1	1		
	6	28	3	2				
	9	28	4	2				
	15	24	5	2				
	16	29	2	2				
	13	41	3	1				
	19	33	5	1				
	3	45	3	2				
	7	40	3	2				
	18	38	4	2				
	1	25	5	1				
	4	30	2	1				
	5	36	4	1				
	8	42	1	1	0	3		
	10	37	1	1	1	3		
	14	44	4	1	1	3		
	11	32	5	2	0	3		
	20	30	5	2	1	3		

Correlation dialog box:

Input
Input Range: $B$1:$C$21
Grouped By: ● Columns / ○ Rows
☑ Labels in First Row
Output options
○ Output Range:
● New Worksheet Ply: Correlation
○ New Workbook
[OK] [Cancel] [Help]

6. Click **OK** to generate the correlation coefficient table as below:

	A	B	C
		Age	Family Size: # Person(s)
	Age	1	
	Family Size: # Person(s)	-0.2588241	1

Based on our fake data, the result shows a weak negative correlation (r=−.259) between age and family size, meaning young respondents are more likely to have more family members. Unfortunately, Excel does not compute the significance value or P value for the correlation coefficients as SPSS or STATA. You will need to check critical values of Pearson's r table in any statistical textbook based on the number of cases to determine whether the correlation coefficient is significant. For n=20, the degree of freedom is n=20−2, which is 18. The table tells us the correlation coefficient would be statistically significant at .05 level, if it is .444 or higher in absolute value. Therefore, our result is not considered significant.

7. To create a scatter plot for the two variables, follow the steps below:
   - Select the two variable columns, including variable name and data.
   - Click the **Insert** tab. You'll see various choices in terms of charts.
   - Click the **Scatter** icon and select the one with marks only.

- You'll have the following:

- You see the range of Age is from 0 to 50. To make the plot easier to interpret and match our data, you can adjust the data range.
- To do this, double-click on any number on the horizontal axis for Age that ranges from 0 to 50. You'll see a **Format Axis** dialogue box.
- For minimum and maximum, you may select 20 to 50 as shown below:

- Then click **OK**.
- You can also add a scatter plot title, and titles for the horizontal and vertical axis through **Chart Tools→ Layout**.

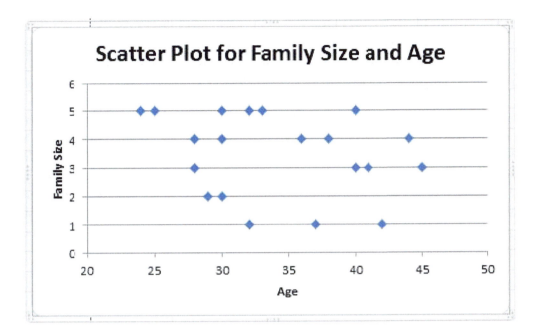

- Finally, add the regression line. To do so, at the **Chart Tool,** select **Design**. Click **Layout 3**. You'll have the negative linear regression line as shown below:

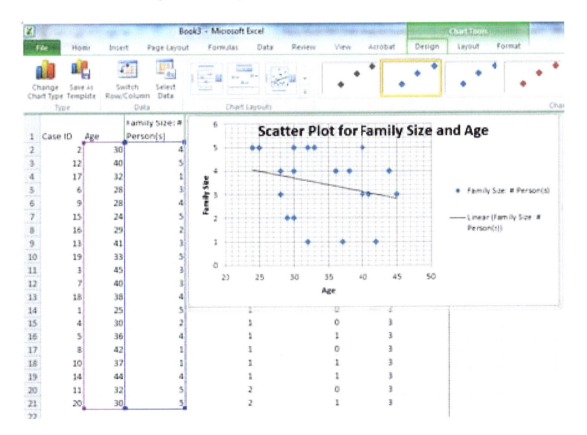

HOW TO PERFORM REGRESSION ANALYSIS WITH EXCEL

In this example, we run a multiple regression analysis of Family Size (y) on Age (x1) and Sex (x2). Note that in regression analysis, the dependent variable (y) must be a continuous variable. The independent variables (x's) can be both continuous and categorical; however, categorical must be transformed into a binary (dummy or indicator) variable with 1 or 0. You can transform a categorical variable into binary variables using the Recode procedure in SPSS or STATA, but Excel does not have this function. You will have to manipulate your variables manually before you can perform an analysis. In this example, Sex is already a binary variable with two values or two categories (Female vs. Male); you can either code 1 for Female and 0 for Male or keep it as it is now. When you interpret the result, you compare with the reference group as listed on the output. For example, in this analysis, since Female was coded 1 and Male was coded 2, the reference group is Female. If the Sex variable was coded 0 for Female and 1 for Male, then Female is also the reference group.

Here are the steps:
1. Open the data set or data sheet.
2. Click on **Data Analysis**, select **Regression**, and then click **OK**.
3. Highlight the Family Size column to insert into **Input Y Range.**
4. Highlight Age and Sex columns to insert in **Input X Range.**
5. Check **Labels**, **Confidence Level**, and **New Worksheet PLY** boxes and type a meaningful name such as MRA (multiple regression analysis).

6. Then click **OK** to execute the analysis.

A	B	C	D	E	F	G	H	I
Multiple R	0.303545							
R Square	0.09214							
Adjusted R Square	-0.01467							
Standard Error	1.442244							
Observations	20							
ANOVA								
	df	SS	MS	F	Significance F			
Regression	2	3.588841	1.79442	0.862674	0.439705399			
Residual	17	35.36116	2.080068					
Total	19	38.95						
	Coefficients	Standard Err	t Stat	P-value	Lower 95%	Upper 95%	Lower 95.0%	Upper 95.0%
Intercept	4.500041	2.269487	1.982845	0.063782	-0.28815751	9.28824045	-0.2881575	9.288240449
Age	-0.05005	0.053353	-0.93816	0.361301	-0.162619493	0.06251167	-0.1626195	0.062511672
Sex: 1=Female; 2=Male	0.456415	0.665087	0.68625	0.501809	-0.946794612	1.85962533	-0.9467946	1.859625333

Interpretation of regression analysis output:

At the top of the output, the **R-squared** of .09 means approximately 9% of the variance of the dependent variable—family size is accounted for by the model, in this case, age and sex. The adjusted R-square attempts to yield a more conservative value to estimate the R-squared for the population. The value of R-square was .09, while the value of adjusted R-square was close to 0.

The **ANOVA** table in the output provides the source of variance, regression model, residual, and the total. The total variance is partitioned into the variance, which can be explained by the independent variables (model) and the variance that is not explained by the independent variables. The P value associated with this F value is .439, much larger than .05, indicating the model is not statistically significant. These values are used to answer the question "Do the independent variables reliably predict the dependent variable?" The P value is compared with your alpha level (typically 0.05) and, if smaller, you can conclude that "Yes, the independent variables reliably predict the dependent variable." In our case, it is just the opposite.

The last section of the output shows the regression coefficients from each independent variable. These are the values for the regression equation for predicting the dependent variable from the independent variables. The negative coefficient for age, −.05, means when Sex is controlled, a one-year increase in age is associated with a .05 decrease in family size. The t value (-.09) and its related P value (.36), however, tells us its effect is not statistically significant. For Sex, since male=2, the regression coefficient of .45 means that compared with female, male respondents' average family size is .45 higher than females when Age is controlled. Again, based on its t value and P value, its effect is not significant, either.

GLOSSARY

AB design: The simplest *single-subject design* that includes one baseline phase (A) and one intervention (or treatment) phase (B). This is widely used among practitioners and researchers because it is conducted with only one baseline phase, thus saving time and expenses. But it has less control for history than most alternative single-case evaluation designs.

Accidental sampling: A nonrandom sampling method in which the researcher includes the most convenient cases in his or her sample.

Acculturation: The process in which a group or individual experiences changes in its language, values, attitudes, and lifestyles after being exposed to and in contact with a majority culture.

Alpha (α): The probability of error, or the probability that a confidence interval does not contain the population value. Alpha levels are usually set at 0.10, 0.05, 0.01, or 0.001.

Alpha level (α): The proportion of area under the sampling distribution that contains unlikely sample outcomes, given that the null hypothesis is true. Also, the probability of Type I error.

Alternative hypothesis: Used in hypothesis testing, it's the hypothesis we accept if we are able to disprove the null hypothesis. For example, if the null hypothesis is "There is *no* difference between immigrant and US-born Americans," our alternative hypothesis would be "There is a difference between immigrant and US-born Americans."

Analysis of variance (ANOVA): A test of significance appropriate for situations in which we are concerned with the differences among more than two sample means.

Anonymity: An arrangement that makes it impossible for a researcher to link any research data with a given research participant. Distinguished from *confidentiality*, in which the researcher is able to identify a given person's responses but essentially promises not to do so publicly.

Association: The relationship between two (or more) variables. Two variables are said to be associated if the distribution of one variable changes for the various categories or scores of the other variable.

Attributes: Characteristics of persons, events, or things.

Attrition: A threat to the validity of an experiment that occurs when participants drop out of an experiment before it is completed. Also called experimental mortality.

Availability sampling: A sampling method that selects elements simply because of their ready availability and convenience. Frequently used in social work because it is usually less expensive than other methods and because other methods may not be feasible for a particular type of study or population.

Average: An ambiguous term that generally suggests typical or normal. *Mean, median,* and *mode* are specific examples of mathematical averages, or measures of central tendency.

Bar chart: A graph used for discrete variables. Categories are represented by bars of equal width, the height of each corresponding to the number (or percentage) of cases in the category.

Baseline: The phase of a single-subject design that consists of repeated measures before a new intervention or policy is introduced.

Beta weights: See standardized partial slope.

Between-groups sum of squares: The sum of the squared deviations of every sample mean from the total mean.

Bias: (1) That quality of a measurement device that tends to result in a misrepresentation of what is being measured in a particular direction. For example, the questionnaire item "Don't you agree that the president is doing a good job?" would be biased because it would generally encourage more favorable responses. (2) The thing inside a person that makes other people or groups seem consistently better or worse than they really are.

Bimodal distribution: A frequency distribution containing two modes.

Bivariate analysis: The analysis of two variables simultaneously to determine the empirical relationship between them. The construction of a simple percentage table or the computation of a simple correlation coefficient would be examples of bivariate analyses.

Box plot: A graphic method for simultaneously displaying several characteristics of a distribution.

Case study: An idiographic examination of a single individual, family, group, organization, community, or society using a full variety of evidence regarding that case.

Causal inference: An inference derived from a research design and findings that logically imply that the independent variable really has a causal impact on the dependent variable.

Central tendency: What is average or typical of a set of data; a value generally located toward the middle or center of a distribution.

Central limit theorem: A theorem that specifies the mean, standard deviation, and shape of the sampling distribution, given that the sample is large.

Chi-square: A nonparametric test of significance whereby expected frequencies are compared against observed frequencies.

Closed-ended questions: Unlike in *open-ended questions*, the respondent is asked to select an answer from among a list provided by the researcher.

Codebook: The document used in data processing and analysis that tells the location of different data items in a data file. Typically, the codebook identifies the locations of data items and the meaning of the codes used to represent different attributes of variables.

Coding: The process whereby raw data are transformed into a standardized form that is suitable for machine processing and analysis.

Coefficient of determination: Equal to the Pearson's correlation squared, the proportion of variance in the dependent variable that is explained by the independent variable.

Column percent: In a cross tabulation, the result of dividing a cell frequency by the number of cases in the column. Column percentages sum to 100 for each column of a cross tabulation.

Computer-assisted telephone interviewing (CATI): Interviewing over the phone by reading questions from a computer screen and immediately entering responses into the computer.

Concept: Naming things, events, persons, and thoughts. Or a mental image that symbolizes an idea, an object, an event, or a person.

Conceptualization: The mental process whereby fuzzy and imprecise notions *(concepts)* are made more specific and precise. So you want to study prejudice. What do you mean by "prejudice"? Are there different kinds? What are they?

Concurrent validity: A form of *criterion-related validity* examining a measure's correspondence to a criterion that is known concurrently.

Confidence interval: The range of mean values (proportions) within which the true population mean (proportion) is likely to fall.

Confidence level: A frequently used alternate way of expressing alpha, the probability that an interval estimate that will not contain the population value. Confidence levels of 90%, 95%, 99%, and 99.9% correspond to alphas of 0.10, 0.05, 0.01, and 0.001, respectively.

Confidentiality: A promise by the researcher not to publicly identify a given research participant's data. Distinguished from *anonymity*, which makes it impossible for a researcher to link any research data with a given research participant.

Consent form: A form that subjects sign before participating in a study that provides full information about the features of the study that might affect their decision on whether to participate—particularly regarding its procedures, potential harm, and *anonymity* and *confidentiality*.

Construct validity: The degree to which a measure relates to other variables as expected within a system of theoretical relationships, and as reflected by the degree of its convergent validity and discriminant validity.

Content analysis: A research method for studying virtually any form of communication, consisting primarily of *coding* and tabulating the occurrences of certain forms of content that are being communicated.

Control group: In experimentation, a group of participants who do *not* receive the intervention being evaluated and who should resemble the *experimental* group in all other respects. The comparison of the control and experimental groups at the end of the experiment points to the effect of the tested intervention.

Content validity: The degree to which a measure covers the range of meanings included within the concept.

Continuous variable: A variable with a unit of measurement that can be subdivided infinitely.

Contingency table: Any table format for presenting the relationships among variables in the form of percentage distributions.

Control variable: In multivariate statistical analysis, an extraneous variable whose values are held constant throughout the experiment.

Convenience sampling: See *availability sampling*.

Convergent validity: The degree to which scores on a measure correspond to scores on other measures of the same construct.

Correlation: The strength and direction of the relationship between two variables. See Figure 8.1 for illustrations of correlation. (p. 105)

Correlation coefficient: Generally ranging between −1.00 and + 1.00, a number in which both the strength and direction of correlation are expressed.

Correlation matrix: A table that shows the correlation coefficients between all possible pairs of variables.

Cramer's V: A chi-square–based measure of association for nominally measured variables that have been organized into a bivariate table with any number of rows and columns.

Critical region (region of rejection): The area under the sampling distribution that, in advance of the test itself, is defined as including unlikely sample outcomes, given that the null hypothesis is true.

Cross-sectional study: A study based on observations that represent a single point in time. Contrasted with a *longitudinal study*.

Cross tabulation: A frequency and percentage table of two or more variables taken together.

Cumulative frequency: The total number of cases having any given score or a score that is lower.

Cumulative percentage: The percentage of cases having any score or a score that is lower.

Cultural bias: A source of measurement error or *sampling error* stemming from researcher ignorance or insensitivity regarding how cultural differences can influence measurement or generalizations made to the entire population when certain minority groups are inadequately represented in the sample. A measurement procedure is culturally biased when it is administered to a minority culture without adjusting for the ways in which the minority culture's unique values, attitudes, lifestyles, or limited opportunities alter the accuracy or meaning of what is really being measured.

Cultural competence: A researcher's ability to obtain and provide information that is relevant, useful, and valid for minority and oppressed populations. Cultural competence involves knowledge about the minority culture's historical experiences, traditions, values, family systems, socioeconomic issues, and attitudes about social services and social policies; awareness of how one's own attitudes are connected to one's own cultural background and how they may differ from the worldview of members of the minority culture; and skills in communicating effectively, both verbally and nonverbally, with members of the minority culture and establishing rapport with them.

Culturally competent research: Being aware of and appropriately responding to the ways in which cultural factors and cultural differences should influence what we investigate, how we investigate, and how we interpret our findings—thus, resulting in studies that are useful and valid for minority and oppressed populations.

Curvilinear relationship: A *relationship* between two *variables* that changes in nature at different values of the variables. For example, a curvilinear relationship might exist between amount of social work practice experience and practice effectiveness, particularly if we assume that practitioners with a moderate amount of experience are more effective than those with none and at least as effective as those nearing retirement.

Cumulative frequency: An optional column in a frequency distribution that displays the number of cases within an interval and all preceding intervals.

Cumulative percentage: An optional column in a frequency distribution that displays the percentage of cases within an interval and all preceding intervals.

Degrees of freedom: In small sample comparisons, a statistical compensation for the failure of the sampling distribution of differences to assume the shape of the normal curve.

Dependent variable: That variable that is assumed to depend on, or be caused by, another (called the *independent variable*). If you find that income is partly a function of amount of formal education, then income is being treated as a dependent variable.

Descriptive statistics: Statistical computations that describe either the characteristics of a sample (i.e., frequency, mean, and standard deviation) or the relationship among variables in a sample. Descriptive statistics merely summarize a set of sample observations, whereas *inferential statistics* move beyond the description of specific observations to make inferences about the larger *population* from which the sample observations were drawn. *Descriptive statistics* is also a branch of statistics concerned with (1) summarizing the distribution of a single variable or (2) measuring the relationship between two or more variables.

Deviations: The distances between the scores and the mean.

Dichotomous variable: A variable that has only two categories.

Direct observation: A way to operationally define variables based on observing actual behavior.

Direct relationship: A multivariate relationship in which the control variable has no effect on the bivariate relationship.

Discrete variable: A variable with a basic unit of measurement that cannot be subdivided.

Dispersion: The amount of variety, or heterogeneity, in a distribution of scores.

Dummy variable: A nominal-level variable dichotomized so that it can be used in regression analysis. A dummy variable has two scores, one coded as 0 and the other as 1.

Effect size: A statistic that portrays the strength of association between variables. Effect-size statistics might refer to various measures of proportion of dependent variable variation explained, or specifically to the difference between the means of two groups divided by the *standard deviation*. The latter is usually called the effect size, ES, or Cohen's *d*.

Equal probability of selection method (EPSEM): A sample design in which each member of a population has the same chance of being selected into the sample.

Experimental design: A research method that attempts to provide maximum control for threats to *internal validity* by: (1) randomly assigning individuals to experimental and control groups, (2) introducing the *independent variable* (typically a program or intervention method) to the experimental group while withholding it from the control group, and (3) comparing the amount of experimental and control group change on the *dependent variable*.

Experimental group: In experiments, a group of participants who receive the intervention being evaluated and who should resemble the control group in all other respects. The comparison of the experimental group and the *control group* at the end of the experiment points to the effect of the tested intervention.

External validity: Refers to the extent to which we can generalize the findings of a study to settings and populations beyond the study conditions.

Face validity: That quality of an indicator that makes it seem a reasonable measure of some variable. That the frequency of church attendance is some indication of a person's religiosity seems to make sense without a lot of explanation: it has face validity.

Factor analysis: A statistical procedure that identifies which subsets of variables or items on a scale correlate with each other more than with other subsets. In so doing, it identifies how many *dimensions* a scale contains and which items cluster on which dimensions.

Five percent level (.05) of significance: A level of probability at which the null hypothesis is rejected if an obtained sample difference occurs by chance only five times or less out of one hundred.

Focus groups: An approach to needs assessment in which a small group of people are brought together to engage in a guided discussion of a specified topic.

F ratio: The result of an analysis of variance, a *statistical* technique that indicates the size of the between-groups mean square relative to the size of the within-groups mean square.

Gender bias: The unwarranted generalization of research findings to the population as a whole when one gender is not adequately represented in the research sample.

Generalizability: That quality of a research finding justifying the inference that it represents something more than the specific observations on which it was based. Sometimes this involves the generalization of findings from a sample to a population. Other times it is a matter of concepts: if you are able to discover why people commit burglaries, can you generalize that discovery to other crimes as well?

Grounded theory method (GTM): A *qualitative* methodology for building theory grounded in data by beginning with observations and looking for patterns, themes, or common categories in those observations.

Histogram: A graph used for interval-ratio variables. Class intervals are represented by contiguous bars of equal width (equal to the class limits), the height of each corresponding to the number (or percentage) of cases in the interval.

Hypothesis: A tentative and testable prediction about how changes in one thing are expected to explain and be accompanied by changes in something else. A statement of something that ought to be observed in the real world if a theory is correct.

Hypothesis testing: Statistical tests that estimate the probability of sample outcomes if assumptions about the population (the null hypothesis) are true. The determination of whether the expectations that a *hypothesis* represents are actually found to exist in the real world.

Independent variable: A variable whose values are not problematical in an analysis but are taken as simply given. An independent variable is presumed to cause or explain a *dependent variable*.

Index: A type of composite measure that summarizes several specific observations and represents a more general dimension.

Inference: A claim about a population based on sample data.

Inferential statistics: The body of statistical computations that is relevant to making inferences from findings based on sample observations to some larger *population*.

Informant: Someone who is well versed in the social phenomenon that you wish to study and willing to tell you what he or she knows. If you were planning participant observation among the members of a religious sect, then you would do well to make friends with someone who already knows about the members—possibly even a sect member—who could provide you with background information about them. Not to be confused with a *respondent*.

Institutional review board (IRB): An independent panel of professionals that is required to approve the ethics of research involving human subjects.

Interaction: A multivariate relationship wherein a bivariate relationship changes across the categories of the control variable.

Internal validity: The degree to which an effect observed in an experiment was actually produced by the experimental stimulus and not the result of other factors.

Interval measure: A level of measurement that describes a variable whose attributes are rank-ordered and have equal distances between adjacent attributes. The Fahrenheit temperature scale is an example of this, because the distance between 20° and 21° is the same as that between 50° and 51°.

Interview: A data-collection method in which an interviewer asks questions of a respondent. Interviews may be conducted face-to-face or by telephone.

Interview guide approach: A semistructured form of *qualitative interviewing* that lists in outline form the topics and issues that the interviewer should cover in the interview, but allows the interviewer to adapt the sequencing and wording of questions to each particular interview.

IRB: See institutional review board.

Judgmental sample: A type of *nonprobability sample* in which we select the units to be observed on the basis of our own judgment about which ones will be the most useful or representative. Another name for this is *purposive sample*.

Judgment sampling (purposive sampling): A nonrandom sampling method whereby logic, common sense, or sound judgment is used to select a sample that is presumed representative of a larger population.

Kurtosis: The peakedness of a distribution.

Lambda: A measure of association for nominal data that indicates the degree to which we can reduce the error in predicting values of one variable from values of another.

Leptokurtic: Characteristic of a distribution that is quite peaked or tall.

Level of confidence: How certain we are that a confidence interval covers the true population mean (proportion).

Levels of measurement: A basic characteristic of a variable that determines what statistical procedures can be used with that variable. Variables can be measured at any of four levels.

Level of significance: A level of probability at which the null hypothesis can be rejected and the research hypothesis can be accepted.

Likert scale: A type of composite measure developed by Rensis Likert in an attempt to improve the levels of measurement in social research through the use of standardized response categories in survey *questionnaires*. "Likert items" use such response categories as strongly agree, agree, disagree, and strongly disagree. Such items may be used in the construction of true Likert scales and also in the construction of other types of composite measures.

Line chart: A graph of the differences between groups or trends across time on some variable(s).

Linguistic equivalence (*or* translation equivalence): The result of a successful translation and *back-translation* of an instrument originally developed for the majority language, but which will be used with research participants who don't speak the majority language.

Longitudinal study: A study design that involves the collection of data at different points in time, as contrasted with a *cross-sectional study*.

Margin of error: The extent of imprecision expected when estimating the population mean or proportion, obtained by multiplying the standard error times the table value of z or t.

Mean: An *average*, computed by summing the values of several observations and dividing by the number of observations.

Measurement: The use of a series of numbers in the data analysis stage of research.

Measurement equivalence: The degree to which instruments or observed behaviors have the same meaning across cultures, relate to referent theoretical constructs in the same way across cultures, and have the same causal linkages across cultures.

Median: Another *average*; it represents the value of the "middle" case in a rank-ordered set of observations. If the ages of five men are 16, 17, 20, 54, and 88, then the median would be 20 (the *mean* would be 39).

Mediating variable (or intervening variable): The mechanism by which an *independent variable* affects a *dependent variable*.

Metric equivalence (*or* psychometric equivalence *or* scalar equivalence): Scores on a measure being comparable across cultures.

Mode: The most frequently observed value or attribute. If a sample contains 200 white, 120 Hispanic, 100 African Americans, and 40 other categories, then white is the modal category.

Moderating variable: A variable that influences the strength or direction of a relationship between independent and dependent variables.

Multiple correlation coefficient (R): A statistic that indicates the strength of the correlation between a dependent variable and two or more independent variables.

Multiple regression analysis: A multivariate statistical procedure that shows the overall correlation between a set (or sets) of *independent variables* and an *interval- or ratio-level dependent variable*.

Multistage sampling: A random sampling method whereby sample members are selected on a random basis from a number of well-delineated areas known as clusters (or primary sampling units).

Multivariate analysis: The analysis of the simultaneous relationships among several variables. Examining simultaneously the effects of age, sex, and social class on religiosity would be an example of multivariate analysis.

Mutually exclusive outcomes: Two outcomes or events are mutually exclusive if the occurrence of one rules out the possibility that the other will occur.

Negative correlation: The direction of relationship wherein individuals who score high on the X variable score low on the Y variable; individuals who score low on the X variable score high on the Y variable.

Negative relationship: A *relationship* between two *variables* in which one variable increases in value as the other variable decreases. For example, we might expect to find a negative relationship between racist attitudes and level of education.

Negatively skewed distribution: A distribution in which more respondents receive high than low scores, resulting in a longer tail on the left than on the right.

95 confidence interval: The range of mean values (proportions) within which there are 95 chances out of 100 that the true population mean (proportion) will fall.

99 confidence interval: The range of mean values (proportions) within which there are 99 chances out of 100 that the true population mean (proportion) will fall.

Nominal level of measurement: The process of placing cases into categories and counting their frequency of occurrence.

Nominal measure: A level of measurement that describes a variable whose different attributes differ only categorically and not metrically, as distinguished from *ordinal, interval,* or *ratio measures.* Ethnicity and gender are examples of a nominal measure.

Nondirectional hypotheses: Predicted relationships between variables that do not specify whether the predicted relationship will be positive or negative.

Nonequivalent comparison groups design: A *quasi-experimental design* in which the researcher finds two existing groups that appear to be similar and measures change on a *dependent variable* before and after an intervention is introduced to one of the groups.

Nonlinear relationship: Also called a curvilinear relationship, a relationship that changes direction as the values of the independent variable increase.

Nonparametric tests: Tests of statistical significance that have been created for use when not all of the assumptions of parametric statistics can be met. Chi-square is the most commonly used nonparametric test. This statistical procedure makes no assumptions about the way the characteristic being studied is distributed in the population and requires only ordinal or nominal data.

Nonprobability sample: A sample selected in some fashion other than those suggested by probability theory. Examples include *judgmental (purposive), quota,* and *snowball samples.*

Nonrandom sampling: A sampling method whereby each and every population member does not have an equal chance of being drawn into the sample.

Normal curve: A smooth, symmetrical distribution that is bell-shaped and unimodal.

Null hypothesis: In connection with *hypothesis testing* and *tests of statistical significance*, the *hypothesis* that suggests there is no relationship between the variables under study. You may conclude the two variables are related after having statistically rejected the null hypothesis.

Observations: Information we gather by experience in the real world that helps us build a *theory* or verify whether it is correct when testing *hypotheses*.

Observed frequencies: In a chi-square analysis, the results that are actually observed when conducting a study.

One-tailed tests of significance: *Statistical significance tests* that place the entire *critical region* at the predicted end of the *theoretical sampling distribution*, and thus limit the inference of *statistical significance* to findings that are only in the critical region of the predicted direction.

One-tailed test: A test in which the null hypothesis is rejected for large differences in only one direction.

One-way analysis of variance (ANOVA): Applications of ANOVA in which the effect of a single independent variable on a dependent variable is observed.

Online surveys: Surveys conducted via the Internet—either by e-mail or through a website.

Open-ended questions: Questions for which respondents are asked to provide their own answer, rather than selecting from among a list of possible responses provided by the researcher, as for *closed-ended questions*.

Operational definition: The concrete and specific *definition* of something in terms of the *operations* by which observations are to be categorized. The *operational definition* of "earning an A in this course" might be "correctly answering at least 90 percent of the final exam questions."

Operationalization: One step beyond *conceptualization*. Operationalization is the process of developing *operational definitions*.

Ordinal level: A level of measurement that allows you to order the categories in a meaningful way, but doesn't allow you to do anything else (such as multiply or divide).

Ordinal level of measurement: The process of ordering or ranking cases in terms of the degree to which they have any given characteristic.

Ordinal measure: A level of measurement describing a variable whose attributes may be rank-ordered along some dimension. An example would be measuring "socioeconomic status" by the *attributes* high, medium, and low.

Parametric tests: Tests of statistical significance that assume at least one variable being studied has an interval or ratio level of measurement, that the sample distribution of the relevant parameters of those variables is normal, and that the different groups being compared have been randomly selected and are independent of one another. Commonly used parametric tests are the *t-test, analysis of variance,* and *Pearson product-moment correlation.*

Partial correlation coefficient: A statistic that shows the relationship between two variables while controlling for other variables; $r_{yx.z}$ is the symbol for the partial correlation coefficient when controlling for one variable.

Percentile: A close relative of the median, a percentile has a certain percentage of the cases above or below it. For example, the 90th percentile has ninety of the cases below it and ten above it.

Pearson product-moment correlation *(r):* A *parametric* measure of association, ranging from −1.0 to +1.0, used when both the *independent* and *dependent variables* are at the *interval* or *ratio level* of measurement.

Pearson's *r.* A measure of association for variables that have been measured at the interval-ratio level; ρ (Greek letter *rho*) is the symbol for the population value of Pearson's *r.*

Percentile rank: A single number that indicates the percentage of cases in a distribution falling at or below any given score.

Phi coefficient: Based on chi-square, a measure of the degree of association for nominal data arranged in a 2×2 table.

Pie chart: A graph used especially for discrete variables with only a few categories. A circle (the pie) is divided into segments proportional in size to the percentage of cases in each category of the variable.

Population: The group consisting of all elements from which a sample is drawn. More formally, it is the theoretically specified group of all study elements.

Positive relationship: A relationship between two variables in which one variable increases in value as the other variable also increases in value (or one decreases as the other decreases). For example, we might expect to find a positive relationship between rate of unemployment and extent of homelessness.

Positively skewed distribution: A distribution in which more respondents receive low than high scores, resulting in a longer tail on the right than on the left.

Posttest-only design with nonequivalent groups: A *pre-experimental design* that involves two groups that may not be comparable, in which the *dependent variable* is assessed after the *independent variable* is introduced for one of the groups.

Power of a test: The ability of a statistical test to reject the null hypothesis when it is actually false and should be rejected.

Pre-experimental designs: Pilot study designs for evaluating the effectiveness of interventions; they do not control for threats to *internal validity.*

Pretest-posttest control group design: The classical *experimental design* in which subjects are assigned randomly to an *experimental group* that receives an intervention being evaluated and to a *control group* that does not receive it. Each group is tested on the *dependent variable* before and after the experimental group receives the intervention.

Probability: The relative frequency of occurrence of an event or outcome. The number of times any given event could occur out of one hundred.

Probability sample: The general term for a sample selected in accord with probability theory, typically involving some *random selection* mechanism. In a probability sample, all elements in the population have an equal chance of being selected to the sample.

Probability sampling: The use of *random sampling* techniques that allow a researcher to make relatively few observations and generalize from those observations to a much wider population. All elements have an equal chance of being selected to the sample.

Probe: A technique employed in interviewing to solicit a more complete answer to a question, this nondirective phrase or question is used to encourage a respondent to elaborate on an answer. Examples include "Anything more?" and "How is that?"

Proportion: A method for standardizing for size that compares the number of cases in any given category with the total number of cases in the distribution.

Qualitative analysis: The nonnumerical examination and interpretation of observations for the purpose of discovering underlying meanings and patterns of relationships. This is most typical of field research and historical research.

Qualitative interview: An interaction between an interviewer and a *respondent* in which the interviewer usually has a general plan of inquiry but not a specific set of questions that must be asked in particular words and in a particular order. Ideally, the respondent does most of the talking.

Qualitative research methods: Research methods that emphasize depth of understanding and the deeper meanings of human experience, and that aim to generate theoretically richer, albeit more tentative, observations. Commonly used qualitative methods include participant observation, direct observation, and unstructured or intensive interviewing.

Quantitative analysis: The numerical representation and manipulation of observations for the purpose of describing and explaining the phenomena that those observations reflect.

Quantitative methods: Research methods that emphasize precise, objective, and generalizable findings.

Quasi-experimental design: Design that attempts to control for threats to *internal validity* and thus permits causal inferences, but is distinguished from true experiments primarily by the lack of *random* assignment of subjects.

Quartiles: Percentile ranks that divide the 100-unit scale by 25s.

Questionnaire: A document that contains questions and other types of items that are designed to solicit information appropriate to analysis. Questionnaires are used primarily in survey research and also in experiments, field research, and other modes of observation. A questionnaire refers to a research instrument completed by respondents without any aid from the researcher.

Quota sampling: A type of *nonprobability sample* in which units are selected into the sample on the basis of prespecified characteristics so that the total sample will have the same distribution of characteristics as are assumed to exist in the population being studied.

Random sampling: A sampling method whereby each and every population member has an equal chance of being drawn into the sample.

Range (R): The difference between the highest and lowest scores in a distribution. A measure of dispersion.

Random selection: A *probability* sampling procedure in which each element has an equal chance of selection independent of any other event in the selection process.

Randomization: A technique for assigning experimental participants to *experimental groups* and *control groups* at random.

Recoding: The process of taking a variable's original codes and giving each code a new code. For example, we might recode the Sex variable from 1 = Male, 2 = Female to 0 = Male, 1 = Female.

Reliability: That quality of a measurement method that suggests the same data would have been collected each time in repeated observations of the same phenomenon. In the context of a survey, we would expect that the question "Did you attend church last week?" would have higher reliability than the question "About how many times have you attended church in your life?" This is not to be confused with validity.

Representativeness: That quality of a sample of having the same distribution of characteristics as the population from which it was selected. By implication, descriptions and explanations derived from an analysis of the sample may be assumed to represent similar ones in the population. *Representativeness* is enhanced by *probability sampling* and provides for *generalizability* and the use of inferential statistics.

Regression analysis: A technique employed in predicting values of one variable (Y) from knowledge of values of another variable (X).

Regression line: The single best-fitting straight line that summarizes the relationship between two variables. Regression lines are fitted to the data points by the least-squares criterion, whereby the line touches all conditional means of Y or comes as close to doing so as possible.

Research hypothesis (H_1): A statement that contradicts the null hypothesis. In the context of single sample tests of significance, the research hypothesis says that the population from which the sample was drawn does not have a certain characteristic or value.

Row percent: In a cross tabulation, the result of dividing a cell frequency by the number of cases in the row. Row percentages sum to 100 for each row of a cross tabulation.

Research design: A term often used in connection with whether logical arrangements permit causal inferences; also refers to all the decisions made in planning and conducting research.

r-squared: Also R-squared, or the coefficient of determination. A measure of the proportion of the variation in the dependent variable that can be explained by its relationship to the independent variable.

Respondent: A person who provides data for analysis by responding to a survey *questionnaire* or to an interview.

Response rate: The number of people who participate in a survey divided by the number selected in the sample, in the form of a percentage. This is also called the "completion rate" or, in self-administered surveys, the "return rate"—the percentage of *questionnaires* sent out that are returned.

Sample: One or more elements selected from a population.

Sampling: The process of selecting a sample.

Sampling distribution: The distribution of a statistic for all possible sample outcomes of a certain size. Under conditions specified in two theorems, the sampling distribution will be normal in shape, with a mean equal to the population value, and a standard deviation equal to the population standard deviation divided by the square root of N.

Sampling distribution of means: A frequency distribution of a large number of random sample means that have been drawn from the same population.

Sampling error: The inevitable difference between a random sample and its population based on chance alone.

Sampling frame: That list or quasi list of units that make up a population from which a sample is selected. If the sample is to be *representative* of the population, then it's essential that the sampling frame include all (or nearly all) members of the population.

Sampling interval: The standard distance between elements selected from a population for a sample.

Sampling unit: That element or set of elements considered for selection in some stage of sampling.

Scatter plot: A graph that shows the way scores on any two variables X and Y are scattered throughout the range of possible score values.

Scalar equivalence See *metric equivalence*.

Scale: A type of composite measure composed of several items that have a logical or empirical structure among them.

Scientific method: An approach to inquiry that attempts to safeguard against errors commonly made in casual human inquiry. Chief features include viewing all knowledge as provisional and subject to refutation, searching for evidence based on systematic and comprehensive observation, pursuing objectivity in observation, and replication.

Secondary analysis: A form of research in which the data collected and processed by one researcher are reanalyzed—often for a different purpose—by another. This is especially appropriate in the case of survey data. Data archives are repositories or libraries for the storage and distribution of data for secondary analysis.

Selection bias: A threat to *internal validity*, referring to the assignment of research participants to groups in a way that does not maximize their comparability regarding the *dependent variable*.

Self-mailing questionnaire: A mailed *questionnaire* that requires no return envelope: when the questionnaire is folded a particular way, the return address appears on the outside. The respondent therefore doesn't have to worry about losing the envelope.

Self-report scales: A source of data in which research subjects all respond in writing to the same list of written questions or statements devised to measure a particular construct. For example, a self-report scale to measure marital satisfaction might ask how often one is annoyed with one's spouse, is proud of the spouse, has fun with the spouse, and so on.

Significance level: The probability level that is selected in advance to serve as a cutoff point to separate findings that will and will not be attributed to chance. Findings at or below the selected probability level are deemed to be *statistically significant.*

Simple random sampling: A random sampling method whereby a table of random numbers is employed to select a sample that is representative of a larger population.

Simple random sample (SRS): A type of *probability sample* in which the units that compose a population are assigned numbers. A set of *random* numbers is then generated, and the units having those numbers are included in the sample. Although probability theory and the calculations it provides assume this basic sampling method, it's seldom used for practical reasons. An equivalent alternative is the *systematic sample* (with a random start).

Skewness: Departure from symmetry.

Slope: In regression, the change in the regression line for a unit increase in X. The slope is interpreted as the change in the Y variable associated with a unit change in the X variable.

Snowball sample: A *nonprobability sample* that is obtained by asking each person interviewed to suggest additional people for interviewing.

Snowball sampling: A *nonprobability* sampling method often employed in *qualitative research*. Each person interviewed may be asked to suggest additional people for interviewing.

Social desirability bias: A source of *systematic measurement error* involving the tendency of people to say or do things that will make them or their reference group look good.

Spearman's rank-order correlation coefficient: A correlation coefficient for data ranked or ordered with respect to the presence of a given characteristic.

Spurious relationship: A noncausal relationship between two variables that exists only because of the common influence of a third variable. The spurious relationship disappears if the third variable is held constant.

Standard deviation: The square root of the mean of the squared deviations from the mean of a distribution. A measure of variability that reflects the typical deviation from the mean.

Standard error: The standard deviation of a sampling distribution. It is the average distance all of our sample means are from the population mean.

Standard error of the difference between means: An estimate of the standard deviation of the sampling distribution of differences, based on the standard deviations of two random samples.

Standard error of the mean: An estimate of the standard deviation of the sampling distribution of means, based on the standard deviation of a single random sample.

Standardized slope: Also called a beta, it is a regression slope translated into standard deviations. With the standardized slopes we can compare the effects of the independent variables.

Statistical control: The technique of adding additional independent variables to a regression model to see if this changes the original effect of an original independent variable.

Statistical power analysis: Assessment of the probability of avoiding *Type II errors*.

Statistical significance: A general term that refers to the unlikelihood that relationships observed in a sample could be attributed to sampling error alone.

Statistically significant difference: A sample difference that reflects a real population difference and not just a sampling error.

Straight-line correlation: Either a positive or negative correlation, so that the points in a scatter diagram tend to form a straight line through the center of the graph.

Stratified sampling: A probability sampling procedure that uses *stratification* to ensure that appropriate numbers of elements are drawn from homogeneous subsets of that population.

Strength of correlation: Degree of association between two variables.

Study population: The aggregation of elements from which the sample is actually selected.

Substantive significance: The importance, or meaningfulness, of a finding from a practical standpoint.

Sum of squares: The sum of squared deviations from a mean.

Systematic error: An error in measurement with a consistent pattern of effects. For example, when child welfare workers ask abusive parents whether they have been abusing their children, they may get biased answers that are consistently untrue because parents do not want to admit to abusive behavior. Contrast this with *random error*, which has no consistent pattern of effects.

Systematic sample: A type of *probability sample* in which every kth unit in a list is selected for inclusion in the sample—for example, every twenty-fifth student in the college directory of students. We compute κ by dividing the size of the population by the desired sample size; the result is called the *sampling interval*. Within certain constraints, systematic sampling is a functional equivalent of *simple random sampling* and usually easier to do. Typically, the first unit is selected at random.

Systematic sampling: A random sampling method whereby every nth member of a population is included in the sample.

Test-retest reliability: Consistency, or stability, of measurement over time.

Tests of statistical significance: A class of statistical computations that indicate the likelihood that the relationship observed between variables in a sample can be attributed to sampling error only.

Theory: A systematic set of interrelated statements intended to explain some aspect of social life or enrich our sense of how people conduct and find meaning in their daily lives.

Time-series designs: A set of *quasi-experimental designs* in which multiple observations of a *dependent variable* are conducted before and after an intervention is introduced.

Total sum of squares (SST): The sum of the squared deviations of the scores from the overall mean.

***t* ratio:** A statistical technique indicating the direction and degree that a sample mean difference falls from zero on a scale of standard error units.

t-test: A test of statistical inference used to see if the difference between two sample means is statistically significant enough to say there is a difference between their respective population means.

Triangulation: The use of more than one imperfect data-collection alternative in which each option is vulnerable to different potential sources of error. For example, instead of relying exclusively on a client's *self-report* of how often a particular target behavior occurred during a specified period, a significant other (e.g., teacher, cottage parent) is asked to monitor the behavior as well.

Two-tailed test: A test that is used when the null hypothesis is rejected for large differences in both directions.

Two-tailed tests of significance: Statistical significance tests that divide the *critical region* at both ends of the *theoretical sampling distribution* and adds the probability at both ends when calculating the *level of significance*.

Type I error: The error of rejecting the null hypothesis when it is true.

Type II error: The error of accepting the null hypothesis when it is false.

Unimodal distribution: A frequency distribution containing a single mode.

Unit of observation: The element that is being studied or observed. Individuals are most often the unit of observation, but sometimes collections or aggregates—such as families, census tracts, or states—are the unit of observation.

Units of analysis: The "what" or "whom" being studied. In social science research, the most typical units of analysis are individual people.

Univariate analysis: The analysis of a single variable for purposes of description. *Frequency distributions*, *averages*, and measures of *dispersion* would be examples of *univariate analysis*, as distinguished from *bivariate* and *multivariate analysis*.

Validity: A descriptive term used of a measure that accurately reflects the concept that it's intended to measure. For example, your IQ would seem a more valid measure of your intelligence than would the number of hours you spend in the library. Realize that the ultimate validity of a measure can never be proven, but we may still agree to its *relative validity, content validity, construct validity, internal validation*, and *external validation*. This must not be confused with *reliability*.

Variability: The manner in which the scores are scattered around the center of the distribution. Also known as dispersion or spread.

Variable: Any characteristic that varies from one individual to another. Hypotheses usually contain an independent variable (cause) and a dependent variable (*effect*).

Variance: The mean of the squared deviations from the mean of a distribution. A measure of variability in a distribution.

Weighting: A procedure employed in connection with sampling whereby units selected with unequal probabilities are assigned weights in such a manner as to make the sample representative of the population from which it was selected.

Weighted mean: The "mean of means" that adjusts for differences in group size.

Within-groups sum of squares: The sum of the squared deviations of every raw score from its sample group mean.

X: Symbol used for any independent variable.

Y: Symbol used for any dependent variable.

Y-intercept: In regression, the point where the regression line crosses the Y axis. The Y-intercept is the predicted value of Y for an X value of zero.

Z score (standard score): A value that indicates the direction and degree that any given raw score deviates from the mean of a distribution on a scale of standard deviation units.

Zero-order correlations: Correlation coefficient for bivariate relationships.

APPENDIX B

Proposal: Example 1

Title of Research Proposal:

Confronting Social Isolation and Depression Among Older Vietnamese Americans

PROJECT SIGNIFICANCE

The Institute for Asian American Studies from the University of Massachusetts in Boston reported there are more than 30,000 Vietnamese Americans living in Massachusetts and that they represent the third-largest Asian group in the state, of whom many primarily reside in Boston. According to the US Bureau of the Census in 2000, there are approximately 1.2 million Vietnamese Americans residing in the United States. Vietnamese Americans are the fourth-largest Asian American group, and the seventh-largest immigrant group in the United States. Highlights from the 2000 census indicated that 74.1% of Vietnamese living in the United States are foreign-born. More than 6% of the Vietnamese American population is sixty-five and older. In addition, data from the American Community Survey in 2008 indicated that a large proportion of Vietnamese elders experiences some form of physical disability (44.3%), and a great majority of them cannot speak English well or not at all (73.8%). This background information suggests older Vietnamese Americans are potentially at risk of being socially isolated and depressed (US Bureau of the Census 2000; US Bureau of the Census 2008).

Research examining the correlates of demographic variables and loneliness found that positive marital relationships seem to offer the strongest buffer, while risk factors included male gender, physical health symptoms, chronic work/social stress, small social network, lack of a spousal confidant, and poor social relationships (Hawkley, Hughes, Waite, Masi, Thisted and Cacioppa 2008; Theeke 2009; Adams, Sanders, and Auth 2004). Developing an understanding of these risk factors will facilitate a preventive intervention that may alleviate loneliness and reduce depression for the elderly Vietnamese. Recent research has also shown that spirituality-based interventions can help improve psychosocial well-being (Moritz, Quan, Rickhi, Liu, Angen, Vintila, Sawa, Soriano, and Toews 2006; Rajagopai, Mackenzie, Bailey, and Lavizzo-Mourey 2002; Emery and Pargament 2004). These significant findings indicate that despite the losses and changes experienced in later stages of adult development, people can draw on religion as a source of personal stability (Maton 1989; Pargament 1997), intimacy and belonging, and coping mechanism in later life (Idler and Kasl 1992). It empowers and affirms the sacredness of life and provides the person with a sense of self-efficacy, control, and integrity (Emery and Pargament 2004). With a more positive prospect, individuals have been shown to be happier just by counting their blessings (National Institute on Aging 2009).

– The approach of the proposed intervention emphasizes the enhancement of social connectedness among Vietnamese elders, along with improvement of overall well-being outcomes. Literature identifying effective interventions on reducing loneliness and social isolation among older people appear to be scarce. In a review of literature by Cattan, White, Bond and Learmouth (2005), however, the authors found that effective interventions have several common characteristics. These include modalities such as group intervention focusing on health education (Andersson 1985), social support (Arnetz and Theorell 1983; Caserta and Lund 1993; Caserta and Lund 1996), and physical training (Hopman-Rock and Westhoff 2002; McAuley et al. 2000). Particularly, these types of intervention were successful because they targeted a specific population while allowing participants some level of control in facilitating the group's activities.

More recently, a host of research on the effects of physical activities seems to have found results in helping alleviate the psychological, social, and physical problems that accompany the aging process (Eyigor, Karapolat, and Durmaz 2007; Mather, Rodriguez, Guthrie, McHarg, Reid, and McMurdo 2002; Penninx, Rejeski, Pandya, Miller, Di Bari, Applegate and Pahor 2002; Grant, Todd, Aitchison, Kelly, and Stoddart 2004). As such, low-cost and low-technology exercise programs such as tai chi appear to enhance older adults' life satisfaction and general well-being (Li, Duncan, Duncan, McAuley, Chaumeton and Harmer 2001). In addition, as an alternative form of physical activity, research has found that low intensity physical exercise is rather effective in improving older adults' functional ability and self-esteem (Sung 2009). A group of older Korean women experienced significant health and mental-health improvements when they participated in a group exercise program consisting of gentle stretching and low-impact muscle strengthening. They performed the activity over regular thirty-minute intervals, for a sixteen-week intervention. Thus, the current research findings imply that slow rhythmic and low intensity exercise activities are key considerations to improving health and mental-health status for older adults (Sung 2009; Li et al. 2001).

The overarching goal for our proposed project is to develop a community-based intervention program that is culturally appropriate, feasible, and sustainable for older Vietnamese in the Greater Boston area. There has been little existing prevention and translational research on the topic of social isolation and depression for older Vietnamese Americans. We hope our findings will inform and contribute significantly to the fields of health-care services and mental health by reducing or preventing loneliness, social isolation, and depression of older adults in underrepresented or marginalized populations.

STATEMENT OF OBJECTIVES

Social interaction or social connectedness can be enhanced through group meetings. These may include religious activities and group physical activities, which have been proven to help older people alleviate social isolation and improve psychological well-being (Emery and Pargament 2004). But for many non-English–speaking immigrants or new American groups, opportunities for these types of social interaction seem to be minimal due to an existing language barrier, lack of transportation, and a paucity in social networking. A relatively high percentage of older Vietnamese Americans live in linguistically isolated households where adult household members only speak Vietnamese. This is one of the many major barriers for older adults to social involvement and interaction in a larger community. This proposed study will implement and evaluate a multifaceted intervention to alleviate social isolation and reduce depression for Vietnamese Americans age sixty years or older, recruited from a Vietnamese Catholic community in the Greater Boston area.

This proposed project aims to test two primary hypotheses:

Participants in both the experimental and parallel control groups will have lower feelings of loneliness and depression at the end of the intervention. Participants in the experimental group, however, will reduce their level of loneliness and depression significantly greater than the control group.

Participants in both the experimental and parallel control groups will improve their social support and self-efficacy. Participants in the experimental group, however, will report a significantly greater improvement than the parallel control group.

We will also test two secondary hypotheses:

Participants in the experimental group will increase their social network and their sense of religiosity at the end of the intervention, compared with the parallel control group.

Participants in the experimental group will report a better self-rated health status at the end of the intervention, compared with the parallel control group.

DESCRIPTION OF METHODOLOGY

Experimental Design

We will use the research randomizer software (http://www.randomizer.org/about.htm) to randomly assign eligible participants to either the experimental group or the parallel intervention control group. Both groups will have the same number of females and males. The duration of the interventions will last six months. All participants will be required to complete a bilingual (English–Vietnamese) survey questionnaire designed to collect information on demographic characteristics and baseline information on the outcome measures. The outcome measures will be repeated at the three-month and six-month periods. A list of the items and questions included in the survey questionnaire is presented in Appendix B.

The key elements of the proposed experimental intervention consist of a series of two-hour sessions that utilize attribution-retraining techniques from the field of motivational psychology, in combination with behavioral strategies derived from social cognitive theory, organized religious activities, and physical activity (Hilt 2004; Weiner 1985).

Screening for Social Isolation

We will use version 3 of the UCLA 10-item Loneliness Scale (Russell 1996). The UCLA Loneliness Scale was developed to assess subjective feelings of loneliness or social isolation. It will take five minutes to complete the screening for each participant. Scores between 15 and 20 are considered a normal experience of loneliness. Scores above 30 indicate a person is experiencing severe loneliness. Prospective participants whose scores are 30 or greater will be invited to participate in the proposed intervention.

Sample Size

Sixty Vietnamese (30 men and 30 women), aged sixty and older living in the Greater Boston area will be recruited to participate in this proposed study.

Eligibility Criteria

The participants will need to meet the following eligibility criteria:
- Self-identified Vietnamese and Catholic sixty years and older.
- Have a score of 30 or greater on the UCLA Loneliness Scale.
- Not currently participating in any organized physical activities.
- Have approval from a physician to engage in physical activities such as tai chi.

Exclusion Criteria

Those who meet the above criteria but have one of the following conditions will be excluded from the selection:
- Plans to move from the area in the next twenty-four months.
- Unable to participate in at least thirty minutes a week in a tai chi program.
- Family member already participating in this program.
- Unable to understand and sign the informed consent form to participate in the program.

Experimental Group

Thirty participants (15 men and 15 women) will participate in a series of experimental sessions that will include four sessions a month (weekly) for three months and two sessions a month (biweekly) for another three months. Each session will include: (1) a thirty-minute informal small group social interaction led by a bilingual social worker and peer leaders. Participants will be encouraged to share personal stories, develop common interests, and exchange interesting information or any other issues of the day; (2) a thirty-minute presentation from invited health and human-service professionals. Each week we will invite a bilingual speaker to present from one of the following topics: nutrition, the importance of physical activity, self-care, nursing care, elderly social services, elderly health-care services, and communicating with physicians or health-care interpreters, as well as any topic recommended by participants. The planned presentations also aim to provide participants with useful information they can use to alter and enrich their life situations; (3) a fifteen-minute session of religious activities led by a Vietnamese Catholic priest. The organized religious activities are designed to motivate participants to alter their life situations to achieve the desired outcomes of this intervention; and (4) a thirty-minute tai chi exercise led by a qualified tai chi instructor. The tai chi sessions are designed to improve physical strength and promote social connectedness among participants. Participants will also have a five-minute break between each set of activities.

Parallel Control Group

Thirty randomly assigned participants (15 men and 15 women) in the parallel control group will participate in a series of planned tai chi exercise sessions four times a month (weekly) for three months, followed by twice a month (biweekly) for another three months. The thirty-minute tai chi exercise will be led by the same qualified tai chi instructor of the experimental group. The same set of exercises as that in the experimental group will be held at a different day and time to avoid a diffusion of information among participants.

Intervention Locations, Incentive, and Selection Rationale

Intervention sessions for the experimental group and parallel control group will be conducted at St. Ambrose Church in Dorchester, Massachusetts (see letter of support). This church currently houses the oldest Vietnamese Catholic community in Boston. The P.I. has had a long history of working with the church and the community. We will rent St. Ambrose Church's facility for the intervention sessions. This church is convenient and accessible by public transportation. Members of the experimental and parallel intervention groups will have their sessions at a different day and time. There will be eighteen intervention sessions and each participant will receive a stipend of $15 for each session.

We chose the Vietnamese Catholic community to implement this proposed study due to feasibility and convenience. Among the organized religions in the Vietnamese community, the Catholic community is the only one with the organizational structure to easily draw members together. Due to the nature of the proposed study, the generalizability of outcomes are limited; however, we hope this study can be implemented in other organized religious, racial, or cultural groups. We will document all aspects of this proposed intervention in detail and disseminate the information widely for future replications and implementations in other settings.

Theoretical Foundation

Although the majority of older Vietnamese Americans or immigrants have lived in the United States for more than a decade (US Bureau of the Census 2000), many have remained linguistically isolated. Loneliness and depression can be perceived as an old-age problem by older Vietnamese people. From our focus group meetings, we have noted that older Vietnamese individuals tend to attribute many of their daily problems to their old age—including lack of community supports, lack of language skills, unfamiliarity with public institutions such as hospitals, libraries, and social service agencies—and a host of other external factors. Human emotions including depression and loneliness can be attributed to both internal and external determinants (Weiner 1985). Research has found that older people with functional disabilities and health problems often attributed their disability and health status to old age (Sarkisian, Liu, Ensrud, Stone, and Mangione 2001; Williamson and Fried 1996). Evidence from attribution-retraining techniques and social cognitive behavioral therapy can be used as the theoretical guide for this proposed intervention (Sarkisian, Prohaska, Davis, and Weiner 2007). As suggested by this theoretical foundation, we will brief the participants at the beginning of each session about the benefits of making social contacts through different means. This will include group meetings, physical exercise, and communal prayers. They will also be reminded that they can change their own life situations by learning how to communicate with others, finding public resources for older people, and engaging in social activities.

DETAILED DESCRIPTION OF THE INTERVENTION

The proposed intervention will last six months. During the first three months, members of the experimental group will participate in a two-hour session, four times a month (weekly). In the subsequent three months, members will meet twice a month (biweekly). Each two-hour session consists of a 30-minute group meeting, a 30-minute presentation, a 15-minute meeting of organized religious activities, and a 30-minute tai chi session. The overarching goal for the four components of this intervention is to improve and enhance social connectedness, thereby reducing depression among participants.

Members of the parallel control group will participate in a 30-minute tai chi session four times a month for the first three months, and twice a month for the subsequent three months.

30-Minute Group Meeting: The purpose of this group meeting is to facilitate and encourage participants to connect with one another and build social networks. At the first meeting, the social worker will ask the participants to provide information concerning their phone number, e-mail, and personal interests or hobbies. Participants will be asked to sign a release form to allow the program to distribute their information to all members. They will be grouped into small groups with members who share similar hobbies or personal interests to encourage their interactions outside the group meetings. They will be encouraged to talk with one another as much as they can during the week. At the following meetings, members will be asked to share their life stories and continue to contact one another.

30-Minute Presentation: The purpose of this weekly presentation is to give participants both an incentive to stay in the program and also strengthen their social network infrastructure. For each session we will invite a bilingual speaker to present from one or more of the following topics: nutrition, the importance of physical activity, self-care, nursing care, elderly social services, elderly health-care services, and communicating with physicians or health-care interpreters, as well as any topic recommended by participants. The planned presentations also aim to provide participants with useful information that they can use to alter and enrich their life situations.

15-Minute Organized Religious Activities: The religious activities are to help participants connect to the community, to each other, and maintain an active and healthy life. A Vietnamese Catholic priest will lead this session. The priest will lead members in prayers and discussions of the social teaching of Catholics with respect to reaching out to neighbors and others. The priest will also use this religious session to encourage members to keep frequent contact with one another, family members, and friends or acquaintances. We will remind the participants that they have the power to change their life situations and find happiness.

30-Minute Tai Chi Session: Members of both experimental and parallel intervention control groups will participate in thirty-minute tai chi sessions, at different days and times. Tai chi is described as a series of exercises that are safe and suitable for older adults and those diagnosed with a chronic disease (Birdee, Wayne, Davis, Phillips, and Yeh 2009; Rogers, Larkey, and Keller 2009). The postures in tai chi emphasize balance, flexibility, and musculoskeletal strength training through a series of choreographed movements.

At this time, there are no universally recognized accrediting bodies for tai chi chuan, due to the vast number of teachers from many schools.

The proposed tai chi program will be taught by qualified instructors who have trained in tai chi for many years under a recognized teacher in the community. Fortunately, Boston—as one of the most cosmopolitan cities in the world—has many resources to choose from in terms of instructors who have years of experience in the training and teaching of tai chi chuan.

The proposed tai chi exercise program will begin with light stretching and a series of warm-up exercises derived from the Eight Pieces of the Brocade, also practiced for centuries in conjunction with tai chi chuan. This portion will take approximately ten minutes, and will safely prepare each participant for a series of static postures that focus on breathing, balance, and improving musculoskeletal development, particularly the lower body. Care will be made to ensure that each participant is comfortable and not overly exerted throughout the session. The instructor will work closely with participants to make corrections to postures and balance, while establishing a connection to each person. After ten minutes of static postures, the remaining ten minutes of each session will be devoted to learning the tai chi short form with twenty-four movements. It will very likely require multiple sessions before participants can recall all the choreographed movements in the form. The most important aspect to learning good tai chi, however, comes from the explanation of subtleties in shifting weight from one leg to another, along with correct positioning of the body in each movement. The instructor will work closely with participants to assist them in this process, while focusing on the particular differences of each individual.

DATA COLLECTION

We will collect data using a bilingual English–Vietnamese questionnaire, consisting of basic demographic characteristics such as age, sex, length of residence, along with outcome measures. The baseline data collection will be conducted through telephone interviews by our bilingual research assistant at the participants' residences. The interview will be approximately forty minutes. At three-month and six-month periods, the participants will fill out the questionnaire at home. This method of data collection works well with elderly immigrants (Aroian, Khatutsky, Tran, and Balsam 2001; Wu, Tran, and Amjad 2004). We will change the order of the questionnaire items and use different formats to minimize testing effects or questionnaire familiarity.

OUTCOME MEASURES

The UCLA Loneliness Scale

The UCLA Loneliness Scale was developed to assess subjective feelings of loneliness or social isolation. We will use version 3 of the UCLA Loneliness Scale (Russell 1996). In this version of the scale, the wording of the items and the response format has been simplified to facilitate administration of the measure to less-educated populations. This Loneliness Scale is one of the most widely used measures of loneliness. Scores on the loneliness scale have been found to predict a wide variety of mental and physical health outcomes.

We have already translated this scale to Vietnamese. Scores between 15 and 20 are considered a normal experience of loneliness. Scores above 30 indicate a person is experiencing severe loneliness.

Lubben Social Support Scale

The Lubben Social Network Scale (LSNS) is a brief instrument, designed to gauge social isolation in older adults by measuring perceived social support received from family and friends (Lubben 1988; Lubben 2006). It consists of an equally weighted sum of ten items used to measure size, closeness, and frequency of contacts within a respondent's social network. Dr. Lubben is a faculty consultant for this proposed project. The scores range from 0 to 50.

The Center for Epidemiologic Studies Depression Scale (CES-D)

This twenty-item scale (Radloff, 1977) was developed to measure symptoms of depression in community populations. The CESD scale has been translated into many languages and used in numerous studies as a screening tool for the presence of depressive illness. Scale items were selected to capture the major components of depression including depressed mood, feelings of worthlessness, feelings of hopelessness, loss of appetite, poor concentration, and sleep disturbance. This scale was translated into Vietnamese by the P.I. and has been validated successfully with this population (Tran, Ngo, and Conway 2003). The scale has scores from 0 to 60. The cutoff score of 16 and above is considered clinically depressed.

Religiosity Scale

A seven-item scale of religiosity will be used (Tran, Chan, and Nguyen 2010). This scale captures two dimensions of religiosity in terms of religious activities and coping resources. The scale has good reliability and factorial structure validity in a sample of Vietnamese adults. The scores range from 7 to 28.

Self-Efficacy Scale

We will use a ten-item self-efficacy scale (Jerusalem and Schwarzer 1992). This scale aims to assess a general sense of perceived self-efficacy in the context of daily hassles and adaptations after experiencing stressful life events. The scale has been translated into many languages, and we will translate this scale into Vietnamese for this proposed project. The scores range from 10 to 40.

Social Support Networks and Contacts

We will ask questions on the size of the participants' social support network, which will include family members, friends, neighbors, membership in social organizations, and frequency of contacts with support networks.

Demographic and Background Variables

We will ask questions about age, sex, marital status, education, income, length of residence in the United States, employment status, retirement status, and self-rated heath status.

Statistical Power and Data Analysis

We assessed the statistical power for the proposed sample size of this study using existing pilot survey data on psychological distress along with evidence from previous research by the P.I. on depression (Tran, Ngo, and Conway 2003; Tran 2008). We estimate that with an alpha level at 0.05 for a one-tailed test, and an equal sample of 30 for the experimental and control group, we will have adequate statistical power to perform our analyses. We will employ paired sample t-tests to examine changes in outcome measures in each group for our within-group analysis. We will use t-tests for the two independent samples to compare the changes in scores of the outcome measures between the two groups. Repeated measures through ANOVA will be used to examine the changes in scores in each group from baseline, at three and six months. We will also use graphical analyses using charts, graphs, and figures to summarize and present the outcomes in visual formats.

RESEARCH TEAM

Although this section is omitted here due to space, it is required for all research proposals. You need to present the qualifications of each team member and her or his role in the project. Read the instruction of the proposal carefully because each agency or foundation can have specific instructions you will need to follow.

Human Subjects

The project cannot be implemented without the approval of the Internal Review Board (IRB) of Boston College. At the time that we submit this proposal to the Aging Research Foundation, we will also submit the proposal and our Human Subject Plan to the Boston College IRB for review. In general, our Human Subject Plan will cover the following items: signed informed-consent letter explaining the benefits and potential but minimal harms of the interventions, protection of confidentiality, voluntary participation and termination, health and mental-health referral information, protection of the confidentiality of participation information, and data monitoring and data storage. At the intervention sites, we will provide the emergency contact information for all participants to staff members. The staff members will also have emergency contact information to access local hospitals, police and fire departments, and a mental-health counseling hotline for referrals if necessary. And all members of our research team, including research assistants, will have to complete the required human subject training program offered by the BC IRB.

Project Time Schedule: Detailed 12-Month Activities

We anticipate completing this project within twelve months. The following table illustrates our tasks and time frame:

– Months 1 to 3:
  Preparation
	– Months 4 to 9:
	  Implementation
		– Months 11 to 12
		– Post–Intervention Tasks

– Subject recruitment and screening, renting facilities, recruiting guest speakers, training group leaders, preparing overall implementation logistics, preparing and finalizing the data collection questionnaire, website designing, collecting baseline data	– Implementing and monitoring the interventions, collect outcome data at 3- month/6-month interventions	– Organizing data, cleaning data, analyzing data, preparing the final report, preparing manuscripts

Dissemination

We will present the results at local and national meetings and conferences. We will prepare manuscripts for publications in health, psychology, social sciences, and social work journals. More importantly, we will set up a website to upload detailed step-by-step information of this proposed project from conceptualization to implementation and results. The purpose of this website is to not only report but enable future replications of the proposed intervention model for older adults from various ethnic groups. We hope the proposed model can be a template for a community-based intervention program that is culturally appropriate, feasible, and sustainable for older persons and other marginalized populations.

APPENDIX C

Proposal: Example 2

Title of Research Proposal:

Defending Childhood Initiative Family Nurturing Program[*]

We omitted the Table of Contents and Appendixes. This sample proposal is provided to us by Mr. Nam V Pham, executive director of Viet-AID. He graciously gave us his permission to reproduce this proposal in this book for our readers.

I. PROJECT ABSTRACT

Agency Name, City, State:

Viet-AID
42 Charles Street, Suite E
Dorchester, MA 02122

Program: Southeast Asian Shelter—Basic Center Program
Proposed service area: Greater Boston area, Massachusetts
Amount of Federal funding requested
    – for 12-month period: $188,675
    – Proposed model of program: Bilingual and Bicultural Shelter & Support Services
    – Target population (if applicable):   Southeast Asian Youth & Families
    – POC, name, phone, and e-mail: Long Nguyen, (857) 919-0566
    – long.nguyen@te-enterprise.com
    – Number of youth to receive services
    – during the 36-month project: 100 Southeast Asian youth annually

Over the past few years, police officers, court personnel, parents, and community leaders have expressed concerns over an increasing number of runaway and homeless youth in poor Southeast Asian communities of Greater Boston. These young people have run away from homes due to cultural differences and parental abuse and neglect. Once on the streets, they are at risk of being sexually exploited or abused by adults for pleasure or profit. In addition, they often engage in shoplifting, survival sex or drug dealing in order to provide for their basic needs.

Viet-AID and our Partners seek funding support from the Basic Center Program to launch a Southeast Asian Shelter to provide emergency shelter and support services to runaway and homeless Southeast Asian youth. The overarching goal of the shelter is to help youth transition to safe and appropriate living arrangements where they receive supportive and caring services, build lasting relationships with adults, reconnect with their families, and develop knowledge and skills to become independent, self-sufficient, contributing members of community.

Our approach incorporates youth development principles and provides shelter and support services in a culturally and linguistically appropriate manner. We will conduct a community outreach and prevention education campaign to increase awareness about our services, runaway and homeless issues and prevention strategies. Youth who are interested in our program will receive individualized assessment and develop a service plan to reconnect with their families and to develop skills and knowledge to become self-sufficient. They will receive shelter and support services, which include individual and group counseling, family counseling when appropriate, and referral services to education, employment, health care, housing, recreational, and cultural programs and services.

Our project will increase community awareness among the 30,000 plus Southeast Asian immigrants and refugees living in Greater Boston. They will help at least 100 runaway and homeless Southeast Asian youth transition to a safe and appropriate living arrangement, reconnect with their families and develop knowledge and skills to become self-sufficient and contributing members of their community and families. They will also prevent at-risk from running away from their families.

II. PROJECT DESCRIPTION

A. Objectives and Need for Assistance

Over the past few years, police officers, court personnel, parents, and community leaders have expressed concerns over an increasing number of runaway and homeless Southeast Asian youth in poor Southeast Asian communities of Greater Boston. These young people have had conflicts at home, performed poorly in school, become involved in substance abuse and gang, and eventually run away from homes due primarily to cultural conflicts between parents and youth and parental abuse and neglect. Once on the streets, they are at risk of being sexually exploited or abused by adults for pleasure or profit. In addition, they often engage in shoplifting, survival sex or drug dealing in order to provide for their basic needs.

In response, Viet-AID and our Community Partners have formed a community-family-school partnership consisting of public schools, non-profit organizations, and cultural associations to offer a range of supports and opportunities to Southeast Asian youth and families to prevent youth violence, improve academic achievement and help youth become responsible and contributing members. The partnership includes Viet-AID, Dorchester House Multi-Service Center, Dorchester Youth Collaborative, Vietnamese American Civic Association, Close to Home, the Boston Police Department – Area C11, cultural associations and faith-based organizations, and local middle and high schools. (*Appendix C: Partnership Chart & Program Model*).

1. Project Goals and Objectives

Viet-AID and our Partners seek funding support from the Basic Center Program to launch a Southeast Asian Shelter to provide bilingual and bicultural emergency shelter and support services to underserved runaway and homeless Southeast Asian youth. The overcharging goal of the Shelter is to help youth transition to safe and appropriate living arrangements where they receive supportive and caring services, build lasting relationships with adults, reconnect with their families, and develop knowledge and skills to become independent, self-sufficient, contributing members of society.

We accomplish this overarching goal through the following objectives:

Objective A: Conduct community outreach and education among the 30,000 plus Southeast Asian community in Greater Boston to increase awareness about our services and to prevent youth from running away from home.

Objective B: Provide information about our services as well as how to prevent youth from running away from home to 300 youth and parents who contact our program.

Objective C: Conduct comprehensive individual assessments and prepare service plan for 100 runaway youth.

Objective D: Provide emergency shelter and support services to 100 youth who are enrolled in our shelter program.

Objective E: Provide referral services to connect 75 youth to health care, education, recreational, and cultural programs

Objective F: Provide family counseling to help 75 you to help them reconnect and reestablish relationships with their families.

Objective G: Provide after care services to at least 50 youth who have successfully secured stable and permanent housing and be re-connected with their families.

In Section B of this application, we detail the measurable outcomes and long term results that we expect to achieve through program activities which are tailored to address this critical community issue and accomplish these objectives.

2. Needs for Assistance

Approximately 21% of the 30,000 plus Southeast Asian population in Greater Boston are children and youth between the ages of 5-18 years old, who are living in a state of distress due to two key factors: *impoverished family and disadvantaged community*. Their healthy development and progression into productive adulthood is at a significant risk. They live in a communities riddled with poverty and crime, where the support needed to foster growth and healthy development are either overburdened or scarce. Their parents are under considerable stress as they attempt to provide for essential family needs often facing language and cultural barriers that reverse parent-child roles and create tensions in the family. The lure of the street life (either gangs or other illicit activities) is an ever-present force. As a result, Southeast Asian children and youth have become more prone to youth violence and runaway from homes.

On Aug. 13, 2007, nearly two dozen Vietnamese-American teenagers stomped, kicked, and punched two others, a 13-year-old girl and a 15-year-old boy, behind a church in the Dorchester neighborhood of Boston. The victims were left unconscious. During the fight, the girl's neck was distended and the boy broke a facial bone near his eye[1] (*Appendix C: News Articles*). This was one of a series of youth violent incidents in the community from 2007 through 2008 that brought community attention to a growing youth violence and runaway problem in the Southeast Asian community.

In response to the cry for help by Southeast Asian parents and community leaders, Viet-AID worked with the Boston Police Department, Dorchester Youth Collaborative (DYC), Dorchester House Multi-Service Center (Dorchester House), Vietnamese American Civic Association (VACA), Close to Home (C2O), and the Southeast Asian community-based faith-based organizations to conduct a needs assessment to gain a better understanding of the problems and causes of increased youth violence and runaway teens. The needs assessment included a review of existing literature and studies, three community forums with parents and youth, a survey of 100 Southeast Asian youth in Dorchester conducted by the Harvard Youth Prevention Project[2], and a series of interviews with police officers, juvenile court personnel, and community stakeholders.

The needs assessment revealed that Southeast Asian children and youth today have become more prone to youth violence, poor academic performance, substance abuse, gang involvement, and runaway. Southeast Asian runaway, homeless and street youth share many background characteristics and experience often associated with runaway and homeless youth. They come from low-income communities and their families are disproportionately poor. They have a history of family disruption and many grew up in single-parent households, and a significant number of these youth have not had any contact with their non-custodial parent. They have difficulties in schools; at homes, they experience family conflicts, abuse and neglect due primarily to cultural differences.

The Harvard Youth Survey yielded serious findings about Southeast Asian youth in great Boston. The study found that over 50% of youth reported witnessing one or more acts of violence and/or experienced one or more type of victimization in the past year; over 50% felt that it was somewhat unsafe or very unsafe at home, in their neighborhood or at school; 23% carried a knife and 10% carried a gun; 70% reported that gunshot, gun violence and shooting is a problem; 30% confronted police officers or were with the Department of Youth Service; and 21% used marijuana during the past year, 38% reported substance abuse in the past 30 days. Assisting with the study, we also discovered a sub population of children of Vietnamese Amerasian refugees. Rejected by Vietnamese society and neglected by their parents, an overwhelming majority of Vietnamese Amerasian children and youth are involved in drugs or violence, and face issues of school dropout, teen pregnancy, and runaway. The study also noted child prostitution involving girls and boys aged 11 to 15 years old. In 2007, a covert operation by the Boston Police Department entitled "Polar Express" arrested 23 Dorchester men in the largest Vietnamese drug seizure in US history. In the same year, an Asian gang's "beatdown" video, distributed widely on the Internet, showed 20 gang members beating two helpless teens, aged 13 and 14, in Dorchester.

---

[1]Vietnamese Parents Struggle with Children's Violence and Gangs. New England Ethnic News. March 2008. Grim video lays bare Vietnamese teen violence. Dorchester Reporter. January 2008. Disconnected- The city's Vietnamese population is turning to Harvard for help in understanding the problems its youth are facing - problems that are often manifested through violence. Boston Globe. May 2008.

[2]The Harvard Youth Prevention Project agreed to conduct the youth survey with Southeast Asian Youth to help parents understand youth violence problems that Southeast Asian youth faces.

The assessment further found a steady decline in academic performance among Southeast Asian students. "It used to be that the Southeast Asian students were always the best in my classes....Now, it isn't like that. I still get some good students who are Southeast Asian, but a lot of them seem even worse than the others. And it's weird, because these kids today were all born here and speak good English." These observations seemed to echo opinions we have heard from many professionals in education, law enforcement, and social services in Greater Boston and nationwide. The Harvard Youth Survey found that 36% of the students reported receiving Cs, Ds and Fs in the past 12 months, 33% reported being truant three or more days during this time, and 36% reported having severe depressive symptoms. A 2009 study by the Gaston Institute entitled "English Learners in Boston Public School" found that the drop-out rate among Southeast Asian students in the Boston Public School system increased from 4% in 2003 to 10.3% in 2006 since the elimination of the bilingual education program in 2003[3].

Studies by prominent social researchers as well as police officers, court personnel, social workers, parents, and youth in our interviews and survey attribute three key factors – poor and culturally-conflicted family, lack of culturally and linguistically appropriate services and poor community– to the increase in youth violence, poor academic performance and runaway among Southeast Asian children and youth.

Due to socioeconomic, cultural conflicts and other cultural factors, many poor Southeast Asian children and youth do not receive adequate support from their families. These factors have been found to contribute to drug use, substance abuse, youth violence, and runaway among Southeast Asian children[4]. Census 2000 shows that almost 26% of Southeast Asian families in Massachusetts live below the federal poverty guidelines and over 50% are low-income[5]. For those with children under 17 years old, the percentage of families who live below the federal poverty guidelines increases to almost 35%. Most Southeast Asian adults are first generation refugees; they have low educational attainment, limited language skills and no transferable job skills. As a result, Southeast Asian immigrant and refugee parents must work multiple, low-wage jobs with no benefits and no career advancement. They also often work 12 hours a day and 6-7 days a week and have little or no time to supervise their children during after school hours. Furthermore, Southeast Asian families often find resettlement in the U.S. difficult; they must learn English quickly, find jobs and housing, enroll children in schools, and adjust to new systems, values, and expectations. They often worry about family members left behind in uncertain conditions, and suffer from trauma, depression, and post-traumatic stress syndrome. Because many Southeast Asian families in Greater Boston live below poverty, they tend to live in overcrowded apartments and houses where extended families and more than one family live. The following quotes, taken from our interviews with Southeast Asian families, are illustrative of tensions which exist in many Southeast Asian families:

"My parents are so weird—they don't speak much English, they wear old clothes, and do not know how to do things in this culture. I have to translate and explain basic stuff to them. They don't understand the things I go through at school or what my life is like here—they act like we are still in Lao."

-Laotian Young Person

---

[3]English Learners in Boston Public Schools: Enrollment, Engagement and Academic Outcomes of Native Speakers of Cape Verdean Creole, Chinese Dialects, Haitian Creole, Spanish, and Vietnamese. Gaston Institute. University of Massachusetts at Boston.

[4]Acculturative Dissonance, Ethnic Identify, and Youth Violence. Thao Le and Gary Stockdale (2006). Delinquency and Acculturation in the Twenty-First Century: A Decade's Change in a Vietnamese American Community. Min-Zhou and Carl L. Bankston III. (2006).

[5]Institute for Asian American Studies. University of Massachusetts at Boston.

"I love my son very much, and try to be patient and teach him to behave well. But there are times he just won't listen to me—in Vietnam, I would hit him to let him know I'm serious and I love him, but they tell us that is not allowed here. I do not know what to do, and his behavior is getting out of control."

-Vietnamese Parent

Culturally, Southeast Asian parents face numerous challenges that severely limit their capacity to fulfill their roles in guiding, supporting, and disciplining their children. Those with limited English skills are dependent on their children to translate and assist with managing the home and family, creating a role-reversal which undermines parents' authority over their children. Their authoritarian parenting style is found to be the least productive among different parenting styles and to cause delinquency and runaway among Southeast Asian youth[6]. Because they are not allowed to use their traditional disciplining methods such as spanking or scolding, they feel frustrated and powerless and do not know exactly what they should or could do. Many parents are frustrated with the system, upset with the law, the court system, and probation officers. They feel that they often are being accused for abusing their children and question how they can facilitate a system that will cooperate with them to lessen the frustration. They feel that whatever they try to do, there are obstacles. The system tells them that it is "illegal" to discipline according to Southeast Asian cultural mores which makes it challenging for parents to find the best solution to work well with their children. Parents further believe that when their children refuse to listen and/or even talk back to them, their children are "bad children." And they often wrongly expect that their children should understand the meaning of scolding, controlling, or spanking. To parents, scolding, controlling, or spanking conveys a message of love and care. The challenge for the parents in the United States is that their children are being raised in a country and society with different customs, making it challenging for them to understand the intended meaning of scolding, controlling, or spanking that their parents use to convey love and care.

Among Southeast Asian youth, social researchers found a substantial gap between adolescents and their parents with regard to views on traditional values such as obedience to parents and respect for authority[7]. According to Dr. Min Zhou, who has studied both Vietnamese refugee and Vietnamese American youth over the past 20 years, the opposing pressures from parents and peer groups create dilemmas for young people that affect all aspects of their lives. Southeast Asian youth often find themselves straddling two social worlds. At home parents put pressure on children to work hard and achieve academically, while on the street they are advised to rebel against authority, reject achievement goals, and engage in consumption standards higher than those of their parents[8]. In our interviews and focus groups with youth, Southeast Asian youth often complain that their parents are too strict, while parents complain that they are not receiving filial piety and respect and feel threatened by their children's embrace of Western culture and values.

Despite major problems and challenges facing Southeast Asian youth and parents, there are no culturally and linguistically appropriate shelter and support services that are available to help runaway and homeless and at-risk youth and families. In our focus groups, both parents and youth identified the lack of culturally

---

[6]Lily Lam (2002). The effects of Parental Involvement on the Academic Achievement of Low-income Asians. The Berkeley McNair Research Journal. Tran, Lieu A., Spring 2003, Factors leading to incarceration among Southeast Asian youth, UC Berkeley. Thao Le and Gary Stockdale (2006). Acculturative Dissonance, Ethnic Identify, and Youth Violence.

[7]Nguyen, N.A., & Williams, H.L (1989). Transition from East to West: Vietnamese adolescents and their parents. *The American Academy of Child and Adolescent Psychiatry, 28*, 505–515. Southeast Asian Fathers' Experiences with Adolescents: Challenges and Change by Zha Blong Xiong, Ph.D. and Daniel F. Detzner, Ph.D. *Hmong Studies Journal, 2005, 6*: 1-23.

8   Zhou, Min and Carl L. Bankston III. 2006. "Delinquency and Acculturation in the Twenty-First Century: A Decade's Change in a Vietnamese American Community."

and linguistically appropriate services for Southeast Asian youth and parents as one of the top challenges. This sentiment echoes findings from studies by the Urban Institute and the Federal Office of Refugee Resettlement that immigrant and refugee children and youth face even more barriers in accessing quality services and support due to language and cultural barriers. While our Partners have operated afterschool programs, these programs do not have the capability to provide shelter and support services to at-risk and runaway and homeless youth. In addition, there exist no bilingual and bicultural programs that provide family counseling and support services to Southeast Asian parents.

Studies further attribute the growth of Southeast Asian delinquency, youth violence, substance abuse, drug use, and runaway to the influence of socioeconomic marginalization in their neighborhood and community[9]. The majority of Southeast Asian youth and families live in Dorchester, one of the poorest neighborhoods in Boston. Dorchester, dominated by minority communities, has some of the highest poverty and crime rates in Massachusetts and the nation. With a population of approximately 130,000, Dorchester is Boston's largest neighborhood —diverse in terms of language and ethnicity (Spanish, Cape Verdean Creole, Haitian Creole, and Southeast Asian) and social capital (non-profit organizations, small businesses, civic organizations). Seventy-three percent (73%) of Dorchester's residents are people of color and of these 34% (20,823) are under the age of 18. Dorchester has the largest percentage of children under the age of 18, more than any other neighborhood in Boston. Sixty-two percent (62%) of the Boston Public School student population lives in Dorchester; this population is projected to increase 28% by 2010 and 74% of these students are eligible for free lunch.

Given the large number of residents under 18, ethnic diversity that can result in cliques that lead to gangs, and the highest rate of violence that Boston has seen in years, Dorchester's young people are at a high risk of gang involvement, violence and runaway. In 2006, 42% of 900 Boston public high school students surveyed said they knew well or were related to someone who had been killed. Homicides in Boston increased 23% between 2004 and 2006, with an 11-year high of 75 homicides in 2006, according to the Boston Indicators Project of The Boston Foundation, which was published in 2008. During the same period, non-fatal shootings in Boston increased by 48%, with 71% of all the shootings occurring in police districts B2, B3, and C11, which includes Dorchester[10]. Of the 341 shootings in 2005, 50% of the victims were between the ages of 14 and 21 years old. Of the 26 identified homicide offenders in 2005, 46% were under the age of 24, and 65% of fatal and non-fatal shootings in Boston during the first 6 months of 2006 involved gang members[11]. There have been 7 homicides in area C11 and over 140 aggravated assaults since the beginning of 2009. The majority of those homicides were people under the age of 21. The Boston Police Department has designated 4 hot spots – small geographic areas with disproportionately high rates of crime – in our proposed service areas: Ronan Park/Hamilton, Bowdoin/Geneva, Fields Corner, and the Washington Street Corridor.

3. Service Location

The proposed Southeast Asian Shelter is located within walking distance of the facilities and offices operated by Viet-AID and our Partners. The Shelter as well as our offices and facilities are located in Fields

---

[9]Bankston, C.L., & Caldas, S.J. (1996a).Adolescents and deviance in a Vietnamese American community: A theoretical synthesis. *Deviant Behavior,* 17(2), 159–81.

[10]Report of the Special Committee on Youth Violent Crime Prevention: Working Together to Increase the Peace," City of Boston, June 2006.

[11]Understanding Homicide and Non-Fatal Gun Violence Trends in Boston," Braga, Anthony A. John F. Kennedy School of Government, Harvard University

Corner, Dorchester and adjacent to a subway station and several major bus lines, making our services easily accessible by all Southeast Asian families and youth. As described above, Dorchester is home to a majority of low-income Southeast Asian families in Greater Boston and a destination for all Southeast Asian families in Greater Boston as well as in Massachusetts for the following reasons:

– Dorchester is home to hundreds of Southeast Asian businesses such as restaurants, supermarkets, travel and immigration services, etc. Most Southeast Asian families come to Dorchester for food, clothing, and other services.

Dorchester is home to a number of non-profit organizations that provide bilingual and bicultural social services, health care, job training, housing counseling, etc. It is also home to five faith-based organizations that provide services in Southeast Asian languages.

Dorchester is easily accessible by major highways and public transportation.

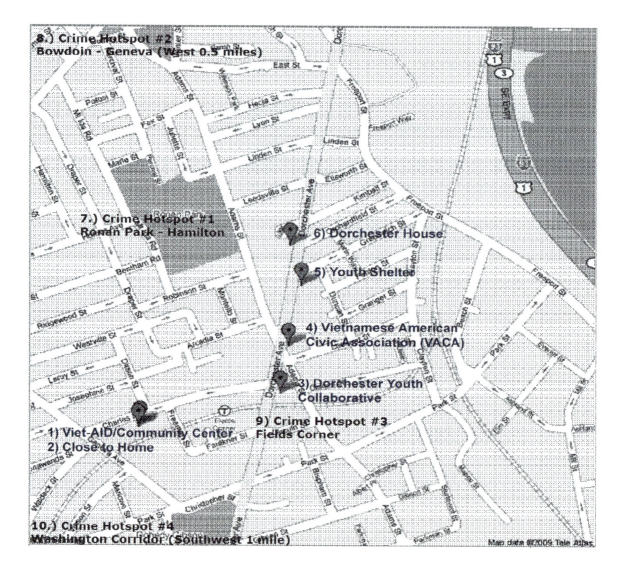

4. Data on Runaway, Homeless and Street Youth

In the past few years, data and reports from the Boston Police Department, our Partner - Dorchester Youth Collaborative and Boston Juvenile Court show an annual average of 200 plus Asian runaways reported along the Dorchester Avenue Corridor in Greater Boston. However, we have learned though our community meetings and one-on-one interviews with parents, religious leaders and community members that the runaway problem among Southeast Asian children and youth is much more severe than reported. The Boston Police Department and the community-based organizations believe that the actual number of runaway is higher than documented since many runaways go unreported. Many times parents do not report their children as runaway due to fear of involvement with law enforcement agencies and shame on their family. Parents are often frightened into silence by the adult leaders of Asian gangs with whom Southeast Asian runaway youth often become affiliated. In addition, the Juvenile Courts have very stringent guidelines regarding what constitutes a "runaway." They will not process a runaway youth, who has not been reported to a law enforcement agency, or a runaway who claims he or she was told to leave home, or a runaway who has returned home voluntarily or involuntarily.

B. Results or Benefits Expected

1. Number of Youth to be Served

A minimum of 100 youth will receive bilingual and bicultural emergency shelter and support services through our Southeast Asian Shelter each year. Our shelter, while available to all runaway and homeless youth, will target Southeast Asian Youth ages 13 through 18 years of age, who are having serious family problems that lead them to leave home or threaten to do so. Further, we will serve 300 youth through non-residential services. Through a comprehensive youth development approach that looks to the young person to set their goals in partnership with professional staff members, youth will receive shelter and support services, build lasting relationships with adults, reconnect with their families, and develop knowledge and skills to become independent, self-sufficient, contributing members of society.

2. Overall Quantitative Outcomes & Relationships between Activities & Outcomes

Through a comprehensive continuum of services, this joint project between Viet-AID and our Partners seeks to accomplish the following qualitative and quantitative outcomes:

– Activities	– Outputs	– Outcomes/Impact
– Conduct community outreach & prevention education. – Conduct street-based outreach to identify and establish relationship with runaway/homeless youth.	– Community outreach and prevention education: – 150 contacts with runaway & homeless youth.	– Outcome 1: 30,000 plus Southeast Asian youth and families increase awareness about our services, issues related to homeless and runaway youth.

– Conduct presentations at community-based organizations, civic groups, courts, etc. – Conduct parenting education workshops. – Distribute program brochures and fliers at Southeast Asian and other business establishments. – Conduct interviews & publish articles on Southeast Asian print and electronic media. – Provide shelter and support services to runaway and homeless youth and their families. – Conduct individual assessment and create service plan. – Provide shelter and support services. – Provide individual and group counseling services to youth. – Provide referral services to connect youth to education, recreational, health care, and other support services: – Sexual/substance abuse counseling and treatment. – Education and/or career development. – Health care (including health, mental health, dental, etc.) – Access to social, recreational and community service activities. – Housing search. – Provide after care services youth who have been discharged.	– Conduct 12 monthly presentations at non-profit organizations, civic associations, etc. – Publish/conduct 12 monthly newspaper articles & interviews. – Distribute 5,000 brochures & fliers. – Conduct 4 quarterly parenting workshops. – Intake, Assessment & Service Plan Development – 100 youth complete intake and assessment and develop service plan. – Emergency shelter and support Services – 100 youth receive emergency shelter service. – 100 youth receive one-on-one and group counseling. – 75 receive family counseling services – 75 youth are connected to services including vocational/educational training, drug/substance abuse counseling, housing search, health care, recreational, and community service. – Aftercare service – 50 youth will receive after care services after discharge.	– Indicators: # of contacts with runaway & homeless youth; # of presentations conducted; # of newspaper articles published and interviews conducted; # of brochures & fliers distributed; # of parenting workshops conducted. – Outcome 2: Youth reconnect with families and return home. – Indicators: # of youth who reconnect with their families and return home. – Outcome 3: Youth secure safe, stable and permanent housing. – Indicator: # of youth who secure long-term, stable and safe living arrangement. – Outcome 4: Youth become independent, self-sufficient, and contributing members of community. – Indicator: # of youth who become engaged in education; # of youth who become employed or participate in vocational training program; # of youth who participate in recreational activities and community service projects. – Outcome 3: Decrease number of youth who run away from home. – Indicator: # and % of reported runaway youth per year; # of at-risk youth who decided not to run away after receiving prevention counseling and support.

3. Evaluation Plan

Viet-AID will use the above logic model as a foundation for our evaluation plan. The logic model describes the relationship between the project's goal, objectives and activities, and the project's short and long-term benefit. To learn about the proposed project's effectiveness and long-term impact, we seek to measure: (i) Process outcomes: Whether we provided outreach and prevention education, shelter and support services; and after care services as planned, and (ii) Outcomes: Did runaway and homeless youth who receive emergency shelter and support services reconnect with their families, secure safe and stable living arrangement, and develop knowledge and skills to become independent, self-sufficient and contributing community members.

The evaluation will focus on collecting two types of information: (i) Information about the project's proposed and implemented activities; and (ii) Information about the project's proposed outcomes and outcomes achieved at the end of the project. We plan to develop new tools to track and measure our results and will also review and collaborate to review existing data collection sources which track longer-term benefits.

The Project Team will initially use the following mechanisms to evaluate the project:

Team Evaluation – Regular team meetings to review progress, ensure we are on target with tasks and milestones, review how well the project design is working, and address any challenges.

Case Management Data – Viet-AID and our Partners will use a common case management tool to track demographic and family data on the youth who receive our services.

Participant Feedback – We will develop systems for "participant feedback" after six months and one year of receiving services. The survey will solicit information about why participants ran away, what were the factors that influenced the participants to decide to access shelter and support services, the effectiveness of the shelter and support services, and benefits of their participation. We will also solicit feedback from our partners, parents and youth.

Program Impact Surveys – We will develop a third evaluation instrument, based on the Colorado Trust Youth Participant Survey, an evidence-based tool used to measure youth development. This instrument will be administered to all program participants. It consists of 46 items addressing six dimensions: sense of self, positive core values, positive life choices, life skills, cultural competency, and community involvement.

Survey and Interview with Partner Referral Agencies – We will periodically meet with or survey agencies or shelters where we make referrals in order to assess the strategies and quality of services received by the young people.

Existing Data Collection and City-Wide Trends – We will annually review crime statistics, school graduation data, and data from referral agencies such as shelters and courts in order to develop a bench line against which we can measure indicators of the mid-term and longer term benefits of the project.

Findings from these team evaluation and participant feedbacks will be used to adjust program design and improve program effectiveness.

Approach

Viet-AID and our Partners will implement a comprehensive approach that helps Southeast Asian youth transition to safe and appropriate living arrangements where they receive shelter and support services, build lasting relationships with adults, reconnect with their families, and develop knowledge and skills to become independent, self-sufficient, contributing members of community. Our approach incorporates youth development principles and provides comprehensive services in a linguistically and culturally appropriate manner.

Youth Development Approach

Viet-AID and our Partners incorporate the Family and Youth Services Bureau's Youth Development Approach in our program design. This program design is holistic, strengths-based, and comprehensive, giving power back to the community to resolve issues. We view children/youth as positive, creative, and resourceful individuals with an amazing ability for emotional resiliency. Services provided by Viet-AID and our Partners have always honored their developmental needs. We will involve youth in all aspects of services, and create positions where youth can be placed in responsible roles guided by responsible adults. We also view communities as being in a developmental process and emphasize that, like people, communities must take ownership of their challenges and opportunities, especially when they concern society's greatest resource: children and adolescents. Members of the community should provide youth with caring and responsible relationships that promote their healthy development.

Viet-AID and our Partners believe that the community must respond to this challenge and seek solutions within the framework of youth development approach. We will help the community develop its existing strengths and enhance and coordinate its resources, creating opportunities to positively engage young people. All communities have within them the potential to develop in a healthy manner. We understand this potential and will engage the community in embracing the responsibility of promoting a healthy attitude toward adolescents, providing youth with mentoring relationships and other opportunities to develop to their greatest potential. We will work with all sectors of the community (youth, parents, businesses, media, schools, community organizations serving youth, civic, volunteer groups, etc.) to implement this youth development approach.

Viet-AID and our Partners will guide the community to shift from a deficit perspective to a strengths-based perspective of youth, families and the community. If adults begin viewing adolescents as resources who are willing to learn and practice skills, youth will develop into responsible for competent individuals. The community must expose adolescents to mentoring and role-modeling opportunities where they can be under the guidance of and encouragement of caring adults. Adolescents need more than brief interventions. Rather, they need nurturing and sustained relationships with adults that will be there for them through their achievements and failings. Therefore, a development approach must be long-term and comprehensive if it is to promote lasting and positive change.

Viet-AID and Our Partners propose to use the youth development approach to engage youth in leadership, social, recreational, cultural and employment activities that will promote their emotional, cultural, social and character development:

Peer-to-peer support services: Viet-AID and our Partners will hire runaway and homeless youth to work with street workers to assist in the design and implementation of the community outreach and education campaign to increase community awareness about the runaway and homeless youth problem, causes, what services are available, and how to access these services. The campaign will consist of presentations at community meetings and other strategies detailed in the "Education and Prevention" section described above.

Leadership on Community Council: Viet-AID and our Partners have recently established a Community Council consisting of youth, Vietnamese teachers, Vietnamese parents, representatives from community-based organizations, and businesses. The Community Council is a forum for exchanging ideas about how to decrease youth violence, decrease runaway, and improve student achievement. Some of the major roles and responsibilities of the Council include: conducting on-going needs assessment to identify problems and challenges facing Vietnamese students and families; conducting on-going research to assess program/ policy and how their impact on the community; promoting leadership development among parents and students so that they can design and implement campaigns to advocate on behalf of the community; and working with Viet-AID to design and implement a sustainability plan. This plan might involve advocating with appropriate agencies for increased funding support for quality afterschool programs, attending meetings with private foundations and corporations to encourage their support, organizing fundraising events, etc.

Leadership on Board of Directors: We will provide opportunities for youth in the program to serve on the Boards of our agencies as well as other non-profit partners in the area. Viet-AID and our Partners will provide training to help youth develop knowledge and skills to effectively become board members of our agencies and the other non-profit agencies in the area. Topics will include basic roles and responsibilities of a non-profit board, financial management, governance, and non-profit programs and strategies. Serving as Board members, youth will be directly involved in leading our agencies to adopt positive youth development approaches, developing programs to effectively address problems and challenges facing runaway and homeless youth, and advocating for more public and private funding for street outreach programs.

Our Voices: Using Artography, youth will work with adults and parents to design and implement an intergenerational art and cultural programs that validate personal histories – refugee experience, explain cultural differences, honor traditions, promote understanding, and link generations and cultures. One of the potential project ideas is to present how cultural difference influences decision by young people to run away from homes through either performance art or digital photography.

Democracy Forum: Teens, with strong adult sponsors, are best able to educate the public and policy makers about the issues that drive teens into running away and homelessness. Interested youth in the Shelter will be trained as community organizers. These teens will conduct research and education campaigns. They will make presentations to the public and meet with elected officials to educate them about runaway and homelessness issues. The Democracy Forum will develop agendas and work with others to improve the lives and futures of runaway and homeless youth.

Language and cultural workshops and events: Youth will have the ability to attend workshops on Saturday whose topics may include Vietnamese culture and tradition, refugee resettlement history (conducted by parents and/or leaders in the community). They may also organize and plan cultural activities in the community and at area schools year round. These can include: Vietnamese "Tet" or New Year, Moon Festival, and International Day celebrations, and other workshops such as storytelling and cooking.

Program Operation (Mandatory Services)

Youth come to Viet-AID through a variety of means – on the recommendation of a friend, parental decision, referral from another agency or institutions, or through another program of Viet-AID and our partners, most notably the street outreach program. Through aggressive outreach and prevention education services, youth and families learn about our program and access our shelter and support services that are inclusive, voluntary, and open to any youth 13 through 18 years of age in the Greater Boston area.

Outreach and prevention education campaign: We will conduct a comprehensive outreach and prevention education campaign to inform youth and families about our services, increase community awareness and response to the problems with runaway and homeless youth, establish and maintain community linkages, expand and develop new resources, and solicit community support. The campaign will consist of the following key activities:

Street-based outreach: Our Partners, DYC and the Boston Police Department – Area C11, has street outreach vans as part of their street outreach services to runaway and homeless youth. The Street Outreach team consists of 2 full-time staff, staff and 4 peer educators who visit places frequented by runaway and homeless youth to develop positive relationships, build trust, and to distribute bilingual literature outlining agency services. Outreach efforts are directed at street youth and potential runaway and homeless youth not under the care of the government such as protective services, foster care and the courts.

Agency-based outreach: We will conduct regular presentations, targeting civic groups, parent groups, faith communities, agencies, and institutions such as schools, and law enforcement. We target under-served Southeast Asian youth and families, especially those who are in alternative education programs and in other facilities such as correctional institutions, shelters, etc. We will also distribute brochures and fliers about runaway and homeless youth risk factors, prevention strategies and resources at over 300 plus Southeast Asian and mainstream business establishments in Greater Boston.

Media-based Outreach: We will conduct monthly media-based outreach activities that reach the 30,000 plus Southeast Asian population in Greater Boston. The monthly media-based outreach activities will include interviews with Southeast Asian radio and TV programs and newspaper articles.

Parenting Workshops: We will conduct four quarterly parenting workshops to increase awareness among Southeast Asian parents about runaway and homeless youth risk factors, prevention strategies and resources, and parenting skills.

Individual Intake Process: Every youth that seeks admission is given an individual, confidential intake interview. In every instance, we seek to help the youth remain in their home and provide resources and referrals to help resolve their problems. However, many of them are already living on the streets or in unsafe living arrangements. Youth are given information on program expectations, and encouraged to come into the program. We can pick youth up or provide a mobile intake for youth at Family Court, hospitals, schools, jails, etc. Admission is available 24 hours a day. The first objective of the intake interview is to address emergency/immediate needs the youth has, such as food, clothing, warmth or medical care. If there is an emergency need beyond the scope of the shelter such as medical/psychiatric emergency, the youth is unwilling to enter the program, doesn't meet eligibility criteria for the shelter, or if no beds are available, appropriate referral services or non-residential services are immediately provided.

If there are no emergency needs, the intake interview commences. The interview usually lasts about an hour and a half and begins with a thorough explanation of the services available through the program, expectations of residents, and a clear message of the voluntary nature of shelter care. The shelter doors are locked from the outside, not the inside. Youth cannot be forced to stay if they are unwilling. We will serve all youth that come to us for help, but the shelter intake criteria are:

– Youth voluntarily desires admission
– In 13-17 years old (under age 13 youth may be accepted based on individual need in an emergency situation, where there are no other safe alternatives)
– Willing to refrain from the use of alcohol and drugs
– Able to accept and understand house rules and guidelines
– Will participate in case planning with staff
– Does not appear to be a danger to self or others
– Understands and agrees to parent/guardian notification

If the youth meets the criteria and is interested in services, general background data is gathered. Youth are asked to provide information on the nature of the problem, describe their relationships with parents, siblings, peers, and teachers. Their medical history, prior counseling experiences, runaway episodes, educational relationships, and use of drugs, alcohol, and other toxic substances is discussed. This process includes a family functioning and drug assessment, and completion of the RHYMIS form. Each youth also establishes their initial goals for our care.

Once the intake is completed, the youth is introduced to staff and residents, given a shelter tour, assigned a bedroom, given any needed personal hygiene supplies, and assigned a case manager that will assist in securing all needed services and provide individual and family counseling. The intake staff member will then contact the parents to gain verbal consent for services and arrange for written consent within 24 hours of admission. The only exceptions are instances where a young person alleges serious abuse or the parents cannot be reached. In the former situation, Child Protective Services is notified immediately, and in the latter, the police are contacted to assist in reaching the parents.

Temporary Shelter: Viet-AID will apply for a state license to provide emergency shelter to runway and homeless youth in our 12-room rooming house facility. Viet-AID developed this rooming house in 2004 to provide quality and affordable housing to low-income individuals. The facility meets and exceeds all licensing requirements required by the Massachusetts Department of Early Education and Care, the state agency responsible for licensing and monitoring child care and residential care facilities which include temporary shelter facility. The facility is conveniently located within walking distance to our offices and facilities, a subway station and major bus lines. We expect to be licensed for 18 youth and reach this capacity during the requested funding period.

The shelter will provide three nutritious meals and two snacks daily, and complies with any special or religious dietary needs of youth served. Further, we offer clothing, personal care items, transportation, supervision, and a weekly monetary allowance. There is a minimum of two staff on duty at *all times* to supervise and guide the youth through their daily routines. When beds are full, we will refer youth to other shelters, if possible, or allow them to stay overnight until arrangements can be made the next day.

Individual and Group Counseling: Each youth is assigned an individual Case Manager at intake, with whom he or she collaboratively develops a service plan to identify needed services and crisis intervention counseling. The service plan is updated regularly with direction from the youth, both at weekly case review and during frequent meetings with their Case Manager, who is available to residents on a daily basis. During individual counseling sessions, the youth and case manager discuss the youth's plans for discharge, goals, and progresses. An asset-based approach is used in individual and family counseling which operates from a foundation that youth and families function effectively most of the time. Young people have relationships and complex lives that go far beyond the old notion of a "presenting problem". The goal is to expand the frequency of their effective behavior, instead of a traditional approach that focuses on deficits. This is a solution-focused, youth development approach.

Youth attend a weekly house meeting to give their input on shelter routines, policies, and procedures. Suggestions and concerns expressed by residents are reviewed by staff members and responded to within 24 hours. Youth participate in educational groups in and outside the shelter an average of 6-7 times per week. Weekly groups include a discussion on current events, social issues; HIV/AIDS prevention, anger control/violence prevention, youth gangs and substance abuse; and substance abuse.

If youth has substance and/or sexual abuse problems, s/he will receive in-house substance abuse treatment services provided by our partner, Dorchester House. If the youth's problems are severe (e.g., cocaine and/or heroin dependence, problems common in area of street youth) these youths are admitted to Rebound, a residential substance abuse treatment program. These services are available to all street-youth and are cost-free. If the youth has a history of sexual abuse, counseling and psychotherapy will be provided in concert with the Sexual Assault Program, another in-house program at DYC. Because running away is closely correlated with sexual abuse Viet-AID and our Partners will work to ensure that youth receive appropriate services to work through the trauma of sexual abuse to prevent further problems associated with sexual abuse such as substance abuse, depression, criminal behaviors, aggression, and running away.

Family Counseling: Family counseling by the family case manager is strongly encouraged for each family as a means to explore family reunification, or if this is not an option, to enlist family support and improve relationships. Parents are often skeptical of family sessions and fear blame for their child's behavior. Our goal is not to lay blame, but to engage the parents, as the experts on their child, in deciding upon a positive disposition for their child. It is our goal to provide resources, support, and referrals to assist them in achieving their goals as a parent.

Family sessions are held on a weekly basis, with participation by other agencies and/or counselors involved with the family. Most families engage in at least two family sessions within the two weeks of shelter care, with some engaging in 2-3 session each week.

Service Linkages: As part of the intake process, in weekly case review and during a youth's residency, staff members assess and inquire if a youth requires additional services. Case Managers make referrals with written consent of youth and families, to involve other agencies in the provision of services whenever possible. In all instances, Viet-AID staff members coordinate with all involved agencies, the youth and family. Viet-AID and our Partners have a solid history and working relationships with other agencies committed to helping youth and their families. These include health, recreational, physical, and fitness activities; youth development activities; education and vocational training; and other legal and support services.

Recreational and fitness activities: Youth will be connected to health, nutrition, fitness, and physical activity programs provided by Viet-AID, DYC, Dorchester House, VACA, and other non-profit organizations in Dorchester. They will have opportunities to play basket ball, swim, and/or participate in traditional martial art classes and programs such as Dragon Dance, Vovinam and Binh Dinh, which are designed to help children/youth develop physical, mental and moral health.

Community service projects: As described in the "youth development approach" section, youth will have opportunities to participate in various community service activities and projects operated by Viet-AID and our Partners.

Mental and Physical Health Care: Youth will have access to mental health and physical care, including individual and group counseling, routine physicals, health assessments, and emergency treatment. These services will be provided by our Partner – Dorchester House.

Education: Youth will be enrolled in public school, provided assistance with application for free lunch and other services, and provided transportation. Youth interested in furthering their education at college or a technical or vocational schools will receive assistance in the application and financial aid processes, and will be provided transportation. In addition, youth will receive academic assistance provided by our Partners, Dorchester House and VACA.

Employment: We will provide services that will assist youth in finding employment, including resume writing and interviewing skills. Eligible youth may apply for job positions through the Workforce Investment Act and be paid by Workforce Solutions while gaining work experience.

Life-skills Training: Training will be provided on skills the youth need to become self-sufficient. Most will be offered on-site, with transportation provided off-site as needed. Each individual learning plan is designed based upon an assessment of the youth's needs.

Mentoring Program: Because social skills are a critical component of success, youth will have opportunity to participate in a formal mentoring program designed to increase their ease in social settings, communication skills and interpersonal relations.

Permanent Housing: Youth at least 18 years old or who have been emancipated will work in conjunction with their Case Manager to contact the local housing authorities and/or private housing, and access utilities etc. Donations will be obtained to assist them with furnishings and other needed household items.

Access to other benefits: Youth will be assisted in obtaining mainstream benefits such as food stamps, WIC and Medicaid.

Case Disposition: Discharge planning begins when the youth develops a service plan with their case manager within 48 hours after admission. The youth, their case manager, the youth's parent (a)/guardian(s), and/or other family member collaboratively explore discharge options and aftercare plans. The discharge plans are revised as needed at weekly case review.

The vast majority of the time youth are picked up from the program at the time of discharge by their parent, family member, or someone that the parent approves. When this is not feasible and the youth is local, staff will transport the youth to their discharge placement. For long distance, transportation, arrangements for the prepayment of tickets by the responsible party are made.

Once the young person has left the program, shelter staff members complete a discharge summary, the RHYMIS form, and parent(s)/guardian(s) are notified, if necessary. Staff members then verify and document youth's safe arrival at their discharge destination within 12 hours of their anticipated arrival.

Aftercare Services – An aftercare plan is developed with each youth to assure continuity of services to youth and their families post-discharge. Aftercare is available through the shelter for as long as needed and includes individual, group and family counseling, advocacy, and referrals. Residents and their parents are told that we are available 24 hours a day, through scheduled, unscheduled visits and telephone calls, including collect calls, to discuss issues and problems that may arise. Whenever possible, resources near the youth/families home are sought for ongoing counseling needs, and referrals are made. However, for approximately half our residents, their family needs are short-term and there is a positive momentum we do not want to disrupt. We continue providing family counseling for up to three months following shelter.

Youth Participation: The program embraces a youth development approach that recognizes a youth's control over their life, so in all elements of the program, youth are active participants in the direction, type and quantity of services. Each resident participates in weekly house meetings to address group dynamics, house rules, and suggestions for improvements. In addition, youth are encouraged and are provided with opportunities to participate in community service projects, serve on the Boards of Viet-AID and our Partners, etc. (*See youth development approach subsection above*)

Ongoing Center Planning: Each year, Viet-AID and our Partners plan to conduct a retreat to review agency and program goals and develop plans for the coming year. This includes a review of crisis counseling, temporary shelter, aftercare needs of youth served, and existing services available to meet those needs. We review the summary of all evaluation surveys completed by parents and youth during the year to ascertain achievement of projected outcomes and recommendations for improvement.

Sub-Grant or Contract

Viet-AID serves as an applicant for this grant and sub-grants a significant portion of the proposed project to our Partners DYC, Dorchester House and VACA. Viet-AID will hold a substantive role in the administration and delivery of services of the project. Viet-AID will be responsible for all contract, fiscal and programmatic management. In addition, Viet-AID will provide emergency shelter; opportunities for youth to participate in community service projects, cultural programs, and career development; and counseling and support to parents. Long Nguyen, Viet-AID's staff, will serve as Project Administrator responsible for communication, programmatic linkages between Viet-AID and Partners' services, scheduling and running project meetings, reporting and evaluation activities.

Outreach Plan to Attract Runaway, Homeless, and Street Youth

Please see Outreach and Education Campaign in Program Operation Above

Outreach Plan to Ethnic and Minority Communities

Our outreach activities and services are designed linguistically and culturally appropriate. Most staff members in the Basic Center Program are of Southeast Asian origin. Further they were runaway youth and have been working with runaway youths for many years. Street-outreach workers, case managers and the program Director have had numerous work and life experiences dealing with Southeast Asian runaways, family conflict, and poverty. All staff members' backgrounds have been checked and they have led productive, responsible life-styles and are eager to communicate their direct experiences to youth. Our outreach activities are designed to target areas where Southeast Asian runaway and homeless youth congregate. In addition, our outreach and education activities target Southeast Asian agencies as well as Southeast Asian language print and electronic media.

Service Linkages with Local Agencies

Viet-AID and our Partners have established written cooperative working agreements with community agencies, most of which are enclosed ion this application. The agreements were developed for the purpose of coordinating comprehensive services for runway, homeless and street youth. The agreements describe the services community agencies will provide as well as the procedures to refer youth to the Shelter. (*Appendix C: Agreement and Letters of Support*)

We also work very closely with the Boston police department, the Boston School Police, and Juvenile Court. These agencies refer all runaway and homeless youths to us that come into their custody. When a youth is in juvenile detention center for running away, the Juvenile Department contacts DYC's Street-Outreach Worker who travels to the detention center to do an assessment and transport youth to the shelter. The Police and Probation Officers also contact DYC's Street-Outreach workers and help transport all youths that are runaway and homeless to the facility.

Finally, Viet-AID and our Partners have formed relationships with other non-profit agencies to provide appropriate career development, education, legal services, housing services, and other services and support that are essential to help runaway and homeless youth reconnect to their families and communities.

School Coordination

Viet-AID and our Partners have strong relationships with several local schools that have high numbers of Southeast Asian students. These schools have agreed to work collaboratively with Viet-AID and our Partners to provide support to help students who are at risk of dropping out and running away from home as well as runaway youth who desire to go back to school and reconnect with their families. As part of case planning for each youth, an educational plan is developed. The best choice is to maintain the current educational plan, augmented by on-site shelter tutorial programming. When the school district of origin is not an option, we work to enroll the student in the appropriate School District, or in an alternative program such as GED classes, Job Corps, employment, etc. Viet-AID staff members visit area schools approximately twice per week to meet with teachers and school administrators to explain our services, to coordinate educational planning for residents, and to ensure that youth stay current with the curricula of the schools to which they will return. Further, our Partners have on-site tutors that are available in the afterschool hours for any youth unable to attend their home school.

Dealing with Runaway Youth Who Have Runaway from Foster Care and/or Correctional Institutions

Viet-AID follows procedures in accordance with Federal, State and local laws in procedures dealing with youth who have run from foster care or correctional institutions. The Boston Police Department is contacted to check for any missing person's reports or arrest warrants for all youth admitted. If a youth has run from the foster care system, the state social worker is contacted so the youth can be placed in an alternative placement.

As part of intake, youth sign a consent allowing Viet-AID to check with the local police juvenile unit for outstanding warrants and missing person's reports. Generally, if there is a warrant, the police, Viet-AID, and the Court decide upon a course of action, depending on the charges. Viet-AID staff informs the youth before he/she signs the consent form as to the possible outcomes. We work closely with health, mental health & social service agencies to obtain needed services for youth.

Parental Contact

Parents are contacted almost immediately upon the completion of the intake interview, and certainly within 24 hours of arrival. The exceptions are when the youth reports serious abuse at home or when their parents cannot be reached. In cases of abuse, Department of Child and Families (DCF) is immediately contacted and consent sought pending an investigation of the abuse. Should the abuse be substantiated, the youth and caseworker work closely with DCF worker to pursue alternative placements. In some cases, where a youth is older and mature enough, we explore independent living options or supervised transition to independence such as with Job Corps or our own limited independent living program.

After Care Plan

Please see After Care Subsection in Program Operation Section above.

Confidentiality of Records

Viet-AID and our Partners will ensure the security of client files as required by state and federal laws regarding confidentiality. We will maintain accurate and current records for each youth receiving residential and non-residential program services. Program staff insures that the youth's records are kept locked at all times when not in use and are inaccessible to unauthorized persons. Our staff does not release any client information to agencies or individuals without written consent of the youth and his or her parents or legal guardian. The only exceptions are program staff, the funding and monitoring agencies and when the courts order the release of records.

Viet-AID and our Partners will gather and submit program and client data as required by FYSB's Runaway and Homeless Youth Management Information System (RHYMIS). The collection of data begins at the intake phase and continue during the time that the youth and family receive services to accurately complete all forms. RHYMIS data is collected and submitted quarterly via computer and also kept in hard copy format in individual client files. We will cooperate with any research or evaluation efforts sponsored by the Administration for Children and Families. All data collected is available for review. We will submit reports twice a year to ACF-HHS and will highlight the number of youth served, the number of youth contacted in the streets, number of youth who accessed shelter services or entered in an alternative living arrangement, accomplishments, local, state and national; partnerships, new program developments, and the number of youth participating at all levels of the service delivery.

Home-base Services

While the program does not provide home-based services, our Outreach and Prevention Education activities are designed to educate parents about appropriate parenting skills to better communicate with their children and to prevent conflicts.

Emergency Preparedness and Management Plan

Viet-AID and our Partners have, as part of our personnel manuals, policies regarding emergency preparedness. As part of the funding for this project and particularly because the project provides shelter services to the youth, we plan to conduct an assessment using the questions and checklists in the Department of Health and Human Services Administration for Children and Families' disaster planning manual for runaway and homelessness youth programs, *Ready for Anything.* Based on our assessment, we will develop appropriate disaster and emergency preparedness policies for our clients, which will include written policies and staff training.

Target Southeast Asian Population

Viet-AID and Our Partners target Southeast Asian youth population. As described in the needs section, this population was underserved as there existed no shelter program that has language and cultural capacity to provide linguistically and culturally appropriate services to Southeast Asian youth and parents.

Organizational Profiles

Viet-AID and our Partners collaborate to offer a comprehensive range of supports and opportunities to runaway and homeless Southeast Asian youth and families. Viet-AID and our Partners have in-depth knowledge and understanding of the Southeast Asian community with regard to runaway and homeless youth and their social service, cultural, health, nutrition, housing, and economic needs.

Organizational Capacity & Experience in Managing Federal Grants

Founded in 1994, Viet-AID is the first and only grassroots community development corporation founded and operated by Vietnamese refugees and immigrants in the U.S. Located in the Fields Corner neighborhood (one of the largest Vietnamese concentrations in the East Coast), Viet-AID's mission is to build a strong Vietnamese American community in Boston and a vibrant Field's Corner neighborhood. This mission is anchored by four basic goals: (1) to increase civic participation, (2) to promote economic development and self sufficiency, (3) to build affordable housing for residents, and (4) to foster youth/grassroots leadership.

Over fifteen years, Viet-AID has worked with mainstream organizations and long-time residents to improve the lives of hundreds of Vietnamese immigrants and refugees; increase the participation of Vietnamese residents in civic life; revitalize the once blighted Fields Corner residential area; and contribute to the economic vitality of the neighborhood. Our current programs and their past accomplishments include:

In FY 08, counseled over 140 prospective businesses, and assisted 18 of them to become small business owners through three key business development initiatives: (1) Family Childcare System that creates self-employment for low-income women, many of whom are former welfare recipients; (2) Commercial Cleaning Marketing Cooperative that provides self-employment opportunities for Vietnamese adults; and (3) Small Business Assistance Program that helps community members improve economic security by running a small business. These initiatives also generate over $100,000 annually to support Viet-AID's programs.

Developed a portfolio of 83 rental and homeownership housing units, of which 100% are affordable units, and trained over 500 families in first-time home-buying, counseling and real estate development;

Improved neighborhood quality of life and contributed to neighborhood economic vitality by: (1) transforming former drug houses and abandoned lots into two four unit affordable housing projects, a multicultural community garden and a multi-purpose community center; (2) working with the police department, school department and MBTA to install new lighting systems around the Fields Corner subway station, to close off "crime spots" at the local school, to increase police presence in the neighborhood, and to organize and support a neighborhood crime watch; and (3) organizing an annual neighborhood clean-up and Taste of Fields Corner.

Fostered youth and grassroots leadership development by engaging hundreds of youth and community residents in: (1) Planning and building a community center; (2) designing and installing two mural projects that converted two blighted walls into cultural and racial reflections of the community; (3) planning and developing an Oral History project to promote greater communication and understanding between young and old generations; and (4) planning and implementing a voter education campaign to promote greater civic participation.

<u>Built a $5.1 million Vietnamese American Community Center that created bilingual andbicultural preschool,</u> after-school day care, youth, and senior programs. The Center currently provides home to the following programs:

Preschool: Provides bilingual and bicultural early care and education to low-income parents in the Dorchester area.

Cultural/Youth programs: On weekend, the Center provides space for youth, cultural and fitness programs managed by community cultural/youth associations. These programs are designed to promote social, physical, emotional and character development among Vietnamese children and youth by providing them with opportunities to learn their language and culture as well as to engage in fitness, health and leadership development activities such as playing table tennis, learning martial arts and attending leadership programs.

Viet-AID, as the lead applicant, has over 10 years of experience in managing federal grants as well as has a financial management system that conforms with the uniform administrative requirements under 45 CFR Part 74. Viet-AID successfully received and managed grants totaling more than $20 million from the ACF Office of Community Service and the Department of Housing and Community Development for our community center and affordable housing projects. Indirectly, we received sub-grants from ACF Office for Refugee Resettlement for our refugee small business development program and Department of Environmental Protection Agency for our Nail Salon and Hardwood Floor Health Education initiative. Our financial management system, *managed by a finance manager and a CPA*, provides that the Board of Directors approves the annual budget, receives monthly reports on Actual vs. Budgeted Revenue and Expense Reports prepared by our experienced finance staff, and oversees the annual audit. We have an accounting system that has ability to keep track revenue and expenses by program and by funder, has appropriate chart of accounts and functions for receipts and disbursements. Our accounting policy and procedures require that we follow cash management requirements established by the US Department of Health and Human Services; that annual audits be performed in accordance with the Circular for fiscal years (FY) with expenditures under Federal awards of $500,000 or more; that bank statements be reconciled in a timely manner by someone not authorized to sign checks and that checks are signed by the Chair and Executive Directors; that proper disbursement and procurement procedures be followed; that matching or cost sharing contributions be adhered; and that proper process be followed for selecting outside consultant, travel, timekeeping, indirect costs rate, and credit cards usage, etc.

Viet-AID is a community-based organization. Membership is open to anyone 18 years or older. Members have a right to participate in the business and social meetings of the organization, elect and remove board members and run for board membership. Viet-AID's Board of Directors presently has nine members who set the agency's strategic plan, policies and oversee operations. To promote leadership development and community input, Viet-AID often establishes community advisory committees to help conduct needs assessment and identify unmet needs and community priorities to guide strategic priorities for the organization. Last year, Viet-AID established a Community Advisory Committee (Community Council) consisting of parents, youth workers, youth, business owners, and other stakeholders to help identify needs and recommend strategic priorities and programs for Viet-AID. This collaborative effort between Viet-AID and the Partners is the product of this process.

Close to Home: Close to Home has focused on community organizing and domestic and sexual violence prevention in Fields Corner since 2002. Close to Home has formed partnerships with youth organizations, police officers, local businesses, and service providers that have enabled the organization to deepen its organizing work with youth in Fields Corner. Our Youth Team consists of 15 young people, ages 15 to 21, who work 10 hours a week during the school year and 25 hours a week during the summer. The youth reflect the demographics of the neighborhood, and work to educate and organize Dorchester youth around issues of dating and domestic violence. Through community assessments, peer-to-peer trainings, community-building events, and leadership and skill-building workshops, the Youth Team has mobilized a network of over 300 youth year-round to communicate about the problem of teen dating and domestic violence and develop creative and effective responses. The team reaches an additional 1,000 youth per year with events, brochures and informational flyers, web communications, and Close to Home's annual Public Awareness Campaign. The youth involved in the Close to Home community have many opportunities to collaborate on projects and events with adult residents involved in the network. Close to Home views this multigenerational approach as critical to building trusting, healthy relationships among families and communities.

Close to Home engages local youth and adults as leaders by asking current leaders to reach out to their social networks, engaging residents of all ages that live in the Fields Corner area, and letting the local community know that we are seeking new leaders. Many people become involved after attending one of our events or trainings, or because they are connected to one of our current volunteers. The network of volunteers is diverse—including youth that are in school and out of school—and people of all ages who have lost loved ones or had direct experience with street violence or domestic violence. Close to Home is committed to engaging and working with youth that are or have been system involved, and community members of all backgrounds and will continue to seek out opportunities to engage a diverse group in domestic, dating and sexual violence prevention.

Vietnamese American Civic Association (VACA): VACA was founded in 1984 to help Vietnamese refugees resettle and rebuild their lives in America. VACA's Youth Development Program was established in 1997, with a modest tutoring program. Since then, the program has grown exponentially to include an after-school program consisting of the Peer Leadership Program, college and SAT preparation, Educational and Financial Aid Counseling, a family literacy program, a summer WorkSmart Program, Weekly Educational Field trips, and Sports. In FY 09, VACA has served 78 participants between the ages of 14 and 20 in our summer program alone; on average we have approximately 45 individuals in our after-school program. Between July 1 and December 27, 2008, VACA received 78 walk-ins from seniors interested in obtaining educational and college financial aid counseling, a small percentage of the larger numbers of walk-ins our Youth Development Program experiences. Our outreach and intervention services have served 150-200 students within South Boston High School and 120-150 students in other area schools. Generally, numbers are split evenly between male and female students, although 65% of participants in our youth program this year were girls. All of our previous Peer Leaders have successfully transitioned from high school to college, some having returned to VACA as college students to provide guidance to the current Peer Leaders and to serve the community in other ways. Graduates of the Peer Leader program also become involved in civic activities on their college campuses.

Dorchester House MultiService Center: Dorchester House provides a full range of health care, public health and community services to the poor and underserved community in Dorchester. It operates a community health care center that offers a full range of primary care services to all people, from children to seniors. It also runs a number of public health programs, ranging from HIV education to diabetes and family support services. To improve its community services, Dorchester House formed DotWell in 1998 as a management service organization with Codman Square Health Center. DotWell is charged with the cross-site management and program development of all social service programs, in addition to managing the critical areas of information technology and data base management, finance, development, marketing and communications, public policy advocacy, and research and evaluation. Built on the combined 150 years of our founding health center's commitment to the well being of Dorchester, DotWell initiatives address the social, emotional and educational needs of youth and adults while celebrating the cultural and ethnic diversity of the community and the potential of every individual. DotWell provides services for 500 youth annually.

DotWell supports not only the child, but the parent and family through counseling, financial education, academic support or help accessing benefit programs. They also recognize that to support the youth, they must work with the school to support the teachers and serve as a bridge for student and parent when necessary. Programs include the following: Teen Tutoring Center provides a continuum of academic, social, artistic, technology, and college-prep skills; The Dorchester Youth Council develops significant leadership skills among Dorchester's teens to foster participation in civic activities; ATLAS (Academics Technology LifeSkills Arts and Sports) provides after school and summer academic achievement; FANtastic Kids provides activities promoting physical and nutritional wellness, and parental involvement to high body mass index (BMI) youth; Boston Community Learning Center (CLC) at the Lee Elementary School provides year-round comprehensive after-school services, implementing a mix of academic, recreational, and social activities, for youth. In additional to the programs listed above, DotWell offers teens both recreational and structured sports and fitness activities, including basketball, swimming, and soccer, as well as internship and employment opportunities.

Education Support Safe City partners offer homework assistance, tutoring, and computer labs. School performance is reviewed and monitored regularly. There is specialized tutoring weekly in Mathematics and English to prepare High School students for MCAS and TOEFL, and in both math and verbal skill building to prepare for the SAT. Staff work closely with the schools to collaborate on meeting the specific needs of each student and often assist the school in working with the parents. English literacy tutoring is available to individuals for whom English is not their first language.

Out of School Time Recreational Activities Recreational activities include sports (soccer, basketball, swimming and volleyball) and sports tournaments, dance lessons, fashion shows, jump rope (Chinese and Double Dutch), movies, cultural activities and field trips. Teens can also take classes in Vietnamese, African, and Hip Hop Dance and other performing art activities. Skill Building Programs are offered that provide youth with practical skills in the areas of media, technology, peer leadership, and entrepreneurship.

Life Skills – Leadership Development Life skills activities are integrated throughout all program activities. Special workshops are offered throughout the year, such as conflict resolution and violence prevention, legal rights of youth, conflict, youth development, dangers of substance abuse and refusal skills, and issues related to health/health screenings. Youth are provided with opportunities to develop work skills and each year more than 40 youth are employed during the summer with 30 youth employed by the programs year round. Through specific training and opportunities to serve as counselors in training, tutors, coaches, and youth council members, teens have the opportunity to develop and foster their leadership skills and to act as beacons to others who are willing to reject gangs, drugs, and violence. Internet support, street outreach, counseling, and center based violence prevention is offered, as well.

Community Service Teens are encouraged to participate in regular community service projects and to serve as mentors and role models to younger children in the neighborhoods. By fostering a commitment to take care of their neighbors, and neighborhoods, teens are provided with a chance to develop a strong sense of civic responsibility and a positive self-image.

Dorchester Youth Collaborative (DYC)

See subsection 4: Agency's Experience Working with Runaway and Homeless Youth

2. Proposal to Sub-grant and/or Contract

Viet-AID serves as an applicant for this grant and sub-grants a significant portion of the proposed project to our partners Dorchester Youth Collaborative, Dorchester House Health Center, and VACA. Viet-AID will hold a lead role in the administration and delivery of services of the project. Viet-AID will be responsible for all contractual, fiscal and programmatic management. We will be responsible for all programmatic and financial reports. Viet-AID will work closely with DYC, Dorchester House Health Center, and VACA to ensure that these agencies follow and comply with all programmatic and grant management requirements.

3. Knowledge of State and Local Licensing Requirements

Viet-AID plans to apply to the Massachusetts Department of Early Care and Education to operate a Temporary Shelter Facility for Southeast Asian youth ages between 13-18 at our 12-room rooming house. The facility meets and exceeds all licensing requirements, some of which are:

All staff who have unmonitored contact with residents must have a Criminal Offender Record Information (CORI) check.

A statement of ownership of the program includes financial documentation and evidence of financial capability, tax certification, business management plan, and evidence of contractual agreements for accepting residents. The statement defines the following:

- A program that is safe, clean, comfortable, of adequate size, free from hazards, and has passed all local building, health, fire, and lead paint inspections.
- Identification of the characteristics of the children who will be served by the program. Evidence that all administrative and direct-care staff are qualified for their positions, and that staff are appropriately supervised and evaluated.
- Evidence that the required staff to child ratios are maintained; staff appropriately supervise residents to ensure the health, safety, and growth and development of each child; Staff personnel policies, including plans for mandatory staff orientation and training.
- A plan that defines the rules, policies and procedures for behavior management, including physical restraint that safeguards the emotional, physical and psychological well-being of children in care.
- The ability to provide all intake, service, and discharge planning for the children in car; to provide all necessary case management, family work, nutritional, health, social, psychological and psychiatric services for the children in care; to provide all educational, vocational preparation, and recreational services for the children in care.
- Written records about the children in care include intake, evaluations and assessments, service planning, medical, progress reports, and discharge information plus all required authorizations and consents.

4. Agency's Experience Working with Runaway and Homeless Youth

Our partner, Dorchester Youth Collaborative, has 20 years of experience in working with runaway and homeless youth. DYC was founded in 1981 to reduce fear and hopelessness of low-income urban teens through positive youth development activities and access to educational, recreational and employment opportunities. DYC starts its relationship with these teens through a drop in, Safe Haven teen center where they are only required to give their first name. DYC operates programs during high crime hours and uses community intelligence to divert teens from becoming first victims of crime and often later gang members and perpetrators of violence. DYC specializes in working with the most "at risk" teens from the target area. DYC also has a special focus on multi cultural programming, performing arts and basketball.

DYC has operated a successful culturally competent Asian gang diversion and intervention programs for teens living along the Dorchester Avenue Corridor. The program seeks to reduce Asian gang violence in the Dorchester Avenue corridor in two ways: (i) Operate 4 basketball/mentoring clubs will continue to divert 60 "high profile" Asian teens that live in this high gang crime corridor away from gangs into positive youth development activities during the high crime afternoon and evening hours of 2- 9: PM. DYC's highest priority teens are those that are relatives of active Asian gang members; (ii) Use a bi-lingual street outreach worker and bi-lingual outreach family worker to reach out to teens that are members of Asian gangs following beatings, stabbings, shootings and murders. DYC holds meetings to arrange peace agreements and also provides goal orientated casework to gang members around school, employment, recreation and court issues. DYC operates a "day job" program which hires teens instantly for as little as one day and builds strong relationships with hard-to-reach gang affiliated Asian teens through this work program.

Current Recipient of Funds from ACF for RHY

Viet-AID and our Partners are not current recipients of funds from ACF for services that support RHY.

Sustainability Plan

Viet-AID and our Partners are committed to continue to operate the proposed project once Federal funding for the project has ended. We plan to leverage other sources of funding to supplement the grant award and to support services through collaborative partnerships which results in cost effectiveness, efficiency and increased resources; diverse portfolio of funding sources including government, private foundation, and corporations; and high- quality programs and proven results.

Collaborative partnerships: We believe that family-community-school partnership is essential to long-term sustainability. This partnership reduces redundancies and duplicative services, while improving program and cost effectiveness. It also strengthens our ability to apply for funding from federal agencies and national foundations and corporations.

Diverse portfolio of funding sources: We will approach public agencies, private foundations and corporations to leverage funding support for this project. Funding sources might include the school district budget, Title I, federal child care subsidies, parent fees, AmeriCorps, United Way, and local and national foundations such as the Boston Foundation, the Peabody Foundation, and Smith Family Foundation.

High-quality programs and proven results: We believe that our ability to prove and document the quality of their programs is an asset when seeking support beyond a Street Outreach Program grant. While receiving a federal grant, we will invest in rigorous program evaluation to demonstrate our program effectiveness and potential community impact. This will help our future fundraising effort.

Positive Youth Development Philosophy

Viet-AID incorporates the Family and Youth Services Bureau's Youth Development Approach in our organizational culture. As described in more detail in the Youth Development Approach Subsection above, we view children/youth as positive, creative, and resourceful individuals with an amazing ability for emotional resiliency. Services provided by Viet-AID have always honored their developmental needs. As such, we have an organizational culture that seeks to involve youth in all aspects of our organization. These include serving on the Board of Directors, member of an Advisory or Steering Committee that is responsible for planning and implementing community initiative; involving in planning and implementation of a community service project; and volunteering in one or more of our program activities. For example, we involved youth in the planning and development of the $5 million Community Center project. Recently, we have formed a Community Council, consisting of parents, youth, teachers and other key stakeholders to advocate for the interests of Southeast Asian youth and families. We will launch our Voices – a project that brings youth and elders together to plan and implement an oral history project. Using *Artography*, youth will work with adults and parents to design and implement an intergenerational art and cultural programs that validate personal histories – refugee experience, explain cultural differences, honor traditions, promote understanding, and link generations and cultures. One of the potential project ideas is to present how cultural difference influences decision by young people to run away from homes through either performance art or digital photography.

Staff and Position Data

Key Staff

Viet-AID has assembled an experienced and committed team consisting of staff members and consultant to implement this project. The key staff positions include: One part-time Project Administrator, one part-time Project Director, two Youth Case Managers, one Family Case Manager, and one Youth Worker. The program staff is supported by a team of street outreach workers (DYC), youth workers (all Partners), Clinical Counselor (Dorchester House). As evidenced in the following section, all staff members have extensive experience in working with homeless, runaway, and street youth.

Staff Experience and Qualifications

Project Administrator, Long Nguyen, Viet-AID: Long Nguyen is responsible for the overall program and grant administration. Long has more than 10 years of experience in managing major federal grants. These include a 3-year $500,000 grant from the ACF's Office of Community Service to promote micro-enterprise development; a 3-year grant from the ACF's Office of Refugee Resettlement to provide services to Vietnamese refugee families; and a 3-year grant from Corporation for National and Community Service to engage young people in serving communities throughout the United States. Long has almost 20 years of experience in starting and leading community-based organizations and social purpose enterprises. From 1995 to 2004, Long served as founding executive director of Viet-AID, where he leveraged over $50 million to help build family and community wealth in the Boston Vietnamese community through projects ranging from community facility to affordable rental and homeownership housing, social purpose enterprises, small business development, revolving loan fund, child care, and senior center. From 2006- present, Long served as Te-Enterprise's Founding and Managing Partner where he helped design and secure over $5 million to

Southeast Asian Shelter – Staffing Chart

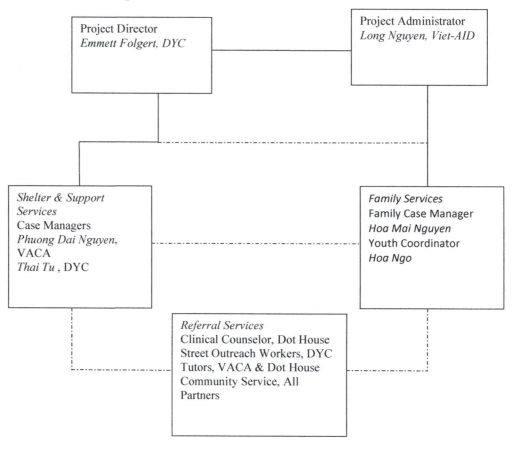

Indicates direct reporting/management

Indicates communication and coordination relationship

implement national and regional initiatives to prepare a new generation of non-profit leaders, build organizational capacity of community-based and faith-based non-profit organizations, and rebuild Gulf Coast communities devastated by hurricanes Katrina and Ike. Since last year, Long has worked with Viet-AID on part-time basis, overseeing the planning and development of a comprehensive youth & family initiative to address increased youth violence and runaway problems in the Vietnamese community. Long has a B.A. in political science and economics and a law degree from Boston University.

Shelter Project Director, Emmett Folgert, DYC: Serving as DYC's Executive Director, Emmett Folgert is responsible for the implementation of the Southeast Asian Shelter. Emmett will oversee program implementation and will provide supervision to the shelter staff. He will provide general supervision and management of the program, including case management services, shelter activities, personnel management, and quality assurance and service delivery. Emmett is will work closely with the Project Administrator to ensure the project be implemented successfully, gather program data according to funding source requirements, compile quarterly reports, and develop yearly report for the program. Emmett has over 25 years experience working with high and proven risk, low income, urban youth and their families. This experience includes direct service such as: street outreach, gang extraction, runaway and homeless youth, substance abuse counseling, residential supervision, court and school advocacy and gang peace negotiations. Emmett has clinical supervision and program development experience. He is a founder of an alternative school for middle school dropouts and co-founder of the Dorchester Youth Collaborative, established in 1981. All of Emmett's work has been with multicultural populations of hard to reach youth. He has specific expertise working with runaway, truant and delinquent Asian youth. Emmett has built strong credibility with the courts, police, schools as well as Asian youth and their families.

Youth Case Managers, DYC& VACA: The youth case managers are responsible for conducting intake and assessment, developing service plan, work collaboratively with youth to implement service plan, and provide after care services. They are also responsible for scheduling and supervising shelter activities and being on on-call duty. They will work closely with the Family counselor to conduct outreach and prevention education activities as well as to coordinate group counseling session with youth and their parents. *Phuong Dai Nguyen, VACA:* Phuong Dai has worked as youth worker at VACA for almost ten years. During that time, she provided advocacy and case management services to help youth identifying their needs and advocate for services and resources to help youth succeed. She also provided translation and advocacy to Southeast Asian families in various settings including schools, community agencies, health centers/hospitals and churches/temples. Thai Tu, DYC: Thai Tu has 4-year plus experience in working with Southeast Asian runaway and homeless youth. Before being hired as a Case Manager, Thai Tu was DYC's youth participant and Peer Leader where he was involved in various street outreach activities, building truce among gang members and coordinating various sport and community service activities for other youth. Thai Tu speaks Vietnamese and Cambodian.

Family Case Manager, Hoa Mai Nguyen, Viet-AID: The family case manager is responsible for providing individualized case management and services to Southeast Asian parents of youth who are enrolled in the Shelter, as well as to coordinate peer support group and recreational activities. Using a strengths-based approach, she will conduct home visits, assess the needs of parents, develop plan to improve parenting skills, facilitate access to community resources and services, and provide counseling services as needed. She will also be responsible for outreach and prevention education activities. Hoa Mai's experience spans over ten years working with the Vietnamese immigrant and refugee population in English language development, job training, counseling, research, health education, social justice and advocacy. She previously held positions at Massachusetts Asian and Pacific Islanders (MAP) for Health, Harvard University's Sociology Department and is currently an adjunct faculty member at the Bunker Hill Community College. Hoa Mai was a teacher in Vietnam and speaks Vietnamese fluently.

Program Service Coordinator, Hoa Ngo, Viet-AID: The Program Service Coordinator is responsible for coordinating all academic and enrichment activities, recruit and supervise tutors and volunteers, plan enrichment activities, and work closely with the parent advocates/case managers/youth counselor to organize activities for students and parents. Hoa Ngo oversees Viet-AID's youth development as well as cultural programs. Hoa has been with Viet-AID for almost 7 years, first as an AmeriCorps member and most recently as youth coordinator.

Staff Ratio

There will always be a minimum of 2 professional paid staff members on duty at all time for a ratio of 1-4 or 1-6 staff to youth ratio.

Agency's Policy for Criminal History or Child Abuse Registry Checks

All staff must agree to be subject to initial and annual Massachusetts CORI, criminal offender record information and CORI- Sexual offender record information checks.

5. Staff Training Plan

Staff training is required of all staff, volunteers, and youth peer counselors at a minimum of 40 hours annually. Many exceed this baseline, but all are required to meet this training goal. Volunteers are treated as the vital co-workers that they are, and are expected at least to complete the orientation and to participate in ongoing training opportunities, as they are available. A myriad of ongoing in-service training is provided internally or by local experts, community, state and national workshops and conferences to ensure each staff member acquires the ongoing education to be of the best possible service to youth and their families. The ongoing training addresses topics such as: youth development, case file reviews, team building, cultural education, sexual minority populations, medication certification, first aid training, CPR, conflict resolution, in-depth analysis of various mental health or behavioral problems, family dynamics, strategies for neutralizing a volatile situation, and others.

The initial training is a rigorous, in-depth orientation for new staff members, conducted by the supervisory team. It is divided into three levels. The first is an overview of services, helping skills, crisis management, youth development strategies and personal characteristics needed to be successful at Viet-AID. The second level addresses family, group dynamics, cultural diversity, documentation, time management, and managing stress. The final phase of the orientation covers the principles of case management and provides greater understanding of the common challenges our young people face, such as abuse, neglect, mental illness, substance abuse, domestic violence, gangs, violence and others. The training is both didactic and experiential and employs different media for communicating the information, addressing the spectrum of learning styles. The initial training and mandatory shadowing for new staff members totals 40 hours of education.

Budget and Budget Justifications

The total annual budget for the Southeast Asian Shelter is $455,038. Viet-AID and our Partners request $188,675 yearly in federal funding and will provide $266,363 in match or 59%. Matching fund consists of in-kind and cash. Viet-AID and our Partners have secured funding commitments from Charles Hayden Foundation, Boston Foundation, Hyams Foundation and Schraffts Foundation. We have proposals pending with the Peabody and Smith Family Foundations to support the case manager position to provide case management services and support to parents of program participants. We also plan to approach state agencies for funding support.

APPENDIX D

List of Formulas

Name	Formula
Proportion	$P = \dfrac{f}{N}$
Percentage	$\% = (100)\dfrac{f}{N}$
Midpoint	$m = \dfrac{lowest\,score\,value + highest\,score\,value}{2}$
Cumulative percentage	$c\% = (100)\dfrac{cf}{N}$
Total percentage	$total\% = (100)\dfrac{f}{N_{total}}$

Row percentage

$$row\% = (100)\frac{f}{N_{row}}$$

Column percentage

$$column\% = (100)\frac{f}{N_{column}}$$

Sample mean

$$\overline{X} = \frac{\Sigma X}{N}$$

Mean from frequency dist.

$$\overline{X} = \frac{\Sigma(fX)}{N}$$

Deviation from sample mean

$$Deviation = X - \overline{X}$$

Range

$$R = H - L$$

Sample variance

$$s^2 = \frac{\Sigma(X - \overline{X})^2}{N-1}$$

Standard deviation

$$SD \text{ or } s = \sqrt{\frac{\Sigma(X - \overline{X})^2}{N-1}}$$

Population variance

$$\sigma^2 = \frac{\Sigma(X - \mu)^2}{N}$$

Population standard deviation

$$\sigma = \sqrt{\frac{\Sigma(X - \mu)^2}{N}}$$

Probability of an outcome $\qquad P = \dfrac{number\ of\ times\ an\ outcome\ can\ occur}{total\ number\ of\ times\ any\ outcome\ can\ occur}$

Z score/standardized score $\qquad z = \dfrac{X - \mu}{\sigma}$

Z score/standardized score $\qquad z = \dfrac{X - \overline{X}}{SD}$

95% confidence $\qquad 95\%CI = \overline{X} \pm 1.96\sigma\overline{x}$

99% confidence interval $\qquad 95\%CI = \overline{X} \pm 2.58\sigma\overline{x}$

Standard error of the mean $\qquad s\overline{x} = \dfrac{s}{\sqrt{N-1}}$

t-test of difference between means of independent samples $\qquad t = \dfrac{\overline{X_1} - \overline{X_2}}{s_{\overline{x}_1 - \overline{x}_2}}$

t-test of difference between means of related samples $\qquad t = \dfrac{\overline{X_1} - \overline{X_2}}{s_{\overline{D}}}$

Partitioning sum of squares $\qquad SS_{total} = SS_{between} + SS_{within}$

Total sum of squares from
Deviation

$$SS_{total} = \Sigma(X - \overline{X}_{total})^2$$

Between-groups mean squares

$$MS_{between} = \frac{SS_{between}}{df_{between}}$$

Within-groups mean square

$$MS_{within} = \frac{SS_{within}}{df_{within}}$$

F ratio

$$F = \frac{MS_{between}}{MS_{within}}$$

Chi-square

$$\chi^2 = \Sigma \frac{(f_o - f_e)^2}{f_e}$$

Chi-square with Yate's correction

$$\chi^2 = \Xi \frac{(|f_o - f_e| - .5)^2}{f_e}$$

Pearson's correlation

$$r = \frac{SP}{\sqrt{SS_X SS_y}}$$

Pearson's r from deviations

$$r = \frac{\Sigma(X - \overline{X})(Y - \overline{Y})}{\sqrt{\Sigma(X - \overline{X})^2 \Sigma(Y - \overline{Y})^2}}$$

Pearson's r from row scores

$$r = \frac{\Sigma XY - N\overline{X}\overline{Y}}{\sqrt{\Sigma X^2 - N\overline{X}^2)(\Sigma Y^2 - N\overline{Y}^2)}}$$

Regression model

$$Y = a + bX + e$$

Regression equation $\qquad Y = b_0 + b_1 X$

X Independent (predictor, explanatory) variable;

Y Dependent variable;

b_1 Slope of regression line

$$b_1 = \frac{n(\Sigma XY) - (\Sigma X)(\Sigma Y)}{n(\Sigma X^2) - (\Sigma X)^2}$$

b_0 y-intercept of regression line

$$b_0 = \overline{Y} - b_1 \overline{X}$$

Residual $\qquad e = Y - Y$

Difference between an observed sample Y value and the value Y that is predicted using the regression equation.

Regression coefficient $\qquad b = \dfrac{SP}{SS_X}$

Regression coefficient from deviations $\qquad b = \dfrac{\Sigma(X - \overline{X})(Y - \overline{Y})}{\Sigma(X - \overline{X})^2}$

Regression coefficient from row scores $\qquad b = \dfrac{\Sigma XY - N\overline{X}\,\overline{Y}}{\Sigma X^2 - N\overline{X}^2}$

Y-intercept $\qquad a = \overline{Y} - b\overline{X}$

Regression line $\qquad Y = a + b\overline{X}$

Spearman's rank order correlation $\quad r_s = 1 - \dfrac{6\Sigma D^2}{N(N^2 - 1)}$

Phi coefficient $\qquad\qquad \phi = \sqrt{\dfrac{\chi^2}{N}}$

Contingency coefficient $\qquad C = \sqrt{\dfrac{\chi^2}{N + \chi^2}}$

Cramer's V $\qquad\qquad V = \sqrt{\dfrac{\chi^2}{N(k-1)}}$

ANOVA Analysis of variance: Method of testing equality of three or more population means (by analyzing sample variances)

Step 1: Calculate the mean for each sample ($\overline{X}_1$, $\overline{X}_2$, $\overline{X}_3$, etc.).

Step 2: Find the sum of scores (ΣX_{total}), the sum of squared scores (ΣX^2_{total}), the total number of cases (N_{total}), and the mean for all groups combined ($\overline{X}_{total}$).

Step 3: Find the total sum of squares.

$$SS_{total} = \Sigma X^2_{total} - N_{total}\overline{X}^2_{total}$$

Step 4: Find the within-groups sum of squares.

$$SS_{within} = \Sigma X^2_{total} - \Sigma N_{group}\overline{X}^2_{total}$$

Step 5: Find the between-groups sum of squares.

$$SS_{between} = \Sigma N_{group} \overline{X}^2_{group} - N_{total} \overline{X}^2_{total}$$

Step 6: Find the within-groups degree of freedom.

$$df_{within} = N_{total} - K$$

Step 7: Find between-groups degree of freedom.

$$df_{between} = K - 1$$

Step 8: Find the within-groups mean square.

$$MS_{within} = \frac{SS_{within}}{df_{within}}$$

Step 9: Find the between-groups mean square.

$$MS_{between} = \frac{SS_{between}}{df_{between}}$$

Step 10: Obtain the F ratio.

$$F = \frac{MS_{between}}{MS_{within}}$$

Step 11: Compare the obtained F ratio with the appropriate critical value for F taken from table value. If the obtained F ratio exceeds the tabled critical value, then reject the null hypothesis of no differences among the population means and continue with the Tukey's HSD test. Otherwise, retain the null hypothesis of no differences and stop.

Internal consistency/Cronbach alpha $\qquad \alpha = N / (N-1)[1 - \Sigma\sigma^2(Y_i) / \sigma^2_x]$

where N is the number of items of the instrument; $\Sigma\sigma^2(Y_i)$ is the sum of item variances; and σ_x^2 is the variance of the total composite. If one is working with the correlation matrix rather than the variance-covariance matrix, then alpha reduces to the following:

Internal consistency/Cronbach alpha $\quad \alpha = N\bar{\rho}/[1+\bar{\rho}(N-1)]$

where N is again the number of items and $\bar{\rho}$ is the mean inter-item correlation.

CPSIA information can be obtained at www.ICGtesting.com
Printed in the USA
LVOW01s1752060914

402677LV00004B/27/P